The Bloc
That
Failed

Charles Gati

THE BLOC THAT FAILED

Soviet–East European
Relations in Transition

Published in association with the Center
for Strategic and International Studies,
Washington, D.C.

Indiana
University
Press
Bloomington & Indianapolis

The paper used in this publication meets the minimum requirements
of American National Standard for Information Sciences—
Permanence of Paper for Printed
Library Materials, ANSI Z39.48–1984.

⊗™

Manufactured in the United States of America

Library of Congress Cataloging-in-Publication Data

Gati, Charles.
The bloc that failed : Soviet–East
European relations in transition / Charles Gati.
p.   cm.
Includes bibliographical references.
ISBN 0–253–32531–5 (alk. paper). — ISBN 0–253–20561–1 (pbk. :
alk. paper)
1. Europe, Eastern—Foreign relations—Soviet Union. 2. Soviet
Union—Foreign relations—Europe, Eastern, 3. Europe, Eastern—
Foreign relations—1945– 4. Warsaw Treaty Organization.
I. Title.
DJ45.S65G37   1990
327.47—dc20   89–36971
                                                CIP

3   4   5   94   93   92

To Daniel and Adrienne,
with love for what they are
and envy for what they can be

CONTENTS

PREFACE   ix

Part One: **Looking Back**

I. STALIN AND SOCIALISM IN ONE REGION   3
Strange Bedfellows, 3 / Satellization, 9 / Early Problems, 13 / Soviet-ization, 18 / What Did Stalin Achieve? 23

II. FROM KHRUSHCHEV TO CHERNENKO: AN OVERVIEW   29
Post-Stalin Soviet Concerns, 29 / Recasting Policy toward Eastern Europe, 32 / Yugoslavia and National Communism, 35 / Crises in the Bloc: Hungary, Czechoslovakia, Poland (1956–81), 39 / From Khrushchev to Chernenko: What Changed? What Didn't? 55

Part Two: **The Era of Reform, 1985–88**

III. POLITICAL RELATIONS   65
The Early Gorbachev Era: Cure or Relief? 65 / The Gradual Demise of the "Brezhnev Doctrine," 71 / The Institutional Framework, 79 / The Ties They Are A-Changin', 87 / Summing Up, 99

IV. ECONOMIC RELATIONS   104
The Elusive Concept of Socialism, 104 / The Urgency of Change, 106 / The Economics and Politics of Trade, 113 / Why CMEA Does Not Work, 124 / Summing Up and Looking Ahead, 132

V. MILITARY RELATIONS   136
Defense against Whom? 136 / The East European Militaries, 143 / Causes of Tension in Military Relations, 147 / Gorbachev's Choices, 150 / Courting Trouble, 154

Part Three: **The Era of Revolutionary Change, Since 1988**

VI. MOSCOW RETREATS   161
From Reform to Revolution, 161 / From Poland to Romania, 167 / Summing Up, 185

VII. THE BRAVE NEW WORLD OF EASTERN EUROPE   191
The Soviet Factor, 191 / East European Prospects, 197 / Western Concerns, 201

APPENDIX: A Soviet View of Eastern Europe   205
SOURCES AND SUGGESTIONS FOR
   FURTHER READING   220
INDEX   223

Preface

REVOLUTION SWEPT each of the six Warsaw Pact countries of Eastern Europe in 1988–89. The dramatic events began somewhat gradually in Poland and in Hungary, then continued in rapid succession during the fall and early winter of 1989 in East Germany, Czechoslovakia, Bulgaria, and finally Romania. Amazingly, the region's old communist guard stepped aside, peacefully, except in Romania where a tragic and gruesome civil war claimed hundreds and perhaps thousands of lives. Equally surprising is that the East European revolutions have far outstripped the reforms Mikhail S. Gorbachev introduced in the Soviet Union. This will lead to increased popular demand for more drastic and comprehensive changes within the Soviet Union itself in the 1990s.

With Moscow unwilling to use force to protect the East European communist parties from their own people, these unpopular and mostly corrupt parties have lost their monopoly of power. Popular expectations in all six Warsaw Pact countries now suggest a desire to adopt Western-style political and economic institutions and practices. Thus, the Soviet bloc as it has existed since Stalin has in effect disintegrated; the countries of Eastern Europe are now on their own.

With the collapse of the region's one-party communist regimes, the first stage of Eastern Europe's remarkable revolution has ended. The second stage, which will involve the creation of new institutions of political and economic pluralism, will take several years. The third stage will be an even slower process, during which a variety of internal measures and international guarantees will consolidate the gains of the revolution, allowing Eastern Europe to rejoin the European community of nations.

When these stages of the revolutionary process will pass cannot now be known; predictions about the region's more distant future remain hazardous. In one or more East European countries even a partial reversal of the enormous changes of 1988 and 1989 is conceivable; revolutions tend to produce new problems and spark new uncertainties. I examine these uncertainties throughout this book, particularly in Part III, where I consider the key questions they raise for the final decade of this century. The first set of questions concerns *Soviet policy in Eastern Europe*:

1. How will Moscow define the new threshold of Soviet tolerance toward Eastern Europe? Can the example of Soviet-Finnish relations serve as a model for Soviet–East European relations? Can there be an Eastern Europe that in its relations with the Soviet Union is cordial but not subservient, independent but not inhospitable, and thus influenced but not dominated by its large and powerful neighbor?

2. On what means will the Soviet Union rely in order to exert influence over Eastern Europe? As it withdraws its forces from the region, as the East European economies turn West, and as Marxist-Leninist ideology ceases to underlie common policy and joint action, will the Soviet Union become but a "pitiful giant" to its closest neighbors?

3. Will Moscow permit East Germany, the keystone of the Warsaw Pact and the Soviet Union's leading trading partner, to enjoy free choice in domestic policy and foreign relations as well? If so, will the next decade witness the establishment of a reunited or otherwise reassociated Germany? Will the division of Europe and the cold war thus end and Europe become one, with its eastern and western parts living peaceably in what Gorbachev has called a "common European home"?

4. Will the upsurge of national assertiveness in East-

ern Europe hasten the efforts of the nations of the Soviet Union—from Estonia to the Ukraine to Armenia—to press for a more autonomous existence under Soviet rule or to demand complete independence? In either case, how will Moscow respond to nationalist challenges to its authority? Can it grant independence to Poland but deny it to Lithuania?

5. If the Soviet leadership resorts to the use of massive force either within the borders of the Soviet Union or in Eastern Europe, how will it affect the future of perestroika, glasnost, and Gorbachev's own political life?

6. If, for whatever reason, Gorbachev fails, will the end of his rule stall or reverse the trend toward political and economic pluralism in Eastern Europe?

Of course, much depends on developments in Eastern Europe itself. Uncertainties over the *prospects within Eastern Europe* center around a second set of questions:

1. Will the region's crumbling communist parties and internal security forces—the KGBs of Eastern Europe—acquiesce in their own demise without attempting either a comeback or at least a bid to sabotage the transition to predominantly Western values and institutions?

2. Will the emerging mixed economies—state-owned and free-market—succeed and economic performance improve so that free, Western-style democracies can take root? If not, will frustration and despair prompt the peoples of Eastern Europe to escape from freedom and embrace populist, nationalist, or military rule—or even drift toward anarchy?

3. Will the end of Soviet domination of Eastern Europe lead to the escalation of old nationalist rivalries—as between Romania and Hungary, or between Poland and Germany, for example?

4. Will any of the region's countries withdraw from the Warsaw Pact and opt for neutrality? Will they give up their membership in the Council for Mutual Economic Assistance and seek to join Western economic institutions?

Finally, a third set of questions addresses the *role of the West* in general and that of the United States in particular:

1. How should the West help to make permanent the changes that have occurred in Eastern Europe and the Soviet Union?

2. Will the redefinition of the role, or the possible dissolution, of the Warsaw Pact—and therefore of NATO—affect Western security? How will the United States and its allies protect their security interests when the Soviet threat to Western Europe appears to have diminished?

3. How should the West respond to the unification of Germany? Should it be directed only by the principle of national self-determination, or should it be guided also by a historically justified concern over the role a strong Germany might play in European politics?

Given the magnitude of the problems ahead, it is tempting to draw unduly *pessimistic* conclusions about the future. Those who are inclined to do so should keep in mind that in 1988 and 1989 the unexpected became the norm in Eastern Europe. Why couldn't Poland and Hungary move from dictatorship to democracy in the 1990s in more or less the same way as Spain and Portugal did in the 1970s and 1980s? Conversely, those impressed by the momentous change that has already taken place may be tempted to draw unduly *optimistic* conclusions about the future. They should remember that the road ahead is very difficult. History offers too many examples of unfinished revolutions and, alas, failed ones as well.

Because of the uncertainties of the moment—because this

book is an assessment in the midst of such fast-changing times—I have selected as the subtitle "Soviet–East European Relations in Transition."

Part One reviews the evolution of Soviet policy in Eastern Europe from Stalin to Chernenko. Part Two examines the "early" Gorbachev reform era (1985–88) and its effect on Eastern Europe. Part Three considers the revolutionary upsurge of 1988–89—the extraordinary events of the recent past that will shape the future of Europe, East and West. The three chapters in Part Two that deal with the reformist, pre-1989 Gorbachev era are written largely in the present tense. This is partly because some of the information they contain is still pertinent, partly because most of Part Two was drafted just prior to or during the 1989 revolutions. I kept the present tense in order to stress the dramatic difference between the early Gorbachev era of 1985–88 and the revolutionary developments since then. Indeed, my main purpose is to explain how these events came to pass and to examine their implications for the rest of this century.

I am pleased to acknowledge the generous financial support of the Ford Foundation and of the National Council for Soviet and East European Research. Grants received from these two sources were initiated and administered by the Soviet and East European Studies Program of the Center for Strategic and International Studies (CSIS) in Washington. Successive directors of the program, Thane Gustafson and Stephen Sestanovich, nudged me along in a friendly but persistent way. Professor Gustafson was also responsible for creating and organizing a study group of leading scholars who reviewed my work over a period of two years and helped clarify what should and what should not be included int his essay. I wish to thank Sarah Terry, who chaired the panel of experts, and my colleagues who participated at its meetings: Madeleine Albright, Ed Hewett, Ross Johnson, Andrzej Korbonski, Ronald Linden, and Angela Stent. The coordinator of the program at CSIS, Alice Young, was helpful all along. Claire Rosensen of CSIS was my most able research assistant.

I am also indebted to my friends Paul Marer and Ivan Volgyes for their detailed critique of an earlier version of Chapters 4 and 5, respectively, and to students at Georgetown University (where I was a visiting professor in the fall of 1988) who read and evaluated the manuscript.

I am grateful to Anne Mandelbaum, editor and friend extraordinary, for being there at the end when I needed her advice most. I will say it in Slakan, the immortal East European language invented by Malcolm Bradbury and reserved for special occasions: Multo grussi!

Any errors of fact and interpretation are, of course, mine.

January 1, 1990

Part One

—————

LOOKING
BACK

I

STALIN AND SOCIALISM
IN ONE REGION

Strange Bedfellows

AS TIMES CHANGE, new terms come into currency—or old
terms acquire new meanings. Take "Eastern Europe." Before
1945 geographers had seldom identified such a region; when
they had, the region so described was the European part of
the Soviet Union, the area west of the Ural Mountains. Of the
six states of what is *now* called Eastern Europe, four—(East)
Germany, Poland, Czechoslovakia, and Hungary—had been
recognized to be in *Central Europe*, while two—Romania and
Bulgaria—in *Southeastern Europe* (or the Balkans).

The map provides ample justification for questioning
Eastern Europe as a geographic entity. Look at a map. While
Prague (the capital of Czechoslovakia) is to the north*west* of
Vienna (the capital of Austria), Czechoslovakia is now said to
belong to Eastern Europe and Austria to Western Europe. Curious, isn't it? More confusing yet, in some accounts Greece
is now placed in Western Europe despite the fact that it is located to the south*east* of every state that has been assigned
to Eastern Europe. It doesn't make sense, does it? In terms
of geography, it certainly does not; yet, politically, the new
terminology has served a purpose.

The Soviet Union perpetrated a hoax in the aftermath of
World War II. When it forcibly reoriented the politics and eco-

nomics of these six states in Central and Southeastern Europe at that time, it began calling them the "people's democracies" of Eastern Europe. Its apparent goal was to make it appear that the Soviet Union had more in common with them than it in fact did. If all *seven* were in Eastern Europe, did they not all have a common heritage, and hence was it not natural and logical that they should be marching together toward the same destiny?

In point of fact—and despite similarities among the Slavic languages and cultures of Bulgaria, Czechoslovakia, Poland, and Russia itself—the six countries of "Eastern Europe" had not had much in common with their large eastern neighbor or even with one another. For example, their foreign trade had been oriented largely toward Germany, certainly not toward Russia. The political tradition of such Slavic neighbors as the Czechs and the Poles was no more similar than that of the very different Hungarians and Bulgarians. Moreover, though they had all belonged to the sphere of influence of one hegemon or another before World War I, they had nonetheless exercised considerable internal autonomy; some of them were particularly skillful at maneuvering between such contending empires as the Habsburg Monarchy, Russia, and Prussia, playing off one against the other. Later, between the two world wars and hence on the eve of the communist takeovers, they enjoyed full independence.

In the domestic realm, it is true that Western-style democracy, with its insistence on institutionalized pluralism and the merits of diversity, had not taken root in pre-communist Eastern Europe—except in Czechoslovakia and Germany. The practice of limiting executive power by constitutional means had remained but a legal fiction. The treatment of national and religious minorities had reflected widespread intolerance toward these minorities' "unusual" habits and life styles. It is revealing that in most languages of the area, then as now, the word "compromise" has always signified something unprincipled and perhaps even shameful.

Yet even as they belonged to or operated in the shadow of a powerful empire, these transitional or borderland states between East and West used to have functioning legislatures and indeed very lively and contentious parliamentary debates. As recorded in the parliamentary diaries of Hungary in the late nineteenth century or of Poland and Romania in the interwar years, such debates were also serious and at times significant. The rights of parliament were seldom violated. Within limits, the region's major parties could always be heard in their countries' legislatures.

There was also considerable freedom of the press, private enterprise, and religion throughout Eastern Europe during much of the nineteenth and twentieth centuries. That these freedoms were not absolute need not be interpreted to mean that they did not exist. Living in what may be called *semi-authoritarian* environments, Poles and Romanians, Bulgarians and Hungarians enjoyed access to information in their newspapers, pursued individual economic ambitions, and practiced religious beliefs. In short, the pre-communist domestic order in the area—no doubt more so in Central Europe than in Southeastern Europe—had signified strong parliamentary traditions as well as certain limited freedoms granted by a normally powerful executive.

Given the semi-authoritarian tradition of Eastern Europe prior to 1945, it is therefore misleading to speak about a shared heritage and parallel development in Russia and the countries of Eastern Europe. They used to be (and still are) strange bedfellows indeed. It is equally misleading to suggest that the harsh and (at least in 1945) totalitarian Soviet model of socialism fell on fertile soil in Eastern Europe. After all, Poland's political past had been no more authoritarian than Finland's and Hungary's no more authoritarian than Austria's— and yet both Finland and Austria have grown to become properly functioning, pluralistic democracies. The postwar evolution of Poland and Hungary on the one hand and Finland and Austria on the other—or, indeed, of East and

West Germany—has had little or nothing to do with their traditions; it was the imposition of the Soviet pattern on Poland, Hungary, and East Germany and the absence of similar measures against Finland, Austria, and West Germany that account for their markedly different postwar development.

In another sense, however, postwar conditions did favor the extension of Soviet power into the heart of Europe. For one thing, it had become clear during the course of several wartime conferences of the allies—notably in Teheran (1943), Moscow (1944), and Yalta (1945)—that neither the United States nor Great Britain was prepared to challenge Soviet primacy in Eastern Europe. With the Red Army liberating almost the whole region from Nazi Germany, the West could not easily counter Soviet expansion. Also favoring the Soviet side was the change of guard—the extensive turnover of the political elites—throughout Eastern Europe. With the exception of Czechoslovakia, the pre-war regimes, having lost whatever legitimacy they might have enjoyed previously, had collapsed and hence there was to be no continuity with the past under any circumstances.

Moreover, some of the programs that the communists managed to champion did have considerable popular appeal at first. Land reforms proposed and largely implemented by them and their political allies could at least partly neutralize the peasantry in Poland, Hungary, and elsewhere. As even in Western Europe, the nationalization of large banks and industries was another popular issue the communists could promote—and claim credit for. They could also stimulate Polish nationalism by identifying themselves with the new Polish-German border and with the postwar expulsion of ethnic Germans from "new Poland." Although popular acceptance of such policies did not necessarily translate into active political support for the local communist parties, let alone for the Soviet Union, some of the highly cherished changes were nevertheless seen as a result of Soviet victory in World War II.

It was especially because of the absence of countervailing power in the international system, but also because of the domestic power vacuum that came to exist, then, that the communists enjoyed such an extraordinary positional advantage in postwar Eastern Europe. The lack of Western interest or will to contain the Soviet Union so soon after World War II provided Stalin's historic opportunity to transform the Red Army's momentous victories into an unparalleled expansion of Soviet power and influence. Having followed an essentially defensive foreign policy course in the interwar period, a time when a weak Soviet Union had focused on protecting "socialism in one country," Stalin presently perceived a power vacuum in Eastern Europe and hence a chance to create "socialism in one region."

It should be recalled that back in the mid-1920s Stalin had been the main advocate of the concept of "socialism in one country." In his heated debates with Leon Trotsky, Stalin had cautioned that the new Soviet state should first solidify itself, overcome internal opposition and deflect external hostility, and only when the correlation of forces in the world would favor such a policy should the Soviet Union extend significant support for revolutionaries abroad.

By contrast, Trotsky's concept of "permanent revolution" signified a more immediately militant position. In Trotsky's view, Moscow should make it a priority to press for communist revolutions for two reasons. One was that, according to Marxist-Leninist theory, the revolutionary process cannot be confined to victory in one country; it must be followed by others. The other, more pragmatic reason had to do with the defense of the Soviet homeland, which in Trotsky's view required the establishment of communist regimes that would help protect the world's first socialist state. Unlike Stalin, then, Trotsky even at this early date was prepared to take chances and indeed to use Soviet power to promote communism. As he once put it, "Not believing in force is the same as not believing in gravity."

Of course, Stalin also believed in force and in promoting communism abroad; he was no wishy-washy nationalist. He had relied on force at home to consolidate his power. His rise to unquestioned preeminence after 1928 was followed by the death of some twenty million Soviet citizens, many of whom were murdered; his victims had greatly outnumbered Hitler's. Nor did Stalin shy away from helping revolutionary causes abroad. Under Soviet control from the beginning, the Third International or Comintern (1919–43) directed the activities of dozens of militant communist parties in Europe, including Eastern Europe. Without much success, to be sure, these parties had nevertheless worked ceaselessly to overthrow established governments—until the mid-1930s when Stalin's and the Comintern's new party line called for the coalitionary, so-called Popular Front strategy of cooperation with all countries and political forces opposed to nazism and fascism.

In contrast to his brutal policies at home, however, Stalin did not pursue an aggressive or even particularly ambitious foreign policy prior to World War II. He had calculated the correlation of forces in the world and decided against an expansionist course. He had signed treaties and made deals with capitalist states—the "international class enemy"—in the 1930s and of course during World War II. In 1939, when he saw the survival of the Soviet Union at stake, he concluded the Nazi-Soviet Pact. Indeed, his major expansionist drive— the forceful reabsorption of the three independent Baltic states of Estonia, Latvia, and Lithuania in 1940—took place only after Hitler had explicitly consented to it (in exchange for Stalin's consent to the German occupation of Poland in 1939). Even after the war, fearful of Western reaction, he was cautious enough not to attempt the formal incorporation of Eastern Europe into the Soviet Union—even though many in the region and in the West feared he would make just such an attempt.

Yet even this most circumspect guardian of Soviet state interests could not but rejoice when faced with the postwar opportunity to project Soviet power into the heart of Europe. At last, the correlation of forces in the world favored the export of communist revolutions to a large, diverse, and in many ways critical region that was to be known as "Eastern Europe."

Satellization

Initially, the Soviet bloc was made up of the Soviet Union and the eight so-called "people's democracies." In addition to Bulgaria, Czechoslovakia, East Germany, Hungary, Poland, and Romania, it included Yugoslavia and Albania as well. But Yugoslavia, where indigenous communist forces under Marshal Tito's leadership had liberated that country largely on their own, was able to defy Stalin, leave the bloc, and establish an independent communist state in 1948–49—still under Stalin's watch and to his utter dismay. Albania, which was by far the smallest and least developed member of the Soviet orbit, and which has continued to revere Stalin to this day, was to adopt an independent if extremely militant communist course in the early 1960s.

The formation of the Soviet bloc comprised two, frequently overlapping processes. Completed by 1947–48, the first was the process of what is often called *satellization*: the binding of the region's states to the Soviet Union. Increasingly after 1944, key decisions were made in Moscow rather than Warsaw or Sofia. The other process that began in 1944–45 but greatly accelerated only after 1947–48 is often called *Sovietization*: the transformation of the region's domestic political, economic, and social structures, institutions, and patterns according to Soviet norms and values.

While satellization ensured that the East European states would be Soviet allies, Sovietization ensured that they would imitate and even duplicate the Soviet model in their internal arrangements.

Despite differences in timing and circumstances, the process of satellization—of gradually inducing compliance with Soviet objectives in each of the East European countries—followed more or less the same general pattern.

During the *first* phase, the region's communist parties tended to cooperate with other political parties— social democrats, agrarians, liberals—within the framework of broadly based, genuine coalition governments. The aim was to make use of practically all elements in society in order to gain their help in the war still being waged against Germany and in rebuilding the region's war-torn economies.

In the *second* phase, the multiparty governments gave way to bogus or pseudo-coalitions in which the communist parties, already the preponderant force, still allowed for the participation of such non-communists who would do their bidding—mostly feeble opportunists known as fellow-travelers. They were used to help placate Western and domestic critics.

Finally, during the *third* phase, with the process of satellization completed and hence the commanding heights of power already in hand, Sovietization became the primary task. The monolithic communist regimes could thus press for domestic transformation along Soviet lines.

Within this general pattern, details varied from country to country:

The genuinely pluralistic coalition regime lasted longest in *Czechoslovakia*. With the liberal and ambitious Eduard Beneš as president, Czechoslovakia sought a special role for itself—that of becoming a "bridge" between East and West. Mindful of Soviet preferences, Beneš was prepared to reject what he called "the purely political conception of democracy in a liberalistic [Western] sense." But his concessions failed to appease Stalin long, at least partly because the Czechoslovak Communist Party—unlike all others in the region—enjoyed widespread support: in the free elections of May 1946 it received 38 percent of the vote. Still, the communists did not seize power until February 1948, a few months after the newly founded Communist Information Bureau (Cominform) had ordered all communist parties in Europe to adopt a more militant strategy.

In *Hungary*, the multiparty coalition government survived until mid-1947. It was dominated by the popular Smallholders' Party, which obtained an absolute majority of the votes (57 percent) in the November 1945 elections—in contrast to the Communist Party's 17 percent. Yet, given the Red Army's intimidating presence and the effective penetration by the communists of all other parties, the communists could have seized full control of the country as soon as the war was over. They decided not to do so. Like its counterpart in Czechoslovakia, the Hungarian Communist Party was under instructions from Stalin to support the pluralistic phase for a few years in deference to Western sensitivities. "The Soviet Union must win the diplomatic battle in order to win decisive influence in Hungary" is how Ernő Gerő, the party's deputy leader, explained the rationale for the coalitionary strategy at a closed meeting of activists in 1945, adding that the Hungarian (and, presumably, Czechoslovak) communists must "not scare the Anglo-Americans" for the time being.[1]

Elsewhere in the region, the pluralistic phase lasted but a few months or not at all—and free elections were never held.

In *Bulgaria*, the government was initially in the hands of Zveno (The Link), a semi-military group that was to do what the Bulgarian communists, lacking in popular appeal, could

---

1. For the source of Gerő's statement, and the circumstances in which it was delivered, see Gati, *Hungary and the Soviet Bloc*, p. 21.

not effectively do: organize Bulgaria's reentry into the war on the Soviet side. Having played that role for a few short months in the late fall and early winter of 1944–45, and then having outlived its usefulness, Zveno was promptly reduced to a supportive role in the emerging pseudo-coalition government thoroughly dominated by the Bulgarian Communist Party.

In *Romania's* first cabinet, formed in August 1944, military men also outnumbered civilians, including representatives of the tiny Romanian Communist Party. The reason was the same as in Bulgaria: Moscow needed the prestige of noncommunist generals to mobilize the Romanian army against Germany. With King Michael as the nominal head of state and with the leader of the Communist Party and the leaders of the three other major parties serving as ministers without portfolio, the first government's composition reflected a measure of continuity with the past. But the days of the coalition were numbered. Soviet deputy foreign minister Andrei Vyshinski presented the king with an ultimatum at the end of February 1945. Either the king would appoint the fellow-traveler Petru Groza as premier or Romania would cease to exist as a sovereign state. Vyshinski is said to have given the king two hours and five minutes(!) to comply. Fearing annexation, the king did what he was ordered to do.

In Germany's Soviet zone of occupation—the area that was to become *East Germany*—a four-party coalition was formed to administer the zone's affairs soon after Berlin's liberation. Its authority was defined, and strictly limited, by the Soviet military command. In less than a year, the coalition composed of the Communist Party, the Social Democratic Party, the Christian Democratic Party, and the Liberal Democratic Party came to an end. In April 1946, the communists forced the social democrats into a new Socialist Unity Party (SED), hoping that the traditional popularity of German social democracy would help the united party to sweep the forthcoming local elections in the fall. The results were indicative of intimidation and cheating: While the SED received about half of the votes cast in the provinces under Soviet occupation, in the three Western sectors of Berlin it could draw only 10.3 percent (British sector), 12.3 percent (U.S. sector), and 21.2 percent (French sector) of the vote.

In *Poland*, then as always the key East European country in Soviet eyes, the actual division in the government formed in June 1945 was between the "Lublin Poles" who were pro-Soviet, and the "London Poles" who were pro-Western. With sixteen of the twenty-one ministries held by members of the "Lublin" group (named after the East Polish city where the first provisional government was formed), the government was a pseudo-coalition from the beginning. The few non-communists included in it were either such fellow-travelers as the social democrat Józef Cyrankiewicz, or were effectively isolated and powerless, such as Stanisław Mikolajczyk, leader of the People's (Peasant) Party. However short-lived the coalitionary game that Moscow had devised for much of Eastern Europe, it was apparently not meant for Poland, by far the largest, most populous, most important, as well as the most volatile country in the emerging Soviet bloc.

Early Problems

In compelling all Eastern European states to submit to his will and turning them into Soviet satellites, Stalin encountered several difficulties.

First, throughout the second half of the 1940s Stalin remained deeply concerned about Western reactions; he could never be sure what the United States and Great Britain might do. Of course, most of Eastern Europe was occupied by the Red Army, and during the war the Western allies had all but conceded the region to Soviet influence. Yet it was not clear whether Soviet *domination* would be accepted; if not, what was the likely course that the West, especially the United

States, would adopt? By 1947 in particular, with the cold war underway, what should Stalin make of President Harry S Truman's promise that the United States would "support free peoples who are resisting subjugation by armed minorities or by outside pressures"?[2] While Truman was apparently referring only to Greece and Turkey, what if his doctrine applied, or would be applied, to Eastern Europe as well? Stalin could not be sure.

Stalin's uncertainty about Western intentions and reactions had prompted him to instruct the Czechoslovak and Hungarian communists to proceed only gradually toward the seizure of power. Among the initiated few, his policy was known as the "Polish trade-off": an attempt to compensate the West for the rapid and often brutal takeovers in Poland— and elsewhere along the Soviet border and in East Germany—by allowing for a somewhat longer pluralistic interlude in Czechoslovakia and Hungary. Zoltán Vas, a Hungarian Politburo member at the time, has since revealed that the Hungarian Communist Party leadership was uncertain *even in 1946* whether "Stalin might not let Hungary [and presumably Czechoslovakia] come under the political influence of the [Western] allies in exchange for Soviet demands on Poland and Germany." Given what is known today, the thought of such "trade-offs" may seem fanciful; yet, at that time, Stalin's concern about Western countermeasures was very real indeed.

Second, learning how to govern—alone or with other parties—proved to be a novel and difficult task for all of the East European communist parties. The "revolutions" exported to the region by the Soviet Union lacked authenticity; they did not arise from domestic circumstances. Although only in Poland was there armed resistance, the communist parties—with the exception of Czechoslovakia's—did not

---

2. The text of the Truman Doctrine of 1947 is reprinted in Gati, *Caging the Bear*, pp. 3–8.

enjoy any significant popular support. As the war came to an end, party membership stood at about 25,000 in Bulgaria, 20,000 in Poland, 2,500 in Hungary, 2,000 in Romania, and probably no more than a few hundred in East Germany (of whom many were so-called "Muscovites": communist exiles returning from the Soviet Union). Thus, Czechoslovakia aside, the Soviet Union could count on no more than only 50,000 or so dedicated supporters in these five countries, whose population was about 75 million at that time.

The communist parties had to work hard to gain new adherents. Intimidation was not enough. They had to prove themselves to be genuine patriots rather than Moscow's agents. Anticipating the problems ahead, Stalin had advised a group of communist leaders in 1944: "Soviet power cannot do everything for you. You must do the fighting, you must do the work." But "doing the work" meant that the parties had to preoccupy themselves with practical, local issues of politics and economics at the expense of fulfilling their revolutionary, so-called "internationalist" duties. The leader of Polish communists, Władysław Gomułka, had to remind some of his puzzled, "sectarian" comrades, who, he said, had failed to understand the "new situation," to "think with the categories of the nation, of the state in which we now cogovern": they should be or should appear to be Poles concerned with Poland rather than communists concerned with the "international class struggle."

Looking inward and thus giving domestic issues rather than international communism top consideration—a tendency Zbigniew Brzezinski would later call the early "domesticism" of the communist parties of Eastern Europe— contributed to the region's incipient diversity. A forerunner of national communism, "domesticism" contained the seeds of conflict between the Soviet Union and its new dependencies. One example of this occurred in the summer of 1947 when, guided by domestic needs, three East European countries—Czechoslovakia, Poland, and Hungary—expressed interest in accepting an American invitation to participate in the Marshall Plan. They saw nothing wrong at first with trying to gain access to hard currency and foreign credits—until Stalin abruptly reminded them that the Marshall Plan was but an "imperialist machination." In this case as in so many others, the East European communists learned the hard way how in the end they must subordinate their domestic concerns to Soviet-dictated internationalist obligations.

Third, the most acute specific problem for Moscow in Eastern Europe was Yugoslavia's defection from the Soviet orbit in 1948–49. As mentioned previously, Marshal Tito's forces had liberated their country without much foreign assistance, certainly without much Soviet assistance. Even then, during World War II, the Yugoslav communists were having some differences with Stalin who had repeatedly cautioned them against a too-rapid seizure of power. Although in the aftermath of the Yalta conference of the Big Three in February 1945, Tito obliged Stalin by coopting a few noncommunists into his government, he still wanted to make Yugoslavia the first "dictatorship of the proletariat" outside the Soviet Union itself. Loyal to Moscow, admiring of Stalin, and yet deeply proud of his own achievements too, Tito resented what Stalin regarded as wise Soviet counsel and assistance and what Tito regarded as unduly cautious advice as well as Soviet interference in the internal affairs of another socialist country.

For its part, to no avail did the Soviet Union mobilize its own and Eastern Europe's armed forces, use so-called "Cominformist" agents—Yugoslavs who were loyal to Cominform—to undermine the Tito regime from within, undertake what amounted to economic warfare, and even excommunicate the "Tito clique" from the communist camp. To no avail did the Soviet and the satellite press engage in namecalling—referring day in and day out to "Judas Tito and his abettors," to "this bankrupt group of sharks," to "dogs tied to American leashes," to these "sinister heralds of the camp of war and death," to "the worthy heirs of Hitler," and to "a gang of spies, provocateurs, and murderers." Backed by an almost completely united Yugoslav leadership and by the Yugoslav people, too, Tito stood firm.

Yugoslavia's ability to withstand such extraordinary pressures and then pursue an independent communist course to be called "national communism" revealed for all to see the limits of Stalin's power even in his own backyard. The Soviet-Yugoslav split shattered both the communist claim and the Western illusion that those who shared the same Marxist-Leninist ideology could not develop significant differences among themselves; that the usual conflict of national interests among sovereign states somehow did not apply to communist states.

Perhaps most important, Yugoslavia's independence offered an alternative to others in Soviet-controlled Eastern Europe. This is why it is all but impossible to exaggerate Yugoslavia's impact on subsequent developments in several East European countries and their relationship with Moscow. Without Yugoslavia it is impossible to understand what the likes of the Hungarian Imre Nagy and the Polish Władysław Gomułka were to do in the mid-1950s or what the Czechoslovak Alexander Dubček would do in the late 1960s. Tito established a precedent for autonomy and, later, reform in the communist world—in Soviet eyes, a very dangerous precedent at that time.

As subsequent developments would amply demonstrate, Stalin did not appear to have drawn the proper lesson from his encounter with Yugoslavia. He could have realized that heavy-handed Soviet policies—particularly the overcentralization of the bloc—were counterproductive. He could have realized that while the region's small- and medium-sized countries might have learned to live with an influential Soviet Union, excessive Soviet interference was bound to breed strong opposition among the East European people and ultimately even among their communist leaders as well. Instead of adjusting Soviet policies to East European realities, however, Stalin was determined to compel Eastern Europe to duplicate Soviet realities. Instead of taking at least a tactical or temporary step backward—as he had done in his dealings with capitalist states before and during World War II—this time Stalin wanted to show that the Soviet way was the only way, that the Soviet model he had shaped at home had universal applicability.

In part, Stalin was dizzy with success. The Soviet bloc was in place, "socialism in one region" was to be his historic accomplishment. Six countries with a population of about 90 million at that time (the same as Great Britain's) and covering an area of 380,000 square miles (over four times the size of Great Britain) were under his control. In military terms, the Soviet Union was the most powerful state in Europe. In part, Stalin was also prompted by his failures and fears: his failure to prevent Yugoslavia's defection and his fear that others would follow Tito's example. In part, finally, his inability to divide and immobilize the West induced his anxiety that the new cold war then underway would lead to a new world war, an anxiety reinforced by the Truman Doctrine of 1947 and then, much later, by the Korean war of 1950–53.

Sovietization

Hence, at the end of 1947, Stalin proceeded to *accelerate* the processes of Sovietization. He attempted to turn the satellites into small replicas of the Soviet Union and in that way further consolidate his hold over his new dominion. The period from about 1948 to Stalin's death in March 1953 also became known as the era of "high Stalinism" in Eastern Europe.

In the political realm, Sovietization entailed substantial changes in East European domestic institutions and policies. The governments were assigned the role of implementing decisions made partly by Moscow, partly by the several communist parties' Politburos, Secretariats, and the offices of the general secretaries. As in the Soviet Union, the head of the government was no longer called "premier" or "prime minister" but "the Chairman of the Council of Ministers." Following the Russian word *soviet*, local governments became "councils." The power of the secret police—"the ears and eyes of the revolution"—so increased as to generate fear among all, communists included. If earlier an average citizen had been harassed and punished for being against the regime, he could now be tortured even for having shown insufficient support for the regime. Formerly that citizen had been told only what not to do; now he was also told what he must do.

Sovietization thus signified the introduction of Soviet totalitarianism into Eastern Europe. One of its features was the repetition on a smaller scale of what had happened in the Soviet Union in the 1930s: the widespread purges—the jailing and killing—of communists. Those who were so purged in Eastern Europe were loyal supporters of the Soviet Union. They showed no signs of favoring "Titoism" or "national communism"—of which they were accused—and they did not deviate from the Moscow-ordained party line. For example, the Czechoslovak Rudolf Slánský, his party's general secretary, or the Hungarian László Rajk, formerly a minister of internal affairs and hence the person in charge of the secret police, were actually thought to have belonged to the more militant wing of their parties. Now they were charged of conspiring with all sorts of countries, including Yugoslavia and the United States, against the Soviet Union and the people's democracies. Years later, when it was publicly admitted that the charges had been fabricated, the victims were posthumously rehabilitated.

Why the Stalinist show trials in Eastern Europe then? Why the killing of fellow communists? The only explanation was, and is, that in the aftermath of the Yugoslav affair Stalin felt compelled to fight "domesticism" and reaffirm his leadership over the international communist movement—and he did it, so to speak, by flexing his muscles. It was a Stalin-style power play, with thousands of victims whose trials were meant to demonstrate who was in charge.

In the economic realm, the postwar nationalization of banks and industry was also followed by measures modeled on Soviet conditions and practices. These measures included the collectivization of agriculture (everywhere but in Poland) and the closing of even the smallest privately owned services and retail outlets as well. The local equivalents of Gosplan, the huge Soviet planning bureaucracy, took control of the East European economies. These new offices were staffed by members of the party apparatus who were devoted to planning and centralization as the rational alternative to the ills of the capitalist marketplace.

Despite the existence of the Council for Mutual Economic Assistance by 1949, and despite much talk thereafter about division of labor and regional integration, CMEA was a dormant institution from the beginning. Indeed, economic Sovietization between 1948 and 1953 meant the opposite of the division of labor; it meant economic autarky or self-sufficiency. For, in practice, each East European country was directed both to duplicate the Soviet experience and develop whatever it needed on its own. Hence the extraordinary build-up of heavy industry in countries that in most cases lacked energy for, say, new steel mills. The same countries also lacked the infrastructure, the personnel, and in all too many instances even the possibility to sell what they made. Stories abound of wasted resources, misplaced investments, and unnecessary products.

If anything, the damage done to agriculture was even greater. In effect, collectivization negated the early postwar achievements—and good will—of the East European peasantry. After the 1945 land reforms had realized the age-old dream of peasants to own their land, they responded by bringing food to the cities; they made a significant contribution to postwar reconstruction. After collectivization deprived them of their land, however, the peasants responded by withholding food; they obstructed in a major way the policies of the emerging Stalinist economic order.

Why such centralization, autarky, and rapid collectivization? The simple answer is that Stalin knew no economic alternative. The more complex answer is that, in addition, he sought to synchronize the region's economies with the Soviet Union's in preparation for World War III. As he was presently doing in his own country, he squeezed consumption below reasonable levels, increased investments in heavy industry beyond realistic levels, and hence, in effect, militarized the East European economic systems. This can be presumed to have been his intention. In practice, his economic policies made Eastern Europe neither stronger nor more self-sufficient. Not incidentally, these policies only served to further discredit the ideals of socialism in Eastern Europe.

Sovietization in the cultural realm has been called "Zhdanovshchina," so named after the Kremlin's cultural watchdog and ideological czar at the time, Andrei Zhdanov. In Eastern Europe the period marked the introduction of "socialist realism" and the Leninist notion of *partinost* or "party-mindedness" in literature, music, and the arts. Writers and artists—whom Stalin had called "the engineers of human soul"—were told to produce works featuring "positive heroes" the people would want to emulate. The positive heroes worked hard for the common good and admired the wise Stalin.

The period also marked the celebration of Soviet achievements, real or imagined, in every possible area of human activity, from science to culture to sports. For one example, high school students were taught that a Russian scientist had discovered the x-ray before the German physicist Wilhelm Roentgen had ever thought of it. At the same time, the region's educational system was changed to correspond to the Soviet pattern. Admission to the universities was based less on talent and promise than on social origin, meaning that the sons and daughters of workers and so-called "poor peasants" received highly preferential treatment.

In ideology, Stalin's main contribution was the theory of the "constantly sharpening class struggle." His point was that, contrary to what Marx and Lenin had expected, socialist construction did not signify the gradual disappearance of the class enemy. Though it was said to have been defeated, its "remnants" continued to work ceaselessly to recapture their old power and reverse the gains of socialism. The class enemy was to be found both at home and abroad. At home, which is to say in the Soviet Union and Eastern Europe, it included not only former capitalists and rich peasants but also all others who were still influenced by a reactionary, petit-bourgeois mentality. Abroad the class enemy included the reactionary, capitalist states, notably the United States. East Europeans were told day in and day out to be vigilant against the machinations of domestic and foreign enemies. Thus the new theory served to draw the sharpest possible distinction between the forces of light (led, of course, by the Soviet Union) and the increasingly dangerous forces of darkness (led, of course, by the United States). In the Manichean image of Stalin and Zhdanov, the world was divided into "two camps."

All in all, Sovietization in the late 1940s and early 1950s signified the penetration of Eastern Europe by Soviet institutions, policies and values. It also signified what, after his death, would be called Stalin's "personality cult." Indeed, with Stalin's pictures and statues everywhere, with the most prominent boulevards and squares named after him, with poets saving their best lines for odes devoted to him, with people forced to rise at the mention of his name (and of the local party leader's) and burst into long and rhythmic applause—Long live Stalin! Long live Gottwald! *or* Rákosi! *or* Bierut!—what with all that and more Stalin made himself at home in Eastern Europe. This was Sovietization. Conversely, the East European people felt decreasingly at home in their own countries. This, too, was Sovietization.

What Did Stalin Achieve?

The long-held, historical dream of czars and commissars, the postwar conquest of Eastern Europe served a number of Soviet military, economic, and political objectives. Alas, proper understanding of the nature and scope of these objectives could not be gained from Stalin's or other Soviet or East European officials' self-serving statements, which tended to conceal more than they revealed. Denying the role of coercion, of course, these statements pointed to a natural historical evolution that was said to have transformed the region from its "semi-feudal" condition into "people's democracies," a transitional political order on the road to socialism.

In the realm of Soviet–East European relations, Soviet as well as official East European writings claimed that relations were basically harmonious from the beginning, that "international relations of a new type" came to characterize the region's inter-state relations. Such harmony could be achieved, it was said, because the "wise Stalin"—his name was seldom mentioned without this and other flattering adjectives—properly understood the dynamics of history and offered "fraternal advice" rooted both in Marxist-Leninist ideology and the momentous experiences of the world's first socialist state.

Nothing could be further from the truth.

While it is admittedly difficult to ascertain what combination of interests guided Soviet policy, it is clear that *geopolitical* interests—concerns about security—topped Stalin's list. However, security signified full control; Stalin was not satisfied with the prospect of an Eastern Europe that would not become an anti-Soviet Eastern Europe. Because of the peculiarities of Russian history, Leninist ideology, and his own psychological make-up, Stalin believed that those who were not with him were against him, that those who did not actively and even blindly support the Soviet Union were "objectively" the enemies of socialism and the Soviet state.

Thus, to repeat, the Stalinist notion of security signified Eastern Europe's complete subordination to Soviet geopolitical interests. To Stalin, these interests meant that the region must be turned into something more than a mere defensive buffer zone; it was also to be used as a staging ground from which Western Europe could be politically and even militarily intimidated and indeed kept off balance.

In Stalin's time, the region's *economic* exploitation was certainly another Soviet objective. In part, this was accomplished by demanding and receiving large reparations from such wartime enemies as East Germany, Hungary, and Romania. In part, Soviet economic benefits accrued from the Red Army's theft of whatever could be moved, including whole factories and technical personnel; from the so-called joint companies whose output, instead of being shared by the Soviet Union and an East European country, was largely transferred to the Soviet Union; and, after the East European economies had come to life, from buying the region's products at unreasonably low prices. According to Paul Marer, a leading American expert on the subject, the total value of Soviet economic benefits so obtained in the second half of the 1940s and early 1950s approached a stunning $14 billion. In effect, Eastern Europe was forced to subsidize the Soviet Union's postwar economic recovery and its preparation for World War III.

Soviet *political and ideological* interests seem to have mattered as much as or more than economic considerations. For with the gradual decline and eventual collapse of every other European empire, the Soviet Union emerged from the war not only as a military but as a political arbiter of the old continent. Gaining ground in Eastern Europe also pointed to the wisdom of Stalin's prewar circumspection ("socialism in one country") *and* his postwar expansion ("socialism in one region"); after all, his postwar success proved him right on the issue of when communist revolutions should be attempted (i.e., only when the correlation of forces in the world favored them).

Moreover, with the Soviet model transferred there, Eastern Europe could also serve as a more relevant example for others to follow—in the West, perhaps, but especially in the former Western colonies of Asia and Africa. Finally, by having generated considerable pride in Soviet power and prestige abroad, Moscow's postwar gains appeared to strengthen the Soviet system at home. As these gains conferred a measure of legitimacy to Stalin's domestic order, they also reinvigorated the revolutionary zeal and enhanced the momentum of the communist movement everywhere.

Guided by these interests, how did Stalin manage to obtain such an extraordinary military, economic, and political/ ideological gain for the Soviet Union? The question is important because victory in war, the intimidating presence of the Red Army, and Western reluctance to confront Moscow over Eastern Europe made Soviet expansion possible. While these were necessary conditions, there were other factors, techniques and circumstances that mattered as well.

For one thing, the region's communist parties, however small at the beginning, turned out to be more united than their social democratic or agrarian political opponents. Here and there in the communist parties there was tension between those who had spent the war years in the Soviet Union (the "Muscovites") and those who had stayed behind participating in the resistance movements (the "native" communists), and of course there were the usual personal rivalries everywhere, but on the whole the communist parties were more disciplined and cohesive than their political adversaries. There were few communists at the beginning, but Stalin could count on their blind loyalty. Some of their leaders even retained their Soviet citizenship.

Second, the early capture throughout the region of the secret or political police—all of whom had been aided by high-level Soviet advisers—provided an opportunity to intimidate all who dared to criticize or even express reservations about communism or the Soviet Union. In the aftermath of World War II, any critic called "fascist" or "anti-democratic" could be charged, detained, and tortured. Tens of thousands of innocent people simply disappeared. Later on, during the years of high Stalinism, many more disappeared without being charged at all.

Third, Stalin held extraordinary authority among communists everywhere. For the admittedly few but energetic "true believers," his name was synonymous with Marxism, Leninism, progress, the communist utopia. No one questioned his version of Marxism or Leninism. Of course, he ruled by terror. Of course, his terror eventually aimed at leading communist officials too. Yet even in those years of Stalinist tyranny there remained an idealistic orientation among communists who believed in Stalin and in his promise of a harmonious socialist future. Blind fanatics, perhaps, but their seemingly unshakable confidence and faith were inspired by Stalin's charisma. Under the spell of communist fundamentalism, many of those who served Stalin in Eastern Europe genuinely believed that the sacrifices he had asked for were needed to purify the movement; only then could the sacred goal of communism be realized.

This is why Stalin's apparent lack of interest in establishing proper *institutional ties* between the Soviet Union and Eastern Europe did not yet matter. Of course, there was the Cominform after 1947 and the CMEA after 1949, and there were numerous bilateral treaties and agreements that constituted the formal foundation of the Soviet bloc. But the institutions that Stalin created were few and hollow. What mattered was Stalin's will and his immense personal authority among communists everywhere (even, to an extent, in Yugoslavia). This is what made it possible for Soviet interests to be implemented either directly through Stalin's agents or indirectly through his band of loyal and fanatic East European supporters.

What did he achieve then? What did he leave behind for his successors? What does the balance sheet show?

On the positive side of the ledger:

(1) Anticipating another conventional war, Stalin endowed the Soviet Union with an impressive dominion of considerable geopolitical worth. He enhanced Soviet power both by the territory he gained and even more by the impression he created that the Soviet Union was a great power capable of, and perhaps even entitled to, having client states under its control.

(2) He extracted substantial economic benefits for the Soviet state at a time of great need.

(3) To his own people, he demonstrated that Leninist systems can be built outside the Soviet Union and that the Soviet system therefore represented the wave of the future.

(4) He significantly advanced the process, begun in the 1920s, of subordinating international communism to Soviet state interests. With the exception of Yugoslavia, he prevented defections from what was then the world communist movement.

On the negative side of the ledger:

(1) Stalin failed to establish a workable system of political and economic inter-state relations in the Soviet bloc. Because of his highly personalized and centralized style of running it, he deprived the communist leaders of Eastern Europe of self-confidence, self-respect, and self-reliance in making decisions. They did not learn how to govern under conditions prevailing in their own countries. They could never know which decisions should be made by them and which ones should be made by Stalin.

(2) The rigid imposition of the Soviet economic model not only entailed excessive reliance on Soviet natural resources,

it also signified the inhibition of proper East European economic specialization in areas of local strength. The result for all of Eastern Europe, and ultimately for the Soviet Union, too, turned out to be catastrophic.

(3) Because of his policy of satellization and Sovietization, Stalin stripped the people of Eastern Europe of even the illusion of autonomy and of a decent standard of living.

(4) Most important, the way Stalin brought the East European communist parties to power deprived them of any claim to legitimacy. Its absence then, and the inability of the East European communist regimes to obtain legitimacy subsequently, remained the underlying source of the region's chronic instability.

Less inflicted by ideological imperatives and the black-and-white dichotomies of the Russian tradition, another hegemon might have interpreted his country's interests so as to seek only extensive influence rather than complete domination over Eastern Europe. But, given the geopolitical opportunity that presented itself, the political culture of which he was a product, and his personal predilection for controlling others, Stalin could do no less than what he did.

By the time of Stalin's death in March 1953, his policies had led to high tension among the elite and widespread popular dissatisfaction in several East European countries. To cope with Stalin's legacy, it remained for his successors in the Kremlin to look for new solutions and to initiate remedial action.

II

FROM KHRUSHCHEV
TO CHERNENKO
An Overview

Post-Stalin Soviet Concerns

AT STALIN'S FUNERAL, Foreign Minister and Politburo member Vyacheslav Molotov paid homage to the man "whom we have all loved so much and who will live in our hearts forever." All the others who spoke on the occasion expressed similar sentiments. They also underlined the need for unity and continuity. Did they mean what they said? Did Molotov recall that his own wife had been exiled to Siberia by Stalin for no apparent reason except that she was born Jewish? Did the others recall that while Stalin was around their own lives were never safe, that a show trial was an ever-present possibility?

What Stalin's heirs thought or felt cannot be known, of course, but subsequent actions would show their awareness that with the old tyrant gone things would not be the same again. It was also obvious, though, that they did not agree what should be changed and how much, and above all they did not agree on who should lead the pack.

During the course of Byzantine maneuverings for power between 1953 and 1957, the Soviet Union was first run by the triumvirate of Georgi Malenkov (Stalin's designated successor), Lavrenti Beria (the security chief), and Molotov; then -

by Malenkov, and then by Khrushchev (both, supposedly, as only first among equals). Only in May 1957 did Khrushchev emerge as the Kremlin's preeminent boss. Having won the struggle for power after four long years, he and his supporters immediately labeled the opposition as the "antiparty group." In point of fact, that group was made up of the Politburo *majority* that the Central Committee had defeated under highly unusual circumstances. The group included Malenkov, Molotov, Lazar Kaganovich, and others (but not Beria, who had been shot in 1953). While applying the term "antiparty group" to Khrushchev's opponents recalled Stalin's sharp rhetoric, it was a sign of changing times that, with Beria out of the way, obscurity rather than death awaited the losers.

Thus, the major domestic innovation of the post-Stalin era was the reduction of political terror aimed against the ruling elite. Called de-Stalinization only in the West, the new Soviet approach was officially designated as "socialist legality," a more accurate term because the Soviet leadership certainly did not reject all of Stalin's legacy. For example, in his momentous speech at the 20th Congress of the Communist Party of the Soviet Union (CPSU) in 1956, Khrushchev attacked Stalin but almost exclusively for the show trials of the 1930s (as well as for his "personality cult"), declaring that the charges against the victims had been total fabrications. Those who had survived the trials would be released, he added, while those who had not would be posthumously rehabilitated. At the same time, the new Soviet leaders continued to praise Stalin for his many other contributions, including his effort to build and protect the first socialist country in the world and to expand its power and influence. What the Kremlin did reject, then, was Stalin's seemingly permanent and certainly excessive terror against the Soviet leadership itself, the effect of which was the demoralization and hence the weakening of the CPSU.

Of course, the Kremlin's focus on "socialist legality" did not obviate the necessity of dealing with other pressing problems. In the economic realm, a so-called "New Course" signified a modest effort—soon shelved and then reinstated—to stress light industry and the vastly underdeveloped consumer sector. In the cultural realm, Stalin's death was followed by an early version of glasnost called "thaw"—the term taken from Ilya Ehrenburg's novel by the same name—that was intended to ease cultural rigidities and broaden the scope of intellectual discourse.

In foreign policy, the Kremlin's new emphasis on the Leninist notion of "peaceful coexistence" with the West, combined with the now publicly stated recognition that nuclear wars were not inevitable, indicated a desire to reduce international tension in order to gain a breathing spell. In 1955, the surprising withdrawal of the Soviet Army from the Soviet zone of occupation in Austria, coupled with the signing of a peace treaty that guaranteed that country's neutrality, raised new hopes—in both the East and the West—of finding a similar solution for divided Germany and hence reviving the spirit of good relations during World War II between the Soviet Union and the West.

Though the evidence is inconclusive, there were reports in 1953 and even later of a Soviet interest in modifying the status of the two Germanies. (In March 1952, similar reports had circulated under Stalin, too.) Presently, Khrushchev claimed that, after the bloody East Berlin riots of June 1953, Beria had considered the abandonment of East Germany—an unlikely tale. The Kremlin had no clear idea of what to propose, if anything, and what to take for what it might give if it were to propose something. If nothing else, the acute power struggle then underway excluded the adoption of any proposal of historic significance. Moreover, Soviet interests were not likely to have been served by changing the German status quo under any circumstances. As Adam Ulam has noted, the Kremlin merely hoped that the Austrian treaty "would have an educative effect on the [West] Germans," who would then consider removing themselves from NATO and "settle down to enjoy opera, beer, and tourists" instead. Still, such unexpected developments in Austria—a neighbor of both Czechoslovakia and Hungary in Eastern Europe—and the first U.S.-Soviet summit in a decade, both in 1955, brought new attention not only to the unnatural division of Germany but to Eastern Europe as well. After all, any consideration of Germany's future was likely to have far-reaching implications for the future of Eastern Europe too.

Recasting Policy toward Eastern Europe

It was the immediacy of reports about tension in Eastern Europe rather than the desire to eventually resolve the German issue that prompted the new Soviet leaders to place the condition of the bloc at or near the top of their agenda. For soon after Stalin's death, some of that long-suppressed tension in the area began to surface, especially in Hungary and Poland, and thus there was no time to waste. Even before the June 17, 1953 riots in East Berlin, which were unceremoniously crushed by Soviet tanks, the Kremlin had called in the Hungarian leadership for what turned into a harsh, even brutal reprimand.

At that unannounced meeting, held on June 13–14, 1953 with every important member of the Soviet Politburo in attendance, the Hungarians were told that the Kremlin was deeply dissatisfied with their performance. Whether similar sessions were held with other East European leaders is not known. If not, it is not clear why the Hungarians were singled out for such criticism. In any case, Mátyás Rákosi, Hungary's Stalinist dictator, was presently ordered to give up either his position as head of the government or his seat at the head of the party. The Kremlin's charges were serious: Rákosi held too much power, the Hungarian economy was on the verge of collapse, the forced collectivization campaign had gone too far, the show trials had decimated the party.

There and then, the Soviet leaders "proposed" the appointment of Imre Nagy as head of the government; Rákosi was to share power with Nagy and take others in the Politburo into his confidence as well. As it was said to be the case in the Soviet Union, there was to be "collective leadership" in Hungary, too. The program that the Hungarians were instructed to pursue also reflected prevailing Soviet priorities: light industry, consumer goods, improvements in the standard of living, rehabilitation of the victims of the purges, greater tolerance for cultural diversity.

The new personnel and the substantive changes introduced in Hungary so early constituted the first indication of the new Soviet leaders' approach to Eastern Europe.

For one thing, by blaming the Hungarians for Stalin's policies, they accepted no responsibility for the past. During the meeting with the Hungarians, neither the Soviet nor the Hungarian leaders present pointed out that whatever Rákosi had done was with the approval and indeed under orders of Soviet authorities. After all, did Rákosi decide on his own to favor heavy industry instead of light industry? Did he conceive of the bloody purges on his own? That the Soviet leaders were silent on this point was due in part to the still-professed infallibility of the CPSU and Moscow's still-professed "leading role" in the world communist movement. As to the Hungarians' silence, their fear of contradicting the Kremlin was no doubt a function of the pervasiveness of what might be called the "satellite mentality."

On the other hand, however, the Kremlin was also delivering a vague if significant message about the future division of responsibility in the bloc. At least some of the Hungarians—Imre Nagy, for sure—understood that in the future the East European communist leaders would be held accountable for what might go wrong in their countries. What they could decide and what would still be decided by the Kremlin was not made clear. But it was understood that from now on the East Europeans were on a longer leash. Presumably within general guidelines set by Moscow, they would be allowed to make more decisions on their own than in the past. They would have greater responsibility and a bit more leeway, perhaps, but not much more power. It appeared, then, that the new post-Stalin leadership in Moscow envisaged a minor shift in the Soviet–East European decision-making process, believing that a somewhat decentralized bloc would become a more stable bloc.

Put another way, the message conveyed to the Hungarians, combined with what the Kremlin was actually doing in the aftermath of Stalin's death, suggested that the modified, post-Stalin Soviet approach to Eastern Europe comprised two basic propositions:

(1) What was *unchanged* was the Soviet Union's continued commitment to the twin goals of bloc endurance and the maintenance of one-party communist regimes in Eastern Europe.

(2) What was *changed* was the Soviet Union's new willingness to make such concessions as were necessary to assure the bloc's endurance and the maintenance of one-party communist regimes.

To say that the new Soviet leaders thus wanted to have their cake and eat it too was, of course, true. To repeat, they were not about to relinquish Stalin's dominion. Yet some of the concessions they were prepared to make indicated considerable flexibility. It was a concession that they would gradually withdraw most Soviet advisors from the region and that they would leave the selection of even some high-level appointments to the discretion of each country's Politburo. It was a concession that they would begin to end Eastern Europe's economic exploitation, not because their own economic conditions had improved so much but because they were apprehensive about the impact of low living standards on the region's stability.

Thus, given their concern about the endurance of the bloc, the new Soviet leaders were hoping to find a solution that would let them save what they had without conceding more than what they deemed absolutely necessary to give up. Between the autonomy that they were unwilling to grant and the old subservient relationship that was proving to be counterproductive, they were looking for a happy middle ground made up of old *hegemonical habits* and slowly evolving *pragmatic flexibility*.

What the Kremlin thus perceived as a "middle ground" was to guide Soviet policy toward Eastern Europe for decades after Stalin's death. The underlying issue of Soviet hegemony was apparently never discussed or debated. The issue discussed and debated was the extent and scope of conciliatory measures needed to *assure* continued Soviet hegemony. How much decentralization in the bloc would provide for effective Soviet control and yet calm the region? What sorts of reform, economic and possibly political, should be tolerated to retain the bloc as a cohesive unit and yet help the region's communist regimes become viable? Could Moscow modify its insistence on communist unity by allowing for "national peculiarities"—and hence diversity—in the bloc?

Yugoslavia and National Communism

Allowing Eastern Europe a longer leash turned out to be too little, and it came too late. By the mid-1950s, there was growing pressure for more substantial economic and political changes in the region, especially in Poland and Hungary. Hungary's intellectuals were particularly vocal in demanding the expansion of "socialist democracy." In Poland, intellectuals and workers pressed for more freedom *and* more bread. The Kremlin's apparent flexibility was, of course, adding fuel to the fire: unwittingly, Moscow encouraged the rise of an atmosphere of national assertiveness.

Whatever the specific issues and demands, the underlying cause of discontent was the denial of nationalist aspirations.

Under prevailing conditions, these aspirations signified opposition to Soviet domination and hence pressure for self-determination. What made the situation different from earlier times was the fact that some of the region's communist leaders themselves responded favorably, if cautiously, to the growing appeal of national assertiveness. Specifically, deep divisions within the ruling elites set the so-called "national communists"—also known as "home communists" or "revisionists"—against the orthodox or dogmatic defenders of the Stalinist past.

The "national communists" could derive some courage not only from Tito's successful defiance of the Soviet Union but also from Moscow's current efforts to normalize Soviet-Yugoslav relations and indeed to entice Yugoslavia to return to the fold. For, in an attempt to contain Tito's radiating influence on Eastern Europe that had the potential to disrupt Moscow's hegemonical relations with the bloc, the Soviet Union took a dramatic step in 1955 to improve relations with Yugoslavia. Going well beyond what had only recently become imaginable, a group of high-level Soviet officials led by Khrushchev descended on Belgrade to apologize for past Soviet behavior.

Although the Soviets blamed Stalin and Beria for the vicious anti-Tito campaign of the recent past, the world was still properly impressed (and East European national communists greatly encouraged) when Khrushchev began his speech at Belgrade airport by saluting "Comrade Tito"—the man whom the Kremlin only a few short months earlier had called "a chained dog of the imperialists." Tito did not bark, though. Behaving like the statesman he had become, he welcomed the Soviet comrades, promised improved relations, and then in no uncertain terms affirmed his country's independent road to socialism. If the Kremlin had hoped to convince Tito to join the Warsaw Pact, formed also in mid-1955, it failed. As one of the distinguished founders of the nonaligned movement, Tito's Yugoslavia would join neither bloc, as it would prefer to benefit from cordial relations with both.

From the Kremlin's point of view, its rapprochement with Yugoslavia was at best a partial success.

On the one hand, it contributed to a growing impression in the West that the new Soviet leadership was seriously reviewing Stalin's legacy and might yet be persuaded to conduct businesslike relations with the rest of the world. On the other hand, however, the Soviet-Yugoslav truce did not stem the national communist tide in Hungary and Poland. To the contrary, Titoist factions around Nagy in Hungary and around Gomułka in Poland interpreted the Moscow-Belgrade accord to mean that they could, and perhaps even should, try to translate into practice the old Soviet theory of "separate roads to socialism"; that, given the example of Yugoslavia, the strict emulation of the Soviet model was no longer obligatory.

In this sense and for this reason, Yugoslavia was to have an extraordinary impact on Eastern Europe in the mid-1950s and even in the 1960s—less on the people who remained skeptical about any form of communism, national or otherwise, than on the region's communist elites. Of all the external influences, it was Tito's national communism that seemed to contribute most to elite divisions, which, in turn, were to prompt some of the major challenges to Soviet authority in Eastern Europe.

Analytically speaking, these challenges were of two kinds.

First, Moscow had to respond to popular, spontaneous movements, riots, uprisings, and revolutions, such as those that erupted in East Berlin (1953), Poznan (1956), Budapest (1956), Warsaw (1968), several Polish cities (1970 and 1976), and most dramatically throughout Poland under the banner of the independent "Solidarity" labor movement (1980–81). When facing such popular movements, the Kremlin invariably and in the end successfully used force to reestablish its authority through direct or indirect interventions. (The "Prague Spring" of 1968, discussed below, does not easily fit into either category of East European "challenges"; it contained elements of both.)

Second, Moscow also had to respond to demands for autonomy advanced by such independent-minded, if otherwise very dogmatic and repressive, communist parties as those of Albania (1961) and Romania (1964). When facing more or less controlled challenges of this kind—initiated and tightly regulated by a ruling communist party–the Kremlin refused to use force and failed to reestablish its authority. Albania left the Soviet bloc altogether, while maverick Romania—still a member of both the Warsaw Pact and CMEA—pursued a semi-independent foreign policy course in the second half of the 1960s.

Challenges of the first kind were more distressing to the Kremlin because they were spontaneous and because they threatened a communist party's monopoly of power. Hence the use of force to counter them. Challenges of the second kind were less alarming because they involved countries in the region's less important southern tier (e.g., Albania and Romania). They were also more difficult to confront because effective resistance could be organized by a regime in power. (The Soviet Union never removed the leadership of a rebellious communist party in Eastern Europe by force if that leadership showed signs of being prepared to defend itself.)

Of the two kinds of post-Stalin challenges in Eastern Europe, it was the Hungarian crisis in 1956 and the Czechoslovak "Prague Spring" in 1968 that prompted Soviet military interventions, while the Polish crisis in 1980–81 was "resolved" with a declaration of martial law by Polish security and military forces. As the Hungarian crisis occurred under Khrushchev's watch, the Czechoslovak crisis under Brezhnev's watch, and the Polish crisis while Brezhnev was formally at the helm (but with Yuri Andropov and Konstantin Chernenko already locked in a struggle for succession), Soviet handling of the three major crises shows aspects of both continuity and change in the Kremlin's post-Stalin approach to Eastern Europe.

Crises in the Bloc: Hungary, Czechoslovakia,
Poland (1956–81)

Hungary, 1956. Because the 1953 East Berlin uprising was confined to one city and because it was crushed in less than 48 hours, the 1956 Hungarian revolution was the first major challenge to Soviet rule in Eastern Europe in the post-Stalin era. Preceded by a reformist prelude in 1953–55 led by Imre Nagy, who lost his premiership in March 1955, the revolution itself began on October 23, 1956, with a peaceful demonstration by students whose demands centered on Nagy's reinstatement, and ended with Soviet military intervention on November 4, 1956.

The Hungarian revolution was largely a function of long-repressed popular opposition to the Soviet Union and to communism. The Hungarians sought cordial and even friendly but not servile relations with Moscow. The students and intellectuals and workers, who were promptly joined by the military as well, succeeded in returning Nagy to his old position as head of the government—a body that was to include representatives of several political parties. While the much-hated collective farms quickly disintegrated, there was no talk at all of returning large factories to their former owners. To the extent that the revolution had time to develop a domestic program, it was social-democratic in character and purpose.

The Kremlin displayed considerable hesitation about the Hungarian events. It dispatched two high-level emissaries, Politburo members Anastas Mikoyan and Mikhail Suslov, to Budapest twice. Between October 24 and 31, they spent four days there. Looking for a political solution, they seemed to assume that Nagy, a Titoist or "national communist" who genuinely welcomed the post-Stalin changes in the Soviet Union, could still save the "cause of socialism" if not Moscow's preeminent position in Hungary. During the course of frantic and chaotic negotiations with the Nagy government, the Soviet emissaries agreed to the withdrawal of Soviet troops from Hungarian territory, approved the replacement of the party's Central Committee with a small executive committee more attuned to the country's mood, and—in yet another major concession—supported Nagy's decision to re-create the 1944–47 multiparty system. Radio Moscow praised "the newly formed Hungarian government headed by Imre Nagy," and the Soviet government formally declared its willingness to settle all outstanding issues by negotiations. With all Soviet forces withdrawn from the capital city of Budapest and the hated political police (ÁVO) dissolved, the revolution appeared victorious.

On October 30 or 31, however, the Kremlin reversed itself. During the night of October 31, new Soviet forces entered Hungary and invaded the country. Khrushchev would subsequently recall in his memoirs that the Soviet leadership had vacillated between "crushing the mutiny" and "getting out of Hungary." "I don't know how many times we changed our minds back and forth," he added. In the end, having consulted with leaders of the neighboring Warsaw Pact states and Yugoslavia, too, the Kremlin dispatched its troops, which reached Budapest on November 4, and crushed the revolution. There was some resistance, and many factories remained idle for weeks and months. In 1958, after a secret trial, Nagy was executed and several of his supporters jailed or put to death.

The Soviet intervention was *not* prompted by two of the most radical decisions made by the Nagy government: the decision to withdraw Hungary from the Warsaw Pact and the decision to declare the country's neutrality. They were made only on November 1, the morning after and hence in response to the reentry of Soviet troops into Hungarian territory. Then why the intervention? Why didn't the Kremlin wait a bit longer to allow the Nagy government to work out a political solution that would satisfy at least most of the basic, geopolitical Soviet interests?

Khrushchev provided a plausible if vague answer to the question of Soviet motives during his discussions with the Yugoslav leadership on November 2:

> If we let things take their course, the West would say we are either stupid or weak, and that's one and the same thing. We cannot possibly permit it, either as communists and internationalists or as the Soviet state.[1]

By saying "if we let things take their course," Khrushchev seemed to be referring to the future—to what *might* happen. More members of the political police being lynched, perhaps? Capitalism? Nationalism today, NATO tomorrow? What then of the Soviet sphere in Eastern Europe, who's next to go? Whether these developments were or were not likely did not much matter; what mattered was that they might come about. Therefore the Soviet leaders decided to respond by force in order to overcome their fear of all the uncertainties Hungary implied. Most disturbing among these uncertainties was the fear of losing control over the bloc and then being seen in the West as weak.

As the Kremlin's leading anti-Stalinist, Khrushchev knew his power was also on the line. His name was synonymous with the pathbreaking Twentieth CPSU Congress, with de-Stalinization. The Hungarian revolution would not have happened without Khrushchev's policies, which between 1953 and 1956 had the effect of dividing the Hungarian communist elite into Stalinists and "national communists." His col-

---

1. Veljko Mićunović, *Moscow Diary* (Garden City, N.Y.: Doubleday, 1980), p. 133. As the Yugoslav ambassador to the Soviet Union at the time, Mićunović was a participant in—and took detailed notes at—the Yugoslav-Soviet summit on the 1956 Hungarian crisis, held two days before the Soviet intervention in Hungary on November 4, 1956.

leagues knew, and Khrushchev feared they remembered, that he was ultimately more responsible than anyone else for de-Stalinization—for the process that had set in motion the events and currents leading to October–November 1956. Thus the Hungarian revolution found Khrushchev politically vulnerable, so much so that he had to prove anew that he could be firm and indeed brutal. Despite their similar anti-Stalinist sentiments, then, Khrushchev had to desert Nagy to save his own position.

The timing of the Soviet intervention almost certainly had something to do with a concurrent international crisis— Suez— that presently so preoccupied the West. With British, French, and Israeli forces landing in Suez in a move strongly opposed by the United States, the West's attention centered on the Middle East. Would Moscow come to Egypt's defense and thereby possibly precipitate World War III? No, but Moscow did use the opportunity provided by Western preoccupation with Suez to invade Hungary. For whatever chance the Kremlin might have otherwise assigned to Western measures in defense of Hungary was now gone, and Hungary certainly could not defend itself against the Soviet Union on its own.

In retrospect, the initial Soviet concessions—Moscow's search for a political solution—might have implied a willingness to tolerate deviations from Soviet policies and preferences. Yet, in the final analysis, the ultimate decision to intervene must be seen as affirmation of the Kremlin's unwillingness to tolerate significant departures from existing patterns. Early hopes in Eastern Europe and in the West that de-Stalinization in the Soviet Union would lead to a major overhaul of Soviet–East European relations proved unfounded.

In the aftermath of the Hungarian revolution the Kremlin still paid lip service to "equality" in such relations, and the bloc's decentralization—the result of which was called "polycentrism" in the West—also continued. Nevertheless, the Soviet position essentially reverted to old, more rigid formulations and policies. Stressing "socialist internationalism" (code words for bloc cohesion and the CPSU's "leading role" in world communism), a Soviet-sponsored gathering of communist parties declared in 1957:

> The socialist countries base their relations on principles of equality, respect for territorial integrity, state independence and sovereignty, and noninterference in one another's internal affairs. These are vital principles. However, they do not exhaust the essence of relations between them. Fraternal mutual aid is part and parcel of these relations. This aid is a striking expression of socialist internationalism.[2]

Czechoslovakia, 1968. The "Prague Spring" of 1968 differed from the Hungarian revolution in that there was no violence in Czechoslovakia and that Soviet intervention—this time actively supported by several Warsaw Pact states—came after considerable vacillation and long debates in the Kremlin and within the Pact. Despite spontaneous expressions of political sentiments, the Czechoslovak movement for change was directed largely by the Communist Party. Journalists, economists, workers, and others were both active and vocal, but the major goals of the "Prague Spring"— expressed in the reformist slogan of "socialism with a human face"— signified changes sought *within* this communist system rather than—as in Hungary—basic changes *of* the system. For this reason, the "Prague Spring" combined characteristics of the two types of challenge to Soviet authority identified above.

The movement for change began within the party, not in 1953 as in Hungary but—for reasons that remain obscure—in the 1960s. Only then did the winds of de-Stalinization reach Czechoslovakia. Only then did the rehabilitation of the victims of the Stalinist purges get underway and discussions about economic reforms commence.

Unable to resist growing pressures for change, the

---

2. *Pravda*, November 22, 1957.

country's orthodox party chief, Antonin Novotný, made an attempt in December 1967 to silence his critics. His obvious purpose was to put an end to what he regarded as dangerous reformist tendencies in the party. But it was too late to reestablish his rapidly fading authority. Lacking sufficient support both in the party and even in Moscow, Novotný actually lost his position. His successor, Alexander Dubček—a Soviet-trained Slovak party apparatchik known to be interested in reforms but opposed to radical change—was quite acceptable to the Kremlin. (Brezhnev had personally endorsed his appointment.) Yet, between the time of his appointment in January 1968 and the Soviet-led intervention in August 1968, Dubček became the symbol if not the leader of the movement for "socialism with a human face." To what extent he embraced the program of the "Prague Spring" out of conviction or under popular pressure is still unclear.

During the early months of 1968, Moscow was concerned about but not opposed to Dubček's reformist course. The Soviet leaders knew that the previous decades had witnessed a marked decline in the growth of the Czechoslovak economy. They knew that prior to World War II Czechoslovakia had been one of the six or seven leading industrial nations in the world, a position long lost since the late 1940s. Even more than elsewhere, the Soviet model had proved inapplicable to this developed Central European country, and hence economic conditions called for a change of direction. The Soviet leaders also knew (or thought they knew) that, since the people of this country were traditionally pro-Russian, economic reforms would not likely turn into anti-Soviet political demands. They seemed confident that, in contrast to Hungarians, the people of Czechoslovakia would not embrace anti-Russian or anti-communist sentiments. Indeed, what the Czechs and Slovaks at least initially sought in the political realm—"socialist legality"—largely corresponded to that which the Soviet Union was professing to advocate at that time.

International circumstances also pointed to the utility of Soviet restraint. West Germany's new *Ostpolitik*—a more flexible approach to the Soviet bloc after years of little or no economic or political contact—was offering Moscow economic benefits as well as the possibility of dividing NATO—advantages that might be lost in case of intervention. Ongoing SALT negotiations with the U.S. and China's new stance against Soviet "hegemonism" also argued for Soviet restraint. Also at stake was the already nebulous "unity" of the world communist movement, particularly in the area of Soviet relations with some of the more independent-minded West European communist parties. This is why even Mikhail Suslov—the Kremlin's otherwise hard-line pointman in charge of relations with communist parties— reportedly favored a wait-and-see attitude vis-à-vis Czechoslovakia. In short, intervention was not to be without cost or consequences.

A similar view was held in the councils of the Warsaw Pact by Romania and Hungary. Professing to stand on principles of international law, Nicolae Ceauşescu's Romania even refused to attend a meeting of the Pact in mid-July to discuss a common policy toward Czechoslovakia—and then it expressed opposition to intervention in the internal affairs of another socialist country under any circumstances. Guided by more pragmatic considerations, János Kádár's Hungary was concerned lest the suppression of the "Prague Spring" have a negative effect on Hungary's own reformist orientation. (In August, Romanian troops did not join the invading forces of the Warsaw Pact, but 5,000 or so Hungarian troops did.)

The contrary view in the Pact was advanced by Gomułka's Poland and especially by Walter Ulbricht's East Germany. Ulbricht was an early and vehement critic of Dubček's policies, arguing that West German "revanchism" and U.S. "imperialism" were manipulating the Czechoslovak reform movement from behind the scenes. He maintained that "socialism with a human face" was but an empty slogan intended to hide a determined Western attempt at restoring Czechoslovakia's prewar, capitalist democracy.

As for Moscow, it was only after June 27—when a group of Czechoslovak intellectuals issued a manifesto known as the "Two Thousand Words"—that Soviet pressures visibly intensified. The planned withdrawal of Soviet troops that were in Czechoslovakia for "exercises" was suddenly and several times delayed. On July 3, Brezhnev stated, "We cannot remain indifferent to the fate of socialism in another country." On July 11, *Pravda* compared developments in Czechoslovakia with those of Hungary in 1956, thus both warning Dubček and preparing the Soviet public for what the Kremlin might decide to do. On July 15, the Warsaw Pact formally demanded that Prague restore order by reinstating censorship and thus silencing the intellectuals. The Soviet side repeated the same demands, and added others, during the Soviet-Czechoslovak negotiations that followed. Ominously, all but two or three members of the Soviet Politburo attended these negotiations.

Yet the immediate cause of Soviet intervention on the night of August 20–21 was almost certainly not what had already happened but what was about to happen. In August, Dubček called for an Extraordinary Party Congress that was to meet on September 9. Had party officials been elected at that congress by secret ballot, as planned, Dubček would have immeasurably strengthened his position in the Czechoslovak Communist Party. His remaining opponents in the leadership, and perhaps even his reluctant supporters, would have been ousted. The congress would have taken the next steps toward democratization and reform. It would have confirmed the lifting of censorship and included noncommunists in the country's political life. In effect, the congress would have consolidated and legitimized the achievements of the "Prague Spring."

As in Hungary twelve years earlier, then, it was to a large extent the Kremlin's fear of what might happen rather than what had already happened—combined with a strong preference for that which was familiar and hence for the Soviet road to socialism—that tipped the balance in favor of intervention. The subsequent justification for it was also similar to that put forth after Hungary. Called the "Brezhnev Doctrine" in the West and "socialist internationalism" in the East, the Kremlin's position was outlined in an authoritative article pointedly entitled "Sovereignty and the International Obligations of Socialist Countries." Published in *Pravda* on September 26, 1968, it included the following key paragraph:

> There is no doubt that the peoples of the socialist countries and the communist parties have and must have freedom to determine their country's path of development. However, any decision of theirs must damage neither socialism in their own country nor the fundamental interest of the other socialist countries nor the worldwide workers' movement, which is waging a struggle for socialism. This means that every Communist Party is responsible not only to its own people but also to all the socialist countries and to the entire communist movement. Whoever forgets this by placing sole emphasis on the autonomy and independence of communist parties lapses into one sidedness, shirking his internationalist obligations.

These words—the "Brezhnev Doctrine"—signified the two faces of "socialist internationalism" and hence it was an attempt to square the circle. On the one hand, the East European states were said to be sovereign and therefore free "to determine their . . . path of development." On the other hand, however, what they do cannot run counter to the bloc's "common interests." It was also understood without being explicitly stated that the Soviet Union reserved the right to decide both what these "common interests" were and what had to be done to protect them. In short, the "Brezhnev Doctrine" explicitly confirmed the postwar Soviet policy of "limited sovereignty" for the states of Eastern Europe.

The people of Czechoslovakia did not resist the invading forces of the Warsaw Pact. Yet, since 1968, they have taken their quiet revenge by apparently abandoning their traditional Russophile orientation. Since '68, both Czechs and Slovaks have joined most Poles, Romanians, Hungarians, and East Germans in adopting an altogether contemptuous attitude toward almost everything Soviet and even Russian.

Poland. 1980–81. The Polish crisis of 1980–81 began in August 1980 in the coastal city of Gdańsk, where workers struck and established the independent labor union "Solidarity." It ended in December 1981 when Poland's security forces, supported by the military, cracked down on the union and declared martial law. In some very significant ways, the Polish crisis differed from both the "Prague Spring" and the Hungarian revolution.

First, from a small group of workers in Gdańsk, "Solidarity" grew almost overnight to become a national labor union whose membership included one-third of the country's population and whose supporters included almost every Pole. It was organized by the industrial proletariat, the presumed mainstay of communist regimes, and led by Lech Wałęsa, an electrician.

Second, the 1980–81 movement for "socialist renewal" led by "Solidarity" was but the largest of the Polish people's postwar confrontations with the proprietors of power in Warsaw. Alone among East Europeans, Poles had fought against the communist regime in a civil war right after World War II. They rebelled against the authorities in Poznan and indeed throughout Poland in 1956. There were strikes and demonstrations—stressing mainly economic demands—in 1970 and 1976 as well, and in each instance workers played a critical role. The "Solidarity" era of 1980–81 was thus the culmination of many efforts and many sacrifices over the years in the struggle for more food and better housing conditions, as well as for political rights and independence.

Third, the extraordinary significance of Poland for the Soviet Union cannot be compared to the importance Moscow attached to any other East European country. Historically,

Russia or the Soviet Union played a role in the partitions of Poland in 1772, 1793, 1795, and 1939. Russia or the Soviet Union was invaded by or through Poland in 1610, 1709, 1812, and 1941. When toward the end of World War II Stalin instructed the communist parties of Czechoslovakia and Hungary to seize power in ten to fifteen years, the delay was explained to party cadres by the need to draw Western attention away from the rapid takeover in Poland. That country's future was nonnegotiable because, aside from Germany's defeat, its capture constituted the most meaningful wartime or postwar gain for the Soviet Union.

Moreover, today as much as in the past, Poland is at the gateway between Europe and Russia; Polish roads and railroads carry all military and commercial traffic between (East) Germany and the Soviet Union. Poland has the largest territory of all states in Eastern Europe, its population of 37 million makes it by far the most populous in the region, and the size of its military is second only to that of the Soviet armed forces among members of the Warsaw Pact. For reasons of history, geography, and size, as well as a multitude of political and ideological factors, Poland's place in the Soviet bloc was always seen by the Kremlin as crucial to vital Soviet interests.

Under the circumstances, the Kremlin watched the rise of "Solidarity" with deep interest and growing anxiety. Even before the Polish government agreed to the formation of the independent labor union in the Gdańsk Agreement of August 31, 1980, Moscow had resumed the jamming of Russian-language Western broadcasts to the Soviet Union. (They had not been jammed since 1973.) Clearly, Moscow was concerned about the spreading of the "Polish disease." The Soviet press spoke of occasional work stoppages taking place in Poland, not strikes. Even at that early stage, however, references were also made to Western and domestic "antisocialist" forces supposedly hard at work to undermine Poland. By December 1980, the Warsaw Pact formally and ominously declared that Poland "was, is, and will remain a socialist state."

In point of fact, "Solidarity" did not advocate a return to capitalism. It did not advocate the establishment of a multiparty system. It did not advocate either neutralism or Poland's exit from the Warsaw Pact. Instead, it affirmed the "leading role" of the Polish United Workers' [Communist] Party (PUWP). Acknowledging Poland's proximity to the Soviet Union, it also affirmed Warsaw's existing international obligations.

Of course, "Solidarity" stood for radical change—for "socialist renewal." It insisted on the right of workers to belong to a free and independent trade union, not to the company unions run by the PUWP and the government. It demanded higher wages and lower prices for consumer goods, especially food. In the political realm, "Solidarity" sought freedom of the press to guarantee that its voice could not be stifled.

The rapid rise of "Solidarity" and its survival for sixteen long months sparked an extraordinary social upheaval that touched all—organizations, groups, individuals. Though displaying its traditional circumspection, the Catholic Church gave "Solidarity" its blessings. Intellectuals—journalists and writers in particular—welcomed the opportunity to express thoughts long considered taboo. In the countryside, millions joined "Rural Solidarity" in an attempt to extend the gains of "Solidarity" to Poland's agricultural population.

The new spirit of "socialist renewal" left its mark on the leaders and members of the PUWP as well. At an Emergency Party Congress held in July 1981, a new Politburo was elected, only four of whose fifteen members had been in the Politburo before. The majority of the new Central Committee was also made up of newcomers. Though the party's first secretary, Stanisław Kania, was seen as a centrist, he proved to be an opponent of harsh measures against "Solidarity." Despite enormous pressure from Moscow and from Polish hard-liners, Kania reportedly refused to endorse plans prepared in the fall of 1981 to declare martial law and crush "Solidarity."

In the face of what amounted to an almost completely peaceful revolution—a momentous and unparalleled upheaval generated and led by the industrial working class—the Kremlin found itself on the horns of a dilemma. Nothing had prepared it for anything like this. Aside from the ideological problem of how to justify crushing another communist state's proletariat, one had to ask what a Soviet military intervention could accomplish. At least in its immediate aftermath, before the opportunists would climb back on the communist bandwagon, could Moscow find more than a few *hundred* loyal followers? Conversely, if the Kremlin were to let things take their course, what would be next? Would others in Eastern Europe follow suit? What would happen then to the Warsaw Pact? Could it be that the "Polish disease" would even spread to a Soviet republic like Lithuania—Poland's neighbor with a very large Catholic population? Moreover, was it not likely that "Solidarity," having gained recognition as a representative of the workers' economic interests, would soon focus on radical political demands too?

If the Soviet Union needed any specific reasons—or excuses—to move against "Solidarity," it had to wait till the fall and early winter of 1981. In September, the "Solidarity" Congress adopted a message addressed to the workers of the whole Soviet bloc. While rather carefully phrased, the message was nonetheless explosive: "We support those among you who have decided to follow the difficult struggle for a free trade union movement. We have the firm hope that our representatives will be able to meet each other." The Polish government called the message a "demonstrative interference in the internal affairs of other socialist states." The Soviet news agency TASS charged "extremist circles" with turning the congress into an "anti-socialist and anti-Soviet bacchanalia."

Against the background of persistent provocations by Poland's political police and the government's repeated attempts to cancel concessions already made, it would have been surprising to see "Solidarity" retain its composure and relative moderation. Indeed, by the fall of 1981, some of the leaders of "Solidarity" began to think that Lech Wałęsa was too conciliatory. In December, despite Wałęsa's reluctance to support the motion, "Solidarity" called for a national referendum on two highly provocative political questions. One had to do with the military relationship between Poland and the Soviet Union. The other raised the question of whether Poland should continue to have a one-party political system.

Although "Solidarity's" call for a national referendum was issued on December 11, 1981, and the government of General Wojciech Jaruzelski declared martial law on December 13, 1981, the two events were unrelated. Plans for a crackdown had been made months before; the date for the crackdown had been set weeks in advance, probably in October. Thus, Poland's struggle for "socialist renewal" came to a not unexpected, if still sudden and brutal, end.

The Polish crisis of 1980–81 and its resolution by an internal crackdown raised a multitude of questions, of which one stands out more than any other: Why did the Soviet Union wait sixteen long months to suppress "Solidarity"?

The answer should begin with a clear understanding of the Kremlin's unhesitating determination to contain this independent labor union. From the moment of its birth in Gdańsk, "Solidarity" was publicly accused by Soviet leaders and the Soviet press of every imaginable endeavor Moscow had deemed contrary to the "best interests" of Poland and the "socialist community." Its demands were said to be "antisocialist." It sought to subvert the Polish government. It created chaotic conditions. It was but the mouthpiece of U.S. imperialism. Brezhnev himself stated at the Twenty-sixth CPSU Congress in February 1981 that "opponents of socialism supported by outside forces are seeking to channel events in a counterrevolutionary course" in Poland. He added that "Polish communists, the Polish working class and the working people of that country can firmly rely on their friends and allies; we will not abandon fraternal, socialist Poland in its hour of need, we will stand by it." Such charges against "Solidarity" were never-ending; threats to destroy it were ominous.

Moscow had three alternatives.

One was to find a political solution to the crisis. What, precisely, such an arrangement would have entailed cannot be known, but it might have included the following:

1. The Soviet Union would have accommodated itself to the existence of "Solidarity," *provided* that the union focused only on economic matters, and in the expectation that a revived PUWP could gradually arrest the union's momentum.

2. The Soviet Union would have tolerated a relatively free press, *provided* that the PUWP resumed control over television and radio, and in the expectation that the press as a whole would refrain from criticizing Soviet policies.

3. The Soviet Union would have accepted a Polish legislature whose members were chosen in competitive elections, *provided* that the PUWP still retained controlling influence over the nominating process.

4. The Soviet Union would have endorsed even a radical economic reform, *provided* that it was implemented under the party's supervision.

In short, a political solution along these lines would have allowed a more narrowly defined renewal process to continue. However, while attesting to some flexibility in the Soviet position, such a course would have asserted that the issue of ultimate control was not negotiable. The Soviet Union and the PUWP would have been the final arbiter of Poland's future.

Unfortunately, this option was rejected. Efforts by the Catholic Church to bring about a compromise solution proved unsuccessful. Perhaps more important, the aging leaders of the Soviet Politburo could not make a decision substantially different from the precedents set in 1956 and 1968, because their fear that Poland would slip away apparently overwhelmed their hope of gaining a measure of legitimate authority in that country.

The second option was direct Soviet military intervention. According to both U.S. intelligence sources and a high-level Polish defector, this option was close to being adopted in December 1980 and again in March 1981. Why the mobilization of Soviet armed forces on those two occasions was not followed by intervention is not known. One possibility is that mobilization was only part of the ongoing war of nerves—part of the Kremlin's strategy to intimidate the Polish people and "encourage" the Polish government to put its house in order on its own.

In this sense, Soviet intervention was intimately tied to the third option: an internal crackdown to be carried out by Polish security and military forces. The connection was obvious: had the internal crackdown failed to suppress "Solidarity" and return Poland to the Soviet fold, the Kremlin could still have dispatched its own troops. Soviet intervention was thus the "backup option" that Moscow was prepared to use, but preferred not to. Dominant among the many reasons for that reluctance was the fear of protracted fighting pitting the Soviet Union against the whole Polish nation. The risks associated with conducting *two* wars concurrently—one in Afghanistan and one in Poland—were also too high.

Why then did Moscow wait for sixteen months? Because it did not have confidence in a political solution and because direct intervention was but a last resort. Moscow waited for economic conditions to become so desperate and political. conditions so chaotic as to convince someone like General Jaruzelski that "law and order" must be restored. True, initial planning for an internal crackdown began in the fall of 1980, within days after the government had deceitfully signed the Gdańsk Agreement with "Solidarity" on August 31st. Yet, according to circumstancial evidence and the testimony of a high-level Polish defector, Jaruzelski ordered actual preparations for the crackdown only in October 1981. Whether he had stalled because he was hoping for a political and thus peaceful resolution of the crisis or rather he was a simple Soviet stooge waiting for a signal from Moscow is a matter of interpretation. What is clear is that by his actions Jaruzelski once again proved the continued validity of the "Brezhnev Doctrine" in Soviet–East European relations. As a TASS commentary stated in 1981, "The socialist community is indissolvable and its defense is a matter not only for each state but for the entire socialist coalition as well."

From Khrushchev to Chernenko: What Changed? What Didn't?

What do the three case studies reveal about Soviet crisis behavior in Eastern Europe? What about other trends in the bloc between crises—during the long period from Khrushchev through Chernenko?

First, in the area of *crisis behavior*, the case studies suggest important similarities in Soviet conduct. In each case, for example, the Kremlin professed to be deeply concerned about forfeiting the "gains of socialism," maintaining that it was acting on behalf of the "people." According to Moscow, the "people" as a whole did not cause the problem; all would have been well were it not for Western imperialists (and especially their voice, Radio Free Europe) and a few misguided Hungarians, Czechoslovaks, and Poles. This was presumably why the Kremlin kept looking for a political solution, hoping that "healthy elements"— its local supporters—could muster sufficient strength to reestablish the Communist Party's "leading role" and obviate the need for military action.

In each case, moreover, the Kremlin consulted with its East European allies or at least informed them of what it was about to do; in 1956 China and Yugoslavia were also consulted. Then, as the time for intervention or crackdown neared, Moscow greatly exaggerated existing disorder—

"chaotic conditions"—on the scene in order to prepare the Soviet public for what was to come. Before the day of reckoning, it also engaged in a good deal of intimidation and deception.

In each case, finally, the Kremlin was in a weak position when the crisis occurred, with neither of the two Soviet leaders—Khrushchev or Brezhnev—at the height of his power. As for selecting an East European leader once the crisis was over, Moscow appeared to prefer relatively new faces at the top—Kádár, Gustáv Husák, Jaruzelski—to create the impression of change and thus help along the process of "normalization."

There were important similarities in East European perceptions and conduct too.

In all cases, intellectuals played a key role in the events that had led to the crises, while peasants tended to be quite passive. Those who sought change strongly affirmed their belief in a socialist society, though their concept of socialism appeared to be limited largely to the ideal of some form of egalitarianism. Their hope for change turned into widespread euphoria—in Poland in particular—about the chances for lasting change.

In all cases, anti-regime sentiments were there for all to see. Deep divisions within the local communist parties, both before and during the crises, resulted in mixed signals to the population as to what the authorities might or might not do. Such mixed signals only encouraged the open expression of anti-regime sentiments. In the end, the Kremlin could be sure about the loyalty of only the local security forces; party members in great numbers were deserting the Soviet cause everywhere.

Differences in Soviet policy had to do mainly with the timing and means of ending the crises. In Hungary, only the Soviet armed forces intervened and they did so less than two weeks after the revolution had begun. In Czechoslovakia, the "Prague Spring" lasted about seven or eight months, and the Soviet Army was assisted by contingents from other Warsaw

Pact countries, with the exception of Romania. In Poland, the "Solidarity" era came to an end after sixteen months, when the security forces and the military executed a domestic crackdown, an action instigated by the Soviets and to a lesser extent by the East German and Czechoslovak regimes.

As for differences in the outcome in Eastern Europe, Hungary after a few years of terror embarked on a reformist course; the Czechoslovak regime became one of the more loyal Soviet supporters in Eastern Europe; and Poland moved toward a peculiar mixture of military/party rule while Polish society quite remarkably ignored the authorities and managed to live by its own rules.

Concerning *trends in the bloc between crises*, important developments both in Soviet foreign policy and in Eastern Europe affected the course of Soviet–East European relations from the 1950s on.

For one thing, the Soviet Union in the post-Stalin era began to face the classic problem all major powers with global interests and ambitions often face—that of trying to appeal to many diverse states, groups, and other political constituencies at the same time. In the process of trying to reconcile its often conflicting goals, Moscow had to learn that it could not easily have all the benefits of detente and at the same time keep invading other countries; that it could not easily befriend the "moderate" Arab states and at the same time support the "confrontationists" of the Middle East; and, indeed, that it could not easily maintain a stable Eastern Europe and at the same time demand strict adherence to its own, alien norms and policies. Thus, like other great powers with diverse interests, Moscow too was compelled to make painful choices, and in some cases its gains did not outweigh the costs.

In its policies toward Eastern Europe, however, what the Kremlin regarded as vital to Soviet interests did not change. From Khrushchev to Chernenko, there remained an unqualified Soviet commitment to the endurance of the bloc and to the "leading role" of the region's communist parties, a commitment rooted primarily in geopolitical and ideological considerations. Yet, by the 1960s at least, these interests were no longer the only determinants of Soviet policy, nor were they applied uniformly to all countries or on all occasions. At least four additional considerations growing out of Soviet experiences and circumstances, as well as domestic and international pressures, produced a somewhat broader definition of what Moscow would come to seek or at least accept in Eastern Europe.

First, in response to expressions of nationalism and the region's chronic political instability, the Soviet leaders began to recognize some of the particular needs and distinctive features of their East European dependencies. Whereas between 1948 and 1953, Stalin could and did subordinate Eastern Europe to the Soviet state's foreign-policy interests and to his own personal and ideological inclinations, his successors—on encountering open and persistent anti-Sovietism—seemed willing to accommodate adaptations fostered by local conditions, traditions, and customs.

The dilemma was obvious: if Soviet leaders were to follow a Stalinist approach, the expected result might be real or perceived ideological cohesion—but dangerous political instability. Conversely, if the Soviets were to adopt a more circumspect course and allow for national peculiarities, the East European regimes might be more viable—but also more difficult to control. As there was a price to be paid in either case, Moscow at times acquiesced in gradual, controlled change away from Soviet patterns, especially when an East European country could make the threat of instability credible. For example, the hard-earned Romanian, Polish, and Hungarian reputations for national self-assertiveness probably helped *these* countries—rather than their neighbors—to obtain more elbow room in recent years.

The second factor affecting Soviet policies was the deteriorating economies of Eastern Europe. Though there was a time when Moscow, overlooking local needs, could impose its will and exploit these countries for short-term gain, such a Soviet approach in more recent periods tended to exacerbate economic problems and ignite political explosions. With Stalin's apparatus of open terror largely dismantled and its use dysfunctional, the Soviet Union began to develop a genuine, vested interest in the viability if not the prosperity of the region's economies.

This was so because Moscow's trade with Eastern Europe—with East Germany and Czechoslovakia in particular—had become essential to the Soviet economy; because it needed increased East European military contributions to the modernization and general upgrading of the Warsaw Pact; and especially because serious East European economic problems were expected to create political tensions which, in turn, would have necessitated either costly economic rescue operations or military interventions, or both. As Moscow learned, the cost of sustaining an ineffective or nearly bankrupt East European regime could be exorbitant, and the political cost of intervention—in terms of Soviet setbacks elsewhere in the world—even higher.

It might appear, then, that the Soviet Union even before Gorbachev would have best served its interests by actively encouraging gradual and controlled economic reforms throughout the area. With the exception of Hungary's post-1968 New Economic Mechanism (NEM), this did not turn out to be the case. Partly because of political inertia, but mainly because of the Kremlin's conviction that economic reforms, however carefully guided, would likely erode the region's political structures, Moscow generally relied on the old formula: fewer new investments, organizational shake-ups, forecasts of future benefits accruing from regional integration via CMEA, and, in the 1970s, some Soviet subsidies. Inadequate as this old formula proved to be, it nonetheless signified a more accommodating Soviet approach to Eastern Europe than Stalin's policy of outright economic exploitation.

A seldom-recognized third factor affecting Moscow's East European policies was the Soviet leaders' preoccupation with the struggle for power in the Kremlin. The years 1953–56, 1964–68, and 1979–85 marked major succession crises in Moscow—and concurrent trouble in Eastern Europe.

In the first instance, Khrushchev extended the processes of "socialist legality" (or domestic de-Stalinization) to Eastern Europe in the 1950s, partly in order to discredit political opponents (principally Malenkov and Molotov) and partly in order to release regional tension pent up during Stalin's last years. In the second instance, several of the East European regimes, such as Romania, Hungary, and of course Czechoslovakia, exploited the opportunity for maneuver afforded by the Kremlin's absorption in internal political matters in the mid-1960s. When released from these concerns, the Soviet leaders could once again clarify—and implement—policies which culminated in interventions in Hungary and Czechoslovakia. In the third instance, the Polish era of "socialist renewal" in 1980–81 should be understood against the background of Brezhnev's illness in the late 1970s and the brief tenures of Yuri Andropov and Konstantin Chernenko in the early 1980s—a long period of immobilism in the Kremlin, which in turn contributed to weakness and confusion at the top in Poland as well.

While in some cases such immobilism in the Kremlin culminated in a crackdown, in several other cases the East European reaction was to take advantage of the Soviet leaders' preoccupation with the struggle for succession—and make such changes as an attentive and vigorous Kremlin might have opposed. When the cat's away the mice will play.

Finally, the fourth factor influencing Soviet policies toward Eastern Europe was Soviet relations with the West. Although the Soviet Union did not accommodate itself to the prospect of any East European country denying the "leading role" of its communist party or removing itself from the Warsaw Pact for the sake of Western trade and whatever else detente denoted, Moscow nonetheless remained sensitive to the damage its East European policies could cause to the fabric of East-West relations.

Accordingly, while the West could not and did not deter the Soviet Union from protecting its real or perceived interests in Eastern Europe, it made the ultimate option of military intervention somewhat more difficult to adopt. It should be recalled that Moscow intervened in Hungary in 1956 when the West was deeply involved with the Suez crisis, and in Czechoslovakia in 1968 when the United States was thoroughly occupied with the Vietnam war. That the Kremlin waited for an incredible sixteen months in 1980–81, and then tried an "internal crackdown" rather than outright intervention in Poland, was due not only to the Soviets' own immobilism but to the unusual attention the West was paying to the fortunes of "Solidarity." In short, Moscow's perception of Western preoccupation elsewhere in the world appears to have influenced—though presumably never determined— Soviet choices in dealing with its East European dependencies.

The four factors discussed above suggest that changes in the Soviet Union were important enough to temper Moscow's interventionist urge. From Khrushchev to Chernenko, the evolution of Soviet policy in the region pointed toward tolerance for a measure of controlled change, economic experimentation, and even political liberalization. The very fact that Eastern Europe was as diverse as it was showed that decisions of some magnitude—though not the ultimate decisions— had come to be locally made; the Soviet bloc had been decentralized. Stalin's heirs acted on what the old tyrant had once said but did not practice: "Soviet power cannot do everything for you. You must do the fighting, you must do the work."

In short, there was both much continuity and change in the Soviet orbit between Stalin's death and Gorbachev's rise. What Gorbachev inherited in the political, economic, and military realms—and how he has coped so far—are treated in Parts Two and Three.

Part Two

THE ERA OF
REFORM,
1985–88

III

POLITICAL RELATIONS

The Early Gorbachev Era: Cure or Relief?

AFTER THE Soviet Union abandoned its communist allies in the fall and early winter of 1989—after the Berlin Wall was breached, a new "Prague Autumn" burgeoned, and the old dictators of Bulgaria and Romania fell—it is easy to forget the *early* Gorbachev: the man who from his rise to power in 1985 to 1988 held a different conception of and had pursued different policies toward Eastern Europe.

Gorbachev, in 1985–88, appeared to view the East European crisis (to employ Seweryn Bialer's distinction) as a "crisis of performance" rather than a "crisis of the system." True, he understood even then that Eastern Europe was the Soviet Union's Achilles heel, a vulnerable spot that would generate acute problems for, and might even end, his policies in the Soviet Union itself. Yet, even as he realized that the region's political and economic conditions were unhealthy, Gorbachev believed that these conditions could be remedied by a dose of perestroika and glasnost. He seemed to assume that only the *regimes* would have to change their ways, and that although here and there new leaders were needed too, the communist *systems* were eminently capable of rebirth, revival, and even renaissance.

Until 1988, the East European communist elites—with the exception of a very few truly radical reformers in Poland and Hungary—had shared the Soviet view of the essentially limited scope of the crisis they faced and what had to be done about it. They, too, wanted to improve performance—and retain their monopoly of power—rather than change the system by adopting genuine political pluralism and developing market-based economies.

For several years, then, Gorbachev failed to come to terms with the depth of popular East European disillusionment with and opposition to any form of communism, reformed or otherwise. He did not seem to understand, or concede, that what he sought—a more efficient and more humane communist system—was anathema to most of the peoples of Eastern Europe, who rejected the system itself and regarded Gorbachev's reforms as "too little and too late." In a July 1988 interview with *The New York Times*, Polish historian Bronislaw Geremek (then a top political strategist for "Solidarity") gave this view of Gorbachev's imminent visit to Poland:

> I hope Mr. Gorbachev will be able to understand that what is quite satisfactory for Soviet problems is not satisfactory for Polish problems. In Poland you have to confront the real potential for revolt and mass movements for dissatisfaction, and a lack of consensus here [even] creates a danger to his policies.

In a nutshell, the choice confronting Gorbachev in Eastern Europe after 1985 was whether this troubled region needed *relief* only or *cure*, palliatives or surgery, reform or transformation. For several years, Gorbachev opted for relief. He did not recognize what the peoples of Eastern Europe knew all along: that the postwar communist political and economic order imposed on the region by Stalin and sustained by his successors lacked legitimacy and was therefore inherently unstable and potentially explosive. They knew what Gorbachev would not acknowledge—that the seemingly permanent crisis that had bedeviled Eastern Europe for four long decades required cure rather than relief.

The pre-1988 Soviet view that relief *was* sufficient was

supported by the experience of Kádár's Hungary in the second half of the 1960s. At that time, during the era of "goulash communism," that country was stable and its people quite satisfied. There was even a mood of optimism about the future, and Kádár himself enjoyed considerable popularity. Despite its dubious origins, the early revenge against the revolutionaries of 1956, and the absence of genuine political pluralism, the Kádár regime managed to earn a measure of support primarily because of its consumer-oriented economic policies, relative political tolerance, and the occasional distance it kept from some of the unduly harsh features of Soviet patterns and policies.

By the 1980s, such "relief" became insufficient to satisfy growing expectations in most of Eastern Europe, including Hungary. East European public opinion, which once looked at Kádár's "goulash communism" with both envy and admiration, appeared to view even Gorbachev-style reform with skepticism, seeing it as possibly beneficial for the Soviet Union but considerably less so for Eastern Europe. In a 1986–87 survey conducted for the highly regarded Audience and Opinion Research Department of Radio Free Europe, citizens —not emigrés—of Bulgaria, Czechoslovakia, Hungary, Poland, and Romania were asked to respond to these questions: "Do you believe that Gorbachev's leadership is good or bad for the Soviet Union?" and "Do you believe that Gorbachev's leadership is good or bad for [respondent's own country]?"[1]

Each of the tables makes an interesting suggestion:

(1) Against the background of decades of persistent anti-Sovietism permeating Eastern Europe, the Soviet Union under Gorbachev seems to have improved its image and reputation in Eastern Europe, to a small extent even in Poland.

---

1. The results of this survey, including the tables reproduced here, were published in *East European Perceptions of Gorbachev and the Soviet Reforms* (Munich: Radio Free Europe Audience and Opinion Research Department, July 1988).

TABLE 1. "Do you believe that Gorbachev's
leadership is good or bad for the Soviet Union?"

	Bulgaria	Czechosl.	Hungary	Poland	Romania
Good	79%	75%	65%	51%	63%
Bad	4	3	10	7	9
Neither	16	18	17	28	19
Other / no answer	1	4	8	14	9
No. of cases	556	436	385	247	541

TABLE 2. "Do you believe that Gorbachev's leadership
is good or bad for [respondent's own country]?"

	Bulgaria	Czechosl.	Hungary	Poland	Romania
Good	64%	53%	38%	20%	40%
Bad	8	8	23	23	10
Neither	24	34	26	44	38
Other / no answer	4	5	13	13	12
No. of cases	556	436	385	247	541

TABLE 3. Evaluations of Gorbachev's leadership
for the respondent's own country as compared
to the Soviet Union

(Tables 1 & 2 combined)

	Bulgaria	Czechosl.	Hungary	Poland	Romania
Good	−15%	−22%	−27%	−31%	−23%
Bad	+4	+5	+13	+16	+1
Neither	+8	+16	+9	+16	+19
Other / no answer	+3	+1	+5	−1	+3

(2) Still, the vast majority of East Europeans were not
convinced that what was good for the Soviet Union was good
enough for them. One of every four respondents believed that

Gorbachev's reforms were less relevant for Eastern Europe than for the Soviet Union. There were also major differences within the region on this issue. While almost two-thirds of the Bulgarian respondents rated Gorbachev's leadership as "good" for Bulgaria, only one-fifth of Polish respondents thought that he was "good" for Poland.

The reasons for the striking gap between the East Europeans' approval of what Gorbachev was doing in the Soviet Union and their uncertainty about the merit of his leadership for Eastern Europe were not self-evident at that time. Was the gap due to the East Europeans' traditionally cynical attitude toward the Soviet Union (i.e., "It's good for 'them' but not for us")? Was it only that East Europeans, in their lethargic mood, thought their leaders lacked the courage, dynamism, skill, and imagination to be innovative like Gorbachev? Or was it due to a growing conviction that their countries' communist system was beyond repair—that it needed cure? Alas, only in retrospect can the results be interpreted to mean East European popular rejection of anything short of systemic transformation.

(3) Nevertheless, the survey also hinted at considerable political excitement among some East Europeans about the Gorbachev phenomenon. Admittedly, the evidence was slim. But Gorbachev's high approval rating in Table 1, which was surely unprecedented for the leader of a country that had suppressed Eastern Europe for over four decades, implied that there were East Europeans who had become hopeful—"cautiously optimistic"—that Gorbachev would manage to find new leaders for the region and still make a difference.

Reports from Eastern Europe generally confirmed this impression. Gorbachev's very warm welcome from the people of Romania and Czechoslovakia in 1987 was both a protest against local leaders and an expression of hope that Gorbachev would find a way to replace them. In Poland and Hungary, two countries that had already surpassed Gorbachev's perestroika and glasnost by then, his program prompted radical questions about the "next steps"—about measures that would go beyond "democratization" to political pluralism, beyond "restructuring" to a mixed economy, and thus beyond what Gorbachev had in mind for the Soviet Union.

Such questions about the next steps in Eastern Europe could not have been raised without Gorbachev. They were raised because a growing number of Poles assumed that if the spirit of perestroika and glasnost were applied to Polish circumstances, for example, the next step there—the formation of an independent labor union and perhaps even the introduction of genuine pluralism—was no longer unthinkable. If the spirit of perestroika and glasnost were applied to Hungarian circumstances, the reorientation of that country's foreign trade toward the West and a correspondingly reduced relationship with the Soviet-sponsored CMEA would be conceivable. If the spirit of perestroika and glasnost were applied to Czechoslovak circumstances, the next step there—the wholesale removal of that country's Brezhnevite leadership—could be achieved. Indeed, given the expectations Gorbachev aroused, some East Europeans began to believe that even the next big step—the gradual transformation of the Soviet "sphere of domination" in their region into a Soviet "sphere of influence"—was no longer a pipe dream.

While by 1988 the Soviet Union had begun to be tolerant toward and even supportive of Polish and Hungarian experiments along these lines, it was still reluctant to pressure either its Brezhnevite allies elsewhere in Eastern Europe or the Stalinist Ceauşescu regime in Romania to undertake serious reforms. Gorbachev seemed to believe that the era of "stagnation" in the 1970s could be ended, stability restored, and sufficient progress made by improving the system—without attacking its structural, systemic deficiencies. He was concerned that radical change would spark persistent instability. He sought reform, not transformation. By contrast, most East Europeans tended to believe that only more drastic changes—those that would take them beyond Gorbachev's program—could resolve the region's chronic economic and political crisis. In that difference between most Soviet and East European leaders, on the one hand, and the East European peoples, on the other—in their very different perceptions of reality and what had to be done—lay Gorbachev's initial challenge and dilemma. The choice Gorbachev made at first was to prescribe for Eastern Europe no more than what he thought the Soviet Union needed—relief, not cure.

The Gradual Demise of the "Brezhnev Doctrine"

The concept that served as the guiding principle of Soviet–East European relations in the early Gorbachev era was still socialist internationalism. Its two components—professed (Soviet) respect for (East European) sovereignty and (East European) respect for the bloc's (Soviet-defined) common interests—were introduced in the previous chapter. Initially, these components of the old Soviet concept of intra-bloc relations remained essentially unchanged under Gorbachev.

Historically, socialist internationalism derives from the Marxist notion of internationalism, which posits the identity of interests of industrial workers based on class rather than on nationality or ethnic origin. In the Marxist view, the world is divided by the underlying conflict of economic interests between workers and their exploiters and not by national antagonisms. The conflict of economic interests was expected to end only in a communist world.

According to Soviet political writers, internationalism developed in three stages. The first stage was the period before the 1917 Russian revolution, when internationalism was said to have manifested itself in the common struggle of workers against capitalism, and in the assistance that workers in one country were giving to workers elsewhere. The second stage covered the period from 1917 to the end of World War II. As the Communist Party of the Soviet Union (CPSU) was the only communist party in power at that time, Moscow assumed the "leading role" in the struggle against capitalism, helping workers as well as the communist parties that claimed to represent the workers' interests.

During the third stage—the post–World War II era, when several Soviet-type systems came into existence to form "the world socialist system"—internationalism emerged in two forms. When socialist states assisted workers and communist parties in the capitalist world, they did so in the name of *proletarian* internationalism; when socialist countries related to one another, their cooperative association was called *socialist* internationalism. The latter was meant to indicate fraternal relations, the absence of fundamental conflicts of interests. Such harmonious relations could exist, it was explained, because all socialist countries, in the absence of class conflict at home, reflected the common interests of workers in their foreign relations across national frontiers. Hence the repeatedly proclaimed "identity of views" on basic questions among the socialist countries.

Because the theory posits the common interests of socialist states, it was always difficult to find appropriate explanations for existing differences between such states. As their interests were presumed to coincide, what caused the rift between the Soviet Union and Yugoslavia or between the Soviet Union and China? How would a Marxist ideologist come to grips with high tension between Hungary and Romania over the Romanian suppression of the Hungarian ethnic minority in Transylvania? In general, why were intra-bloc relations so seldom harmonious, to say the least?

Even at the beginning of the Gorbachev era, the simple answer given by Soviet and East European ideologists was that as long as capitalism exists, its representatives—particularly U.S. "imperialism"—will instigate conflicts and indeed exploit "contradictions" (i.e., problems) in the socialist world.

The argument was familiar: *We* have a problem and it is (largely) *your* fault. But there was a more sophisticated explanation as well. It was that even in countries where socialism was victorious, remnants of the old, so-called petty-bourgeois mentality survived, and thus external forces could still count on the support of some misguided individuals. According to this more complex version, faulty decisions by the regimes or their leaders could also contribute to or exacerbate such problems; for example, Stalin and Beria were blamed for the Soviet-Yugoslav rift.

Significantly, it was also the concept of socialist internationalism that provided justification for the need to be vigilant in defense of the gains of socialism *everywhere*. Hence the "Brezhnev Doctrine"—the application of the theory of socialist internationalism to contemporary circumstances in Eastern Europe. As Brezhnev once explained it:

> The CPSU has always advocated that each socialist country determine the concrete forms of its development along the path of socialism by taking into account the specific nature of its national conditions. But it is well known, comrades, that there are common natural laws of socialist construction, deviation from which could lead to deviation from socialism as such. And when external and internal forces hostile to socialism try to turn the development of a given socialist country in the direction of the restoration of the capitalist system, when a threat arises to the cause of socialism in that country—a threat to the security of the socialist commonwealth as a whole—this is no longer merely a problem for that country's people, but a common problem, the concern of all socialist countries.
>
> It is quite clear that an action such as military assistance to a fraternal country to end a threat to the socialist system is an extraordinary measure, dictated by necessity. It can be called forth only by the overt actions of the enemies of socialism within the country and beyond its boundaries, actions that create a threat to the common interests of the socialist camp.[2]

Under Gorbachev the Soviet definition of socialist interna-

2. *Pravda*, November 13, 1968. For an English translation, see *Current*

tionalism—and its corollary, the "Brezhnev Doctrine"—was gradually modified. What was new from the beginning was the emphasis on the autonomy of the East European communist parties and Moscow's rather convincing disavowal of its "leading role" in the communist world. Speaking in Prague in 1987 and answering his own question about the "major principles" of the Soviet–East European relationship, Gorbachev himself reiterated some of the old Soviet views and at the same time hinted at intriguing modifications:

> First and foremost we proceed from the premise that the entire system of the socialist countries' political relations can and must be built on the basis of equality and mutual responsibility. No one has the right to claim special status in the socialist world. We consider the independence of every party, its responsibility to the people of its own country, and its right to decide the questions of the country's development to be unconditional principles.
>
> At the same time, we are of the firm conviction that the community of socialist nations will be successful only if every party and country is concerned not only about its own interests, and only if every party and country treats its friends and allies with respect and is sure to take their interests into account.[3]

In his 1987 book *Perestroika*, written for the English-speaking world and phrased accordingly, Gorbachev elaborated on the same points:

> The entire framework of political relations between the socialist countries must be strictly based on absolute independence. This is a view held by the leaders of all fraternal countries. The independence of each Party, its sovereign right to decide the issues facing its country and its responsibility to its nation are the unquestionable principles.

Digest of the Soviet Press 20, No. 46 (December 4, 1968), pp. 3–5.

3. Mikhail Gorbachev, *For a "Common European Home," For a New Way of Thinking,* Speech by the General Secretary of the CPSU Central Committee at the Czechoslovak-Soviet Friendship Meeting, Prague, April 10, 1987 (Moscow: Novosti, 1987), p. 10.

We are also convinced that the socialist community will be successful only if every party and state cares for both its own and common interests, if it respects its friends and allies, heeds their interests and pays attention to the experience of others. Awareness of this relationship between domestic issues and the interests of world socialism is typical of the countries of the socialist community. We are united, in unity resides our strength, and from unity we draw our confidence that we will cope with the issues set forth by our time.[4]

Comparison of Gorbachev's statements with Brezhnev's prompts these observations:

(1) The underlying justification for "fraternal assistance" by the Soviet Union—the "Brezhnev Doctrine"—still remained largely unchanged. The code words were still there: the "socialist community" had a "common responsibility" and "common interests," and the socialist countries "will be successful only if every party and state cares for both its own and common interests." The phrasing was less threatening than Brezhnev's but the argument was similar. What was unclear was whether the Soviet Union, having disclaimed its "leading role," was still ultimately in charge of interpreting the meaning of, and determining when to act on behalf of, the bloc's "common interests."

In a subsequent interview with *The Washington Post* (May 22, 1988), Gorbachev specifically addressed the issue of past Soviet policies toward Eastern Europe. When asked about Soviet military interventions in Hungary and Czechoslovakia, he had an opportunity—on the eve of his Moscow summit with President Reagan—to break with the past. Instead, this is what he said even then:

When you speak about interference, I understand what you have in mind. But when I recall those situations, I had something else in mind. I have in mind that before what you are

---

4. Mikhail S. Gorbachev, *Perestroika: New Thinking for Our Country and the World* (New York: Harper and Row, 1987), p. 165.

talking about happened, another kind of interference had occurred.

Implicit in Gorbachev's reply was an old argument: The Soviet Union extended "fraternal assistance" ("what you are talking about") to Hungary and Czechoslovakia because "another kind of interference"—presumably by the West—had made it unavoidable. In other words, Moscow intervened in order to protect the common cause of socialism not from the likes of Imre Nagy and Alexander Dubček but from the West. With past Soviet interventions so justified, Gorbachev declined to repudiate the "Brezhnev Doctrine."

(2) At the same time, Gorbachev was placing far greater stress than his predecessors on "the independence of each [Communist] Party" in the region. He repeatedly affirmed Moscow's intention to deal with the East European parties "on the basis of equality," effectively disclaiming the Soviet Union's "leading role" in world communism. "No one has the right to claim special status in the socialist world," he said. In a major speech delivered in Moscow in November 1987, Gorbachev added: "We have become convinced of there being no 'model' of socialism to be emulated by everyone."

It was difficult to sort out the precise meaning of the Soviet position; clearly, it was under review.

Some Soviet representatives said that Gorbachev's words about the East European parties' autonomy should be taken at face value. For example. Oleg T. Bogomolov, the reform-minded and influential director of the Institute of Economics of the World Socialist System, told *The Washington Times* (July 8, 1988), "We have completely changed our relations with the East European countries. . . . [Today the] "Brezhnev Doctrine" is completely unacceptable and [its application] unthinkable. . . . We gave too much advice before to our partners, and it was actually very damaging to them. It's time to keep our advice to ourselves." In a similar vein, Fyodor Burlatski, chairman of the Soviet Human Rights Commission, told the Austrian paper *Die Presse* in April 1988, "We

have given our allies so much bad advice in the past that now
we [even] hesitate to give them a piece of good advice."

A few writers went even further, denouncing the history
of Soviet policy toward the communist movement. In the government paper *Izvestia* (July 11, 1987), Alexander Bovin, a
senior foreign policy analyst, blamed the Soviet Union for the
harm it had done to communist parties abroad, including
those in Eastern Europe:

> The prospects for socialist transformation in developed capi-
> talist countries has been shunted into the indefinite future. *The
> situation in a number of countries of socialist persuasion re-
> mains unstable and is susceptible to regression.* And in capitalist
> and Third World countries [most] communist parties . . . have
> been unable to transform themselves into mass organizations
> and secure the support of the bulk of the working class and
> working people. *There are a number of reasons for this and one
> of them is undoubtedly the failures, contradictions, and phenom-
> ena of crisis and stagnation in the development of the Soviet
> Union, other socialist countries, and world socialism as a whole.*
> [Emphasis added.]

Looking at these comments, Western analysts—and probably most East Europeans—were inclined to shake their
heads in disbelief. Could it be that the Soviet Union recognized the sovereignty and independence of the countries of
Eastern Europe? Could it be that the old rhetoric about non-
intervention now actually signified a prohibition not only
against military intervention but even against "good advice"
as well? Was the "Brezhnev Doctrine" really "unacceptable"?
Did socialist internationalism acquire a different meaning?

No one could be sure. It appeared, however, that the concept of socialist internationalism was being modified to
stress the responsibility and autonomy of the East European
communist parties. Moscow was showing more tolerance toward its allies. Clearly, there was more room for experimentation than ever before. Moscow's vision of the Soviet–East
European relationship was not what it had been in the 1960s
and the 1970s, let alone in Stalin's time, when the Kremlin's

Mikhail Suslov could—and did—dismiss East European Politburo members at will.

In effect, Gorbachev was giving the old theory of "separate roads to socialism" a new lease on life. He was telling the communist leaders of Eastern Europe to take charge of their own affairs. The *countries* of Eastern Europe were not (yet) on their own, but the region's communist *parties* were granted far more autonomy than they had before; it was not primarily their responsibility and not the Soviet Union's to improve economic performance under (if at all possible) stable conditions. Gorbachev's apparent intention was to accelerate the bloc's decentralization that had begun after Stalin's death.

All in all, the words emanating from Moscow did not yet point to a radical break with the past; they suggested a gradual evolution in Soviet thinking. On the one hand, Gorbachev's affirmation of the socialist states' "common interests" was a sign of continuity in the Soviet perception of Eastern Europe. On the other hand, his emphasis on the autonomy of the region's communist parties was a hopeful sign of the fading of Moscow's imperial mentality.

On the basis of Soviet statements, most Western analysts could not yet conclude that Soviet hegemony over Eastern Europe was giving way to full respect for the principles of sovereignty and non-intervention. They, and probably most East Europeans, assumed that under certain circumstances Moscow would resort to the use of military force on behalf of its real or perceived security interests, though no longer on behalf of its real or perceived ideological interests. Indeed, the important question was not whether the "Brezhnev Doctrine" was dead. *Saying* that it was—in statements not from Gorbachev but from lesser officials and commentators—did not really answer the question; East Europeans remained skeptical of future Soviet intentions. They wondered how far an East European country could go without inviting Soviet "fraternal assistance." What was the new threshold of Soviet tolerance?

Until 1988–89, one answer was that as long as an East European country remained in the Warsaw Pact and accepted "socialism" or at least called itself "socialist," there would be no intervention. A second answer was that the threshold of Soviet tolerance might be higher for the region's small and strategically insignificant countries (Bulgaria, Romania, and Hungary) than it was for the northern tier countries (East Germany, Poland, and Czechoslovakia). The third answer— the safest and the best—was that only if and when an upheaval occurred would Gorbachev himself (or his successor) know and decide what to do, and therefore the outside world could not know in advance either.

By 1988, growing uncertainty about the "Brezhnev Doctrine," combined with the widely held feeling that Moscow was raising its threshold of tolerance, produced new pressures from the East European people, who wanted their leaders to undertake radical experiments that suddenly seemed to be acceptable to the Soviet Union. Emboldened by the spirit and logic of perestroika and glasnost, by the presumed erosion of Moscow's imperial mentality, by informal Soviet disclaimers of the "Brezhnev Doctrine," and by subtle changes of emphasis in the official definition of socialist internationalism, East Europeans were putting their leaders on the defensive—in Gorbachev's name.

The Institutional Framework

The bloc's extensive institutional network was no barrier to Gorbachev's placing Soviet–East European relations on a more equal footing—but it was of no particular help either. In point of fact, the existing network could be used for all types or kinds of relations.

Throughout the Gorbachev era, as before, most of the political business transacted between the Soviet Union and Eastern Europe has been through *bilateral* ties, including party-to-party and government-to-government relations as well as numerous semi-governmental and semi-official contacts.

In the CPSU, important decisions concerning Eastern Europe have always been made by the Politburo and implemented by the Secretariat. Until mid-1988, a key post in that institutional setting was the Central Committee secretary in charge of relations with the socialist countries, a post Vadim Medvedev occupied for several years. Unlike his predecessors (including Suslov), Medvedev was not a Politburo member at that time. His large staff of specialists on every socialist country in Eastern Europe and elsewhere worked for the awkwardly named Department for Liaison with the Communist and Workers' Parties of Socialist Countries. This department maintained "liaison" with all *ruling* communist parties, but not with those that were *competing* for power in Western Europe and elsewhere.

Prior to the mid-1988 reorganization of the CPSU apparatus (see Chapter 6), two other major departments shared responsibility for Eastern Europe. One was the general International Relations Department, headed at the time by Anatoly Dobrynin, the long-time Soviet ambassador to the United States; the other was the Information and Propaganda Department, led by Politburo member and strong Gorbachev ally Aleksandr Yakovlev. (One of Yakovlev's deputies was Nikolai Shishlin, a veteran East European specialist.) Whether, or to what extent, either Dobrynin or Yakovlev was authorized to supervise the work of the Liaison Department was not known. Nor was it clear how responsibilities for East European affairs were divided among the several Central Committee departments (including Medvedev's) on the one hand, and Gorbachev's very influential "personal advisor" on Eastern Europe (the highly regarded political scientist,

Georgi Shakhnazarov) on the other. However, all the top policy makers mentioned here—Medvedev, Dobrynin, and especially Yakovlev, Shakhnazarov, and Shishlin—belonged to the CPSU's reformist wing.

As for government-to-government relations, they have always constituted the other major channel for bilateral contacts. Most of the business transacted this way involves economic issues—bilateral trade in particular. When the head of the Soviet government—currently Nikolai Ryzhkov—or one of his ministers meets his East European counterpart, the principal subjects under discussion are trade, financial matters, deliveries, and the like.

As for non-economic issues, there are at least four ministries, institutions, or semi-governmental agencies keeping an eye on or maintaining close contact with the region. Until 1989, the most important of them was probably the KGB, the Soviet secret police and intelligence service. The KGB's contacts with its East European equivalents—except the independent-minded, if huge and brutal, Romanian service—were presumed to be extensive and frequent. Its main task was believed to be the collection of information about the reliability of East European leaders. Except in Romania, KGB agents also advised, though no longer supervised, their East European counterparts. Presumably in cooperation with Soviet military intelligence, the KGB was also in charge of coordinating joint East European activities in the West, including the collection of technical intelligence, such as the purchase and theft of high-technology information and blueprints.

Until the 1988 reorganization of the foreign-policy hierarchy, the role of the Soviet Ministry of Foreign Affairs, headed by Politburo member Eduard Shevardnadze, was to facilitate rather than to decide. Under the supervision of one of Shevardnadze's deputies, the ministry dealt only with the formal aspects of diplomatic relations with Eastern Europe, such as protocol; his staff was divided, as are such staffs elsewhere in the world, into geographic divisions and country desks. The ministry staffed the embassies, of course, and it also received most of the cables from the region's capitals and distributed them to appropriate officials throughout the bureaucracy, including party headquarters.

The Soviet Ministry of Defense has maintaineds bilateral, government-to-government contact with the region's ministries of defense. While military relations are conducted largely via the multilateral framework of the Warsaw Pact (see below and Chapter 5), wherever Soviet forces are stationed—in East Germany, Poland, Hungary, and Czechoslovakia at present—there are numerous practical issues that must be settled bilaterally. Normally, these issues relate to the implementation of agreements previously made by the councils of the Warsaw Pact.

Finally, an important role in Soviet–East European relations was reserved for the Soviet Academy of Science's Institute of Economics of the World Socialist System, directed by Academician Oleg Bogomolov. The institute's staff conducts extensive research on contemporary economic, political, and social developments in Eastern Europe; it is by far the largest Soviet think-tank focusing on the region. Aside from research, the institute also advises the party and the government on what policies they should adopt. Members of the staff are frequently assigned to the Soviet Union's East European embassies, where they serve as economic officers, cultural attachés, and the like. The Bogomolov Institute, as it is often called, is known to have long advocated a tolerant Soviet approach to Eastern Europe.

As for *multilateral* ties, there are two major, well-known institutions in the bloc—the Warsaw Pact and the Council for Mutual Economic Assistance. Their respective military and economic roles are discussed in Chapters 4 and 5, while some of the more recent changes are treated in Chapter 6. The Warsaw Pact's political activities and significance can be summarized here as follows:

The Warsaw Pact was formed in 1955. Why it was created

then is still a matter of controversy. Formally, it was presented by its founders—the Soviet Union and its East European allies—as a response to NATO in general and to West Germany's imminent decision to join NATO in particular. The problem with that explanation is that NATO had been in existence for six years, since 1949. Moreover, Moscow did not really need the Warsaw Pact to counter NATO, with or without West Germany as its member, for wartime agreements provided for the stationing of Soviet troops in several East European countries. (The legal rationale for stationing Soviet troops in Poland was that they maintained links between the Soviet homeland and the Soviet occupation forces in East Germany, while Soviet troops in Hungary and Romania were supposed to be there to maintain links with Soviet occupation forces in then-divided Austria.)

Why then was the Warsaw Pact formed in 1955—why at that time? The most likely explanation is that it was created in response to the neutralization of Austria in 1955, the consequence of which was the withdrawal of Soviet forces (as well as of the occupying armies of the U.S., Great Britain, and France) from that country. The new circumstances required Moscow to find a new legal basis for keeping Soviet troops in Hungary and Romania. The Warsaw Pact provided the necessary legal justification: Soviet troops could remain on the territory of any member state to protect all members against foreign (i.e., Western) aggressors.

A second controversy has involved the primary function of the Warsaw Pact. According to its treaty, it is a defensive organization intended to act as a military counterweight to NATO and to offer its members a forum for foreign-policy consultation and coordination.

Many Western observers have seen the *main* role of the Warsaw Pact differently—as an instrument for the Soviet Union to keep Eastern Europe in line. One Western analyst wrote that with the Pact operating as an agent of Soviet control over the region, its "main uses are political rather than

purely military, and it serves as an iron corset to hold together the communist bloc. In a larger sense, the Warsaw
Pact serves as an alliance system through which the Soviet
leaders seek to entangle their unwilling allies in a web of Soviet national interests."[5] Since 1989, as discussed in Chapters
5 and 6, this is a role the Pact has ceased to play.

Still, the Warsaw Pact has brought together the region's
top leaders once or twice a year for meetings of its Political
Consultative Committee (PCC), the Pact's highest organ. Another political channel has been the Pact's Committee of Foreign Ministers. Meetings of both committees have rotated
among the capitals of the member states, with the host country in charge of arrangements and protocol as well as of draft-
ing the inevitable communiqué that is released to the press
after the meeting is concluded.

At these very high-level discussions, foreign-policy issues
and intra-bloc relations used to come up for discussion. For
example, the meetings usually generated some proposals, recommendations, or "appeals" that dealt with arms control and
European security. It is a fair guess that the primary objective was to add weight to a Soviet proposal which would be
presented later as the Warsaw Pact's "new approach" to peace
and security. Only since the formation of a largely noncommunist Polish government in 1989 have East European
representatives begun to debate such routine Soviet proposals at Warsaw Pact meetings.

To discern a new idea in a PCC communiqué dealing with
"peace and security" required extraordinary patience and eru-
dition, as well as considerable familiarity with previous proposals and with the intricacies of communist jargon. At
times, Western analysts confronted what appeared to be a
slightly modified version of an old proposal issued by the
Pact. What followed then was speculation: Does the modifica-

---

5. Roman Kolkowicz, "The Warsaw Pact: Entangling Alliance," *Survey*,
No. 70/71 (Winter/Spring 1969), p. 101.

tion signal a possible new approach or is it only propaganda intended to divide or confuse Western publics eager for change? Generally, to decipher the meaning and possible significance of Warsaw Pact communiqués and documents, it was necessary to solicit more information through diplomatic contact with Soviet and East European officials.

In times of past crises in Eastern Europe, however, the PCC conducted important business. During the 1968 Czechoslovak and the 1980–81 Polish crises, for example, leaders of the Warsaw Pact met on several occasions to figure out what to do. Thanks to the subsequent defection of Gomułka's interpreter, whose testimony has been generally confirmed by other sources, it is known that the July 1968 PCC meeting dealing with the "Prague Spring" was long and contentious. Led by Brezhnev, the Soviet delegation had not indicated what it wanted to do—except that it did not approve of the changes then underway in Czechoslovakia. Because Moscow was not yet ready to propose or undertake intervention, its junior allies felt free to express their own views. According to Gomułka's interpreter, the debate was heated. Hungary's Kádár showed so much "patience" toward Dubček's reformist course in Czechoslovakia that East Germany's Ulbricht could not contain himself. He is reported to have turned to the Hungarian, shouting:

> If you think, Comrade Kádár, that you are helping the cause of socialism with your objections and reservations, you are making a big mistake. And you have no idea what will happen next. Once the American–West German imperialists have got Czechoslovakia in their control, then you will be next to go, Comrade Kádár. But that is something you can't or won't understand![6]

In 1981, at the time of the Polish crisis, there was also heated debate in the councils of the Warsaw Pact. This time, according to another Polish defector—a high-level Polish

---

6. Erwin Weit, *At the Red Summit: Interpreter behind the Iron Curtain* (New York: Macmillan, 1973), pp. 193–217.

military officer—the Romanian representatives expressed various "objections and reservations."[7]

In the early Gorbachev era, too, East European participation continued to depend on the issues under discussion:

(1) "Distant" foreign policy issues having to do with South Africa or Nicaragua were of no immediate concern to East Europeans. Romania, an exception under Ceauşescu, quibbled about the phrasing of a particular Warsaw Pact declaration, but on issues of this sort Moscow generally prevailed. There was little or no payoff for the East Europeans in trying to counter such "distant" Soviet policies.

(2) For both economic and political reasons, issues having to do with intra-European affairs were of more immediate concern to the East Europeans. Even before Gorbachev's rise to power, in 1983–84, as Moscow initiated a harsh campaign against West Germany for permitting American missiles to be deployed there, East Germany demurred. (Still, having expressed "reservations," eventually all East European states fell in line; under Soviet pressure, the East German and Bulgarian leaders at the time, Honecker and Zhivkov, soon cancelled their planned visits to Bonn.) By contrast, when Hungary criticized a Soviet draft resolution that condemned West Germany during the "later" Gorbachev era (in 1989), the text *was* modified to accommodate Hungarian objections.

(3) Issues directly related to Eastern Europe itself—those that are "closest to home"—have always prompted more extensive discussion and debate. The East Europeans expressed strong views, for example, when it came to the possibility of military interventions—as the nasty 1968 debate about

---

7. Former Colonel Ryszard J. Kukliński, who escaped to the West a few weeks before martial law was declared in December 1981, was an officer of the Polish General Staff during preparations for martial law. See his lengthy interview under the title "Wojna z narodem widziana do śradka" in *Kultura* (Paris), April 1987, pp. 3–57. An abridged version appeared in English under the title "The Crushing of Solidarity" in *Orbis* 32, No. 1 (Winter 1988), pp. 7–31.

Czechoslovakia showed. More recently, under Gorbachev, tough bargaining has come to characterize talks especially with respect to the individual countries' contribution to Warsaw Pact military expenditures and with respect to foreign trade among the CMEA countries.

Indeed, while the region's formal institutional structure established in the mid–1950s and refined in the 1960s and 1970s is more or less intact, a little story here and a leak there indicate that in the early Gorbachev era the *atmosphere* at various bilateral and multilateral forums changed in the following ways:

(1) On most issues, Soviet negotiators are said to have entered into discussion with their East European counterparts without dictating the final terms of an agreement or declaration. The arrogance of the past was fading; at times, Soviet officials conceded that they did not know the answer. They wanted to hear not what others imagined they would like to hear, but what the East Europeans really thought.

(2) The East Europeans, in turn, were more inclined to speak up and take exceptions to Soviet proposals — on critical economic issues as well as on political ones. Even before the watershed year of 1989, they were emboldened by Moscow's reluctance to publicly criticize an East European country, an East European leader, or even an East European decision. Apparently, Gorbachev was determined from the beginning to stop public polemics against East European "deviations"—once a regular occurrence and favorite pastime of Soviet ideological watchdogs. As a result, East European officials have become more confident in their opinions and hence more willing to share them with their Soviet counterparts.

The Ties They Are A-Changin'

That neither the ideological nor the institutional structure of the Soviet–East European relationship changed dramatically during the early Gorbachev years was interpreted to mean that a reversal was still conceivable. The same institutions could once again serve a hegemon-satellite relationship as much as they could provide the framework for relations among more or less equal partners.

Yet structure has mattered much less than the hope generated by the Gorbachev phenomenon since 1985. Especially as the end of the 1980s approached, East Europeans were correctly sensing a promising trend toward raising the threshold of Soviet tolerance in their region. While the meaning of this trend escaped precise definition, the following generalization was an approximate guideline to Gorbachev's initial policies:

> Before Gorbachev, Moscow regularly and repeatedly reminded the East European leaders of what they must not do as well as what they should do; it issued both prohibitions and imperatives. Under Gorbachev, Moscow was beginning to be satisfied with indicating to the East European leaders what they must not do; it issued only (non-specific but still well-understood) prohibitions. As seen by East Europeans (until 1988–89), the most important Soviet prohibitions were against leaving the Warsaw Pact, against relinquishing the one-party political order, and against abandoning "socialism."

While, to repeat, the new Soviet attitude thus did not yet offer independence to the *states* or freedom of choice to the *peoples* of Eastern Europe, it did provide the region's *communist parties* a good deal of autonomy or "elbow room" to determine what sort of socialist arrangements would best suit their interests and circumstances. Given what Gorbachev inherited from his predecessors, this was a substantial concession.

There were at least two ways to assess the Soviet decision to undertake this initial step toward decentralizing the bloc. One was a *historical perspective*. Consider a few episodes in the history of Soviet–East European relations and speculate:

Could this have happened in the early Gorbachev years?

• A few years after World War II, Stalin invited a group of Polish leaders to Moscow. One night, in the Kremlin, he decided to have some fun — Stalin-style. He played dance music on his record player and told Bolesław Bierut, the top Polish leader, to dance with Soviet Foreign Minister Molotov. Cheek to cheek or not, they danced. This *could not* have happened in the early Gorbachev years.

• In 1955, Hungarian Prime Minister András Hegedüs attended the founding meeting of the Warsaw Pact and signed the new treaty on his country's behalf. Prior to the elaborate ceremonies in Warsaw, Hegedüs did not even have an opportunity to see the text of the treaty, let alone discuss it with members of his cabinet. This *would not* have happened in the early Gorbachev years.

• In 1968, during the course of his discussions with Dubček, Brezhnev expressed his "disappointment" that the Czechoslovak leader had not cleared some of his decisions with Moscow earlier that year. "I believed in you," Brezhnev began, "and I stood up for you against the others [in the Soviet Politburo]. Our Sasha [Dubček] is a good comrade, I said. And you disappointed us so terribly," remarked Brezhnev as if lecturing a small child. Then he added: "From the outset I wanted to help you against [the Stalinist] Novotný, and immediately in January [after Novotný's ouster] I asked you: Do you want to replace the minister of the interior? And the minister of national defense? And is there anyone else you want to replace?"[8] Such excessive Soviet involvement in personnel matters was still *possible but unlikely* in the early Gorbachev years.

• In June 1981, during the Polish crisis, Moscow addressed

---

8. Zdeněk Mlynář, *Nightfrost in Prague: The End of Humane Socialism* (New York: Karz, 1980), pp. 238–239. The author was a member of the Czechoslovak delegation that negotiated under duress with Soviet leaders in Moscow after the Warsaw Pact intervention in Czechoslovakia. Although Mlynář cites Brezhnev from memory, the quotation rings true.

an "open letter" to the Polish party. Against the background of its growing concern that the "gains of socialism" were in jeopardy, the CPSU stated: "S. Kania, W. Jaruzelski and other Polish comrades expressed agreement with our point of view. But nothing has changed, and the policy of concession and compromise has not been corrected."[9] On another occasion, Brezhnev asserted, "We will not abandon fraternal, socialist Poland; we will stand by it."[10] If such ominous language could be used publicly, it is easy to imagine the tone of warnings and threats voiced behind closed doors. In the early Gorbachev era, given comparable circumstances, the Soviet Union would have been *concerned but would not have publicly chastised another communist party.*

Looking at the four cases from the past suggests both important changes and possible continuities in Soviet conduct *after* 1985 and *before* 1988. The obvious prohibition—i.e., Poland must not leave the Warsaw Pact, must not abandon socialism, and must not give up the party's "leading role"—still remained. But the incessant and irritating lecturing about what the East Europeans should do—the imperatives—was passé. Instead of polemics and admonition, there was far more give and take. (And it was impossible to imagine Gorbachev compelling an East European leader to dance with Foreign Minister Shevardnadze.)

There was of course another way to look at the East European parties' newly granted autonomy—not from a historical but from a *contemporary perspective.* The question then was not "how things changed over the years" but this:

Before 1988–89, were the leaders of Eastern Europe taking advantage of the new "elbow room" to intro-

---

9. The Soviet "letter," dated June 5, 1981, appeared in Polish dailies on June 11, 1981.

10. *Report of the Central Committee of the CPSU to the XXVI Congress of the Communist Party of the Soviet Union on the Immediate Tasks of the Party in Home and Foreign Policy,* delivered by L. I. Brezhnev, General Secretary of the CPSU Central Committee, 23 February 1981 (Moscow: Novosti, 1981).

duce glasnost and perestroika and undertake the "next steps" in their countries' national interests? Alternatively, were they using their expanded authority to circumvent the processes of change for fear of losing their privileges and possibly their power?

The answer to this question was that, Poland and Hungary excepted, the East European regimes were still desperately trying to resist the spirit of perestroika and especially glasnost. The Romanian and East German authorities, in particular, disclaimed any need to follow Gorbachev's path. One East German Politburo member put it this way: Just because one of our neighbors changes the wallpaper in his house, should we all follow his example?

A country-by-country survey showed that *Bulgaria* led the pack in offering daily commentaries on Gorbachev's "historic" economic proposals and their relevance for Bulgaria. In one speech after another, particularly in early 1987, party leader Todor Zhivkov went out of his way to praise perestroika—though he barely mentioned glasnost. Claiming that the Bulgarian Communist Party had followed a correct course since its April 1956 plenum—the first party gathering he dominated—and that the country had since caught up with the industrialized world, Zhivkov still kept insisting on the adoption of literally hundreds of new economic measures. In his own words: "We can and must transform our already transformed Bulgaria."

Unlike Gorbachev, Zhivkov offered no criticism of the past. He could not. In power since 1956, he was responsible for over three decades of Bulgarian history. There was no talk in Sofia of reassessing Bulgaria's poor treatment of its large Turkish minority or of improving relations with Yugoslavia, another neighbor with whom Bulgaria had an uneasy relationship. Nor was there any indication of a cultural thaw; Bulgarian intellectual life continued to reflect conditions similar to those in the Soviet Union under Brezhnev rather than under Gorbachev.

All the same, Zhivkov's rhetoric was still full of plans for economic restructuring, decentralization, self-management, increased independence for the country's industrial plants, agricultural units and banks, "new types of management structures," income differentiation to reward hard work, closure of inefficient enterprises, construction of small- and medium-sized factories, and the like. It was widely assumed that this ambitious rhetoric was no more than hot air. Zhivkov's advanced age, his personal stake in continuity rather than change, the abrupt dismissal in mid-1988—as late as mid-1988!—of his heir apparent, Chudomir Alexandrov (who was reportedly accused of "new thinking"), and the apparent absence of a reformist wing in the party that could challenge him all combined to make it doubtful that this most (and perhaps only) pro-Russian state in the region would experience radical reforms while Zhivkov was at the helm.

Czechoslovakia was a test case for Gorbachev's impact on Eastern Europe. This was so because, having waged war against reformism for over two decades, the post-1968 Czechoslovak regime was particularly vulnerable to the winds of reform emanating from Moscow. Western-oriented advocates of human rights, led by the eminent playwright Václav Havel, were very active. In Alexander Dubček there was also a well-known—reformist and pro-Gorbachev—alternative to the country's Brezhnevite regime.

There was no adequate explanation as to why Gustáv Husák, party leader from 1969 to 1987 and then president for two years, allowed the Czechoslovak economy to slide and its polity to degenerate. Although, prior to World War II, it was a cultural mecca and one of the six or seven most highly industrialized countries in the world, Czechoslovakia under Husák became a showpiece for an economic antique shop while its stifling cultural atmosphere resembled the vibrancy of a political cemetery. According to one theory, Husák —himself a victim of Stalinist purges in the 1950s and an erstwhile supporter of the "Prague Spring"—felt compelled to compensate for his reformist inclinations. A corollary to this theory was that Husák was no more than a figurehead all these years, with the real power being held by Central Committee Secretary Vasil Bil'ak, a man with neo-Stalinist views and close ties to the pre-Gorbachev Soviet leadership. Be that as it may, the fact remained that certain Czechoslovak policies were even more rigid and conservative than those pursued by Brezhnev. In the meantime, Moscow could not yet decide what to do (see also Chapter 6), for any Soviet attempt to ease out this *united* Czechoslovak leadership ran counter not only to Gorbachev's professed principle of noninterference in the internal affairs of the East European countries; as seen at that time, it also entailed the risk of considerable instability.

Under Erich Honecker's leadership, *East Germany*, once Moscow's most loyal ally, approved of perestroika and glasnost—for the Soviet Union. Typically, East German officials expressed agreement with the Soviet Union on all "fundamental issues," endorsed Gorbachev's policy of seeking to raise "the Soviet people's material and cultural living standards"—and denied Western "suspicions of the existence of differences and nuances" between Moscow and East Berlin.

There were, indeed, no significant differences between the two countries on foreign policy issues. Back in 1983–84, before Gorbachev, there *was* a tug-of-war over intermediate-range nuclear weapons, European detente, and intra-German relations. At that time, the Soviet Union was in the midst of an anti–West German campaign, accusing Bonn of becoming Washington's stooge and of reverting to an anti-Soviet, so-called "revanchist" policy (of trying to take revenge, as it were, for German losses in World War II). East Germany, by contrast, continued to act on the basis of its national economic interests, which dictated improved or at least civilized relations with West Germany. With its economy so heavily dependent on West German credits, investments, and trade,

East Berlin was reluctant to join Moscow's campaign against Bonn and echo its belligerent rhetoric. However, after the end of that campaign—after Gorbachev also began to court West Germany—foreign policy issues no longer stood between the two countries.

But East Germany found no reason to adopt Gorbachev's policies at home. Kurt Hager, the East German Politburo's leading ideologist at the time, asserted in 1987 that the "forms and methods" of perestroika were "not transferable to other socialist countries."[11] Officials in East Berlin claimed that since their so-called "streamlined" economy was performing well and since respective conditions differed, East Germany should only continue to "improve" its economic mechanism but should not—need not—experiment with untested, radical reforms. As for glasnost, they said—only half-jokingly—that they had a particular, German version of glasnost: *West* German television that could reach all of East Germany. Indeed, that anti-Stalinist Soviet film *Repentance* was shown only on West German TV in early 1988—and was promptly criticized in the East German official daily *Neues Deutschland* and other papers for its "hostile caricature" of Soviet life. (The film had packed movie houses throughout the Soviet Union, Hungary, and Poland.) Moreover, also in 1988, East German authorities prohibited the distribution of Soviet journals whose content was contrary to their own, orthodox views. Incredibly, many other Soviet publications were *verboten* in East Germany as well.

Honecker and his colleagues also denied that there was an inherent link between economic reform and political liberalization. They argued that political reform especially would mean trouble for a country as exposed to the West as East Germany. When they saw East German youth demonstrate against the Berlin Wall in 1987 by invoking Gorbachev's

11. As quoted on East Berlin radio on April 9, 1987. For an English translation, see *Foreign Broadcast Information Service* (FBIS), April 10, 1987, p. E1.

name, they concluded that the wind of change emanating from Moscow threatened the stability and perhaps the existence of East Germany. Their point was similar to that of Prague's beleaguered leaders—and Moscow's response was nearly the same in both cases. For the time being, Gorbachev was too preoccupied with other matters to do more than to *ask* Honecker to change his ways. The embarrassing gap between Soviet reformism and East Germany's orthodoxy notwithstanding, Gorbachev waited. Only in 1989 did he assert himself (see Chapter 6), apparently telling Honecker to change his ways *or else*.

Hungary's initial reaction to the Gorbachev phenomenon was both complicated and confusing.

Before Gorbachev came to power in 1985, Hungary's János Kádár had already set in motion the most comprehensive economic reform in Eastern Europe. The New Economic Mechanism (NEM), begun in 1968, had introduced a measure of rationality into the economy. By focusing on agriculture, small-scale industry, and the service sector, the reforms succeeded in creating an economy in which plan and market could somehow co-exist and living standards rise as well. Kádár's "goulash communism"—perhaps an early version of perestroika—was also assisted by his regime's relative political tolerance and openness—perhaps an early version of glasnost. In the process, Kádár himself acquired considerable popularity and his country became the envy of East Europeans.

The 1980s witnessed a dramatic downturn in the Hungarian economy as well as a growing sense of hopelessness about the future. In May 1988, at the age of seventy-six, Kádár was forced to resign as his party's general secretary, and his whole old guard in the leadership went with him. In the shake-up, eight of the thirteen members of Kádár's Politburo were ousted; of the eight, six were ousted even from the large Central Committee.

The leadership chosen in 1988 was a curious coalition of

pseudo-reformers, reformers, and radical reformers. What united them momentarily was the desire to get Kádár's old guard out; the new Politburo's average age was only fifty-two. The coalition was led by the party's new general secretary, Károly Grósz, a long-time party functionary with a decidedly "law and order" mentality. Soon after his appointment, Grósz began a harsh campaign against the country's pro-Western, "liberal opposition." When on June 16, 1988, members of the opposition organized a small, peaceful demonstration to commemorate the 20th anniversary of Imre Nagy's execution, for example, Grósz called the demonstration an "incitement toward fascist propaganda, chauvinism and irredentism." Asked why the police had used truncheons to break it up, Grósz replied, "We do not like our policemen to be beaten up. . . ."[12]

Because of actions and statements of this kind, Grósz proved to be unpopular immediately, both among ordinary Hungarians and even within his party. From the beginning, he found himself on the defensive against the *real* party reformers led by Imre Pozsgay, who had openly embraced the goal of democratic socialism years before even Gorbachev ever though of it. Although, as discussed in Chapter 6, Grósz's "holding operation" marked him as a man of the past, Moscow was apparently satisfied for now. According to Grósz, Gorbachev told him in June 1988 that "it is probably the Hungarian endeavors and the Hungarian perceptions that are closest now to those of the Soviet Union."[13]

Poland's General Jaruzelski was the main East European beneficiary of Gorbachev's program and policies. After 1985, Moscow's once grudging approval of Jaruzelski's relatively moderate course turned into enthusiastic support. The Soviet press stopped questioning Jaruzelski's courting of the Catholic Church, the open discussion of controversial issues in Pol-

---

12. *Newsweek* (International Edition), July 18, 1988, p. 24.
13. *The New York Times*, July 10, 1988.

ish newspapers, or the absence of severe punishment for leaders of the Polish opposition. In 1987, the prominent Soviet weekly *Literaturnaya Gazeta* published a long and apparently uncensored interview with Józef Cardinal Glemp.

On numerous occasions, Gorbachev himself endorsed Jaruzelski as "a man of high morality, of huge intellectual capacities," a man "who loves his country." Gorbachev's ringing endorsement of the Polish leader—Jaruzelski's de facto elevation as Moscow's "favorite son" in Eastern Europe—was undoubtedly due to what he did for the Soviet Union in December 1981; his crackdown on "Solidarity" rendered Soviet intervention unnecessary. But because Gorbachev also approved of the Polish regime's policies after 1981, Jaruzelski enjoyed wide latitude to do what he deemed necessary to make Poland stable. Earlier than others could do elsewhere in Eastern Europe, he was free not only to introduce major economic reforms but to experiment with new forms of political participation—such as competitive elections, legislative innovations, consultation with the Catholic Church. The Polish press, already the freest in Eastern Europe, could even deal with such sensitive subjects as Soviet-Polish relations. This is why the general returned Gorbachev's compliments by welcoming the same "historic current of change" in the two countries. "Poland has not experienced such a happy convergence for the whole of the past millennium," Jaruzelski declared in 1987, commenting on the smooth state of his relations with Gorbachev.

Still, until late 1988 and despite the very favorable eastern winds helping with the Polish regime, it was far from certain how far Jaruzelski would go. True, he allowed more glasnost in Poland than there was in the Soviet Union. For several years now, even before Gorbachev, the Polish regime had closed its eyes to the publication of uncensored and illegal books and periodicals, some of which appeared regularly and enjoyed wide circulation. The Catholic Church was an acknowledged and seemingly welcome pillar of the Polish establishment, opposition leaders spoke their minds to Western reporters and visitors, almost any Pole could travel to the West, and even the country's company unions made an occasional effort to represent the workers' interests

However radical by Soviet or East European standards at that time, Jaruzelski's initial measures proved to be insufficient. The public was in no mood to support what the regime regarded as the necessary economic sacrifices unless the regime made what the public regarded as the necessary—more extensive—political concessions. Even more so than in Hungary, the key to economic change in Poland was political pluralism. The institutionalized form it would have to take would surely entail the legalization of "Solidarity," a move which remained perhaps even harder for Jaruzelski to accept —until, as discussed in Chapter 6, his sudden and dramatic change of mind in late 1988—than it was for Gorbachev to advocate in the early years.

Romania, unlike any other member of the Warsaw Pact, openly questioned the ideological soundness of glasnost and perestroika. The Romanian press all but ignored Gorbachev's very important January 1987 speech to the CPSU Central Committee; the party newspaper *Scinteia* printed only a brief, innocuous summary, after a three-day delay. The CPSU's 1988 party conference received almost no coverage at all. While Romania continued to follow a maverick course on some foreign policy issues, the country's economic structure and political atmosphere failed to respond to Gorbachev's call for change; "reform" was but a dirty word in the Romanian political dictionary. Under the brutal tyranny of Nicolae Ceauşescu and his family, and even by comparison with Brezhnevite East Germany, Bulgaria, or Czechoslovakia, Romania remained an isolated, Stalinist holdout—a cruel anachronism—in the Warsaw Pact. When Gorbachev visited Bucharest in 1987, his facial expression strongly suggested that he had no respect for the egomaniacal Ceauşescu.

For his part, Ceauşescu even questioned Gorbachev's adherence to "the invincible principles of scientific socialism." Alluding to the CPSU's new platform, for example, he said that a truly revolutionary party would not let "enterprises or economic sectors manage themselves" and thus abdicate its obligations to society. "Self-management and revolutionary democracy," he declared, "are inconceivable without the leading role of the Party . . . as the vital center from which all creative energies" should originate. Ceauşescu also ridiculed the idea of "improving socialism by developing so-called small private property," asserting that "Capitalist property is capitalist property, be it small or large."

Although there was a marked expansion of trade between Romania and the Soviet Union after 1984, it was not due to political considerations. Ceauşescu was simply determined to eliminate Romania's hard-currency debt as quickly as possible, irrespective of cost or consequences; trade with the Soviet Union was simpler and more advantageous under the circumstances. In the political and ideological realms, however, Ceauşescu defiantly dissociated Romania from glasnost and perestroika, signaling both his contempt for what the Soviet Union was doing and his unequivocal opposition to emulating the Soviet example at home. In the end, as related in Chapter 6, only a massive, bloody revolution in December 1989 finished the tyranny—and this tyrant, on Christmas Day.

Summing Up

A review of the Soviet–East European relationship *during the early Gorbachev era* shows how Soviet policy evolved before the critical year of 1989. This is how the 1985–88 period looked at that time:

(1) "Radical change" in Soviet policy toward Eastern Europe did not yet signify independence for the states and peoples of the region. In comparison to the respect Gorbachev showed

toward China, Eastern Europe remained but a Soviet dependency. China was able to set "three obstacles" that it said must be removed if Sino-Soviet relations were to improve: Moscow must withdraw from Afghanistan, thin out its forces along the Sino-Soviet border, and force Vietnam, its ally, to get out of Kampuchea (Cambodia). Incredibly, Gorbachev promptly reconsidered his predecessors' policies and began to remove the "three obstacles." The change in Soviet policy was radical, even dramatic. Moscow showed that it was prepared to relate to China by shelving, if not stifling, its hegemonic aspirations.

By contrast, no such radical change was yet apparent in the Soviet–East European relationship. True, the situation in many respects was not analogous. But the key question—could Moscow treat other communists as equals?—was similar, and yet, for the time being, the Soviet answer to China was "yes" and to Eastern Europe "no" or "not yet." There were possible scenarios—the abrupt withdrawal of an East European state from the Warsaw Pact, for example—that could spark strong Soviet pressures and (as a last resort) perhaps even Soviet military intervention.

(2) Still, the threshold of Soviet tolerance was markedly raised. Even as late as the beginning of 1989 it was impossible to predict how Moscow would respond to the next East European outburst of popular sentiment. On the one hand, the Soviet Union did not yet repudiate the principle of socialist internationalism and hence the "Brezhnev Doctrine." On the other hand, Gorbachev seemed most anxious not to use military force in defense of the region's "common interests." This was indicated by his own statements, his representatives' comments, the evolution of Soviet foreign policy in general and its emphasis on improved relations with Western Europe in particular, as well as the apparent priority that Moscow assigned to its domestic concerns. According to conventional wisdom in the West at that time, one way to distinguish between the old threshold of Soviet tolerance and Gorbachev's

was to surmise that if another "1956" (Hungary) were to happen the Soviet Union *would*—but if another "1968" (Czechoslovakia) were to happen it would *not*—intervene militarily. That conclusion, between 1985 and 1988, was probably valid; by late 1989 it became, or turned out to be, patently wrong.

(3) The most visible sign of Gorbachev's early policies was the growing autonomy of the East European parties. One of the phenomena clearly observable after 1985 was the disappearance of public Soviet criticisms of the East European parties and their policies. The CPSU's long-standing practice of exercising its "leading role" by lecturing other communist parties about what is or is not an "ideologically correct" policy, approach, or formulation was passé. Moscow ceased to pontificate; its imperial mentality was eroding. The East European parties gained much more "elbow room" than ever before. There was much they could now do in accordance with their judgment and their countries' national interests. Indeed, and somewhat inconveniently, they could no longer blame Moscow for all that went wrong in Eastern Europe.

(4) Four of the East European regimes chose not to take advantage of their newly granted autonomy. The one word that best describes these regimes' response to the Gorbachev phenomenon is "resistance." For the reasons given below, Romania, East Germany, Czechoslovakia, and Bulgaria—the region's gang of four—were all unwilling to follow Gorbachev's path and adopt his perestroika and glasnost.

First, the region's old leaders could not duplicate what Gorbachev was doing: obtain political momentum by turning against the record of their predecessors. After all, Zhivkov had led Bulgaria since 1954; Ceauşescu had led Romania since 1965; and Honecker had led East Germany since 1971. Nor could Miloš Jakeš, Czechoslovakia's party chief since 1987, dissociate himself from the recent past in that country: he had belonged to the leadership since at least 1969 and was still surrounded by the old guard. Even Jaruzelski, who had led Poland since 1981, faced political circumstances quite different from Gorbachev's.

Second, the East European gang of four's resistance to reform was a function of skepticism (widespread throughout the region) about Gorbachev's staying power. Privately, many East European leaders believed that his tenure would not last long. Even reform-minded officials, those who shared Gorbachev's ideas and rooted for him, tended to doubt that the general secretary could decentralize the Soviet economy, modify the present system of subsidies, alter the artificial pricing system, cope with nationalist demands for independence, and enact political reforms. They stressed the limits and dangers of glasnost, pointing especially to growing tension in Armenia, Azerbaijan, and the Baltic republics as signs of more trouble to come. In the meantime, assuming that Gorbachev had only a few years to prove himself, most East European communist leaders preferred to wait and see if his reforms were indeed "irreversible."

Third, and most important, the East European communist regimes were concerned about the risk of instability associated with glasnost and even perestroika. The risks were presumably much higher in Eastern Europe than in the Soviet Union because the Soviet system was seen—perhaps mistakenly—to enjoy a measure of domestic popular support that the East European systems lacked. More than four decades of communist rule did not perceptibly improve the East European regimes' standing with the vast majority of their people, young and old, who appeared to dream of a *European* future. Hence, almost irrespective of what they did, the region's communist leaders were walking on thin political ice. For this reason, they were fearful that any change in the region carried with it the danger of serious political turbulence.

(5) *Policy aside, Soviet perceptions of Eastern Europe were changing.* As the future evolution of Soviet political relations with Eastern Europe were a function of Moscow's perceptions, the reassessment taking place in the early Gorbachev

era foreshadowed the possibility of smoother Soviet relations with the region.

The bad news seemed to be that Moscow continued to underestimate the persistence of anti-Sovietism in Eastern Europe, taking comfort, perhaps, in Gorbachev's personal appeal. While realizing that there was a "crisis" in the region, Soviet spokesmen and analysts showed an apparent lack of understanding about popular East European sentiments, which pointed toward the need to *cure the system*—preferably by replacing it. Moscow appeared to believe, as did some Westerners, that new, one-party regimes headed by reform-minded communist leaders could assure long-term stability.

The good news was that the Soviet Union was beginning to come to terms with the realities of its *past* policies toward the region. A paper prepared in mid-1988 by Soviet scholars at the Institute of Economics of the World Socialist System conceded, for example, that the "administrative-state type model . . . did not withstand the test of time" in Eastern Europe; that changes after Stalin were "of a contradictory character"; that under "the leadership of Brezhnev-Suslov . . . the era of stagnant neo-Stalinism began"; and that "the hegemonic aspirations of the Soviet leadership" contributed to the "deep political crises in Hungary in 1956, Czechoslovakia in 1968, and Poland in 1956, 1970 and 1980." (This paper is reprinted in the Appendix.)

Such self-critical *perceptions* of the past portended different Soviet *policies* in the future. By mid-1988 it seemed possible that some day Moscow would begin to prescribe surgery rather than palliatives and would thus accept systemic transformation instead of promoting only its own version of in-system reform. As related in Chapter 6, that extraordinary change, first in Soviet thinking and then in Soviet policies, occurred much sooner than expected. No one in the Soviet Union, Eastern Europe, or in the West was prepared to predict even at the beginning of 1989 that within less than a year Moscow would step aside and allow Eastern Europe to get on its feet and stand on its own.

IV

ECONOMIC RELATIONS

The Elusive Concept of Socialism

IF THERE was a time when "socialism" had a more or less identifiable meaning in Marxist lexicons, under Gorbachev it is no more. Who is to say what a socialist economy is or should be? Soviet political literature continues to affirm "socialist" goals and decry "anti-socialist" tendencies, but what it is specifically that is being affirmed and decried is unclear. Was Ceauşescu's Romania—with its highly centralized, planned economy—socialist? Is Hungary—with its more market-oriented economy—less so?

Even the word "socialism" came under review in the early Gorbachev era.

In 1985, Gorbachev was reported to have warned East European officials not to abandon socialism:

> Many of you see the solution to your problems in resorting to market mechanisms in place of direct planning. Some of you look at the market as a lifesaver for your economies. But, comrades, you should not think of lifesavers but about the ship, and the ship is socialism.[1]

Yet, by 1988, Gorbachev was praising Hungary's ("market oriented") version of socialism without giving Ro-

---

1. As quoted in Seweryn Bialer and Joan Afferica, "The Genesis of Gorbachev's World," *Foreign Affairs* 64, No. 3 (America and the World 1985), p. 612.

mania's (still "directly planned") version of socialism its due.

The Soviet people were apparently confused as well. Abel Aganbegyan, Gorbachev's economic adviser, related in 1987 that Soviet tourists returning from Hungary in the mid-1980s had questioned that country's socialist character. Why? Because the tourists found that in Hungary people did not have to stand in line for food! The Soviet economist, trying to allay his people's concern, assured them: no, comrades, socialism does not mean shortages; no, socialism does not mean a poor distribution system; yes, Hungary is a socialist country. But he did not say what socialism or a socialist economy was.

Even as they enter the 1990s, the economies of Eastern Europe still have some common characteristics, of course. Their ownership patterns, planning mechanisms, organizational forms, even investment priorities—as well as most of their problems—remain similar. As in Stalin's time (see Chapter 1), almost all the large factories, mines, banks—the means of production throughout the region—are still state-owned. Most smaller plants, agricultural and service units are also either directly owned or—in the case of cooperatives— closely supervised and regulated by the government. Each country has an extensive economic apparatus, too, including the Planning Office and numerous ministries; together, they make plans for the whole economy, determine allocations and most prices, and regulate wages, employment practices, and of course foreign trade.

At the heart of all Soviet-type economic systems is the plan. It sets production goals, the means by which they should be achieved, and the way the products are to be distributed. At its excessive worst, the plan specifies when, how many, and what size nails and screws a particular factory must make, with little or no allowance for changing needs during the course of the plan. The original reason for creating such a centrally planned economic system was to overcome the ups and downs—the fluctuations and "chaos"—inherent in market-oriented or capitalist economies. Instead, even development and central planning were expected to assure steady growth and full employment. Communists long believed that an unplanned economy would signify the absence of political control and even "conditions of anarchy."

To be sure, the "ideal" Soviet-type system was never transferred in full to all of Eastern Europe; there was some divergence even under Stalin. In Poland, agriculture was not collectivized as elsewhere; in East Germany, a number of repair shops and retail outlets of the "Mom and Pop" variety remained in private hands. Existing diversity was justified by the theory of "different roads to socialism."

Since Stalin, and especially since the mid-1960s, the trend toward diversity has accelerated. Most of the region's economic systems have lost some of their once-common characteristics—Bulgaria more so than Romania, Poland more than Czechoslovakia, Hungary more than any other, and—until Gorbachev's perestroika—the Soviet Union less than most. Changes introduced in Soviet-type systems have all sought to rationalize economic policy by making decisions according to economic factors rather than only political criteria. By allowing market mechanisms to play a role in the allocation and distribution of resources, some countries have decentralized economic decision making and hence reduced reliance on the central plan. The reason why more fundamental changes were neither attempted nor accomplished earlier was that the authorities had only tried to make the old system more productive and more efficient—without losing political control. The goal was to reconcile plan and market, to use as few "capitalist" techniques as possible to make "socialism" as viable as possible.

The Urgency of Change

Why changes at all then? And why first in some of the East European countries rather than in the Soviet Union?

The obvious answer to the first question is that all communist or, especially, post-communist regimes are dissatisfied with the performance of their economies. They want to improve them, although they want to improve them without harmful social consequences. The less obvious answer to the second question is that popular demands for a better life have always been greater in Eastern Europe than in the Soviet Union. East Europeans view their conditions more critically, and hence they have always pressed harder for improvements.

The difference between Eastern Europe and the Soviet Union in this respect is paradoxical. According to economic indicators, which are unfortunately seldom comparable and never precise, Eastern Europe as a whole is ahead of the Soviet Union, and its people are better off than the Soviets. In the 1980s, for example, the region's standard of living was probably about a third higher than the Soviet Union's, and the difference was even greater when Soviet living standards were compared to those of East Germany, Czechoslovakia, and Hungary. By Soviet standards, moreover, the availability of food and consumer goods—the distribution system—in Budapest, East Berlin, and Prague is efficient and impressive. Yet it is the East Europeans who keep pressing more vigorously for change because they do not compare their economic conditions to those of the Soviet Union. Czechs have not been known to be happy just because they are better off than the Russians; they are unhappy because they are worse off than their neighbors in Austria and West Germany. For this reason and by *these* standards, economic problems have always been more challenging to the political order in Eastern Europe than in the Soviet Union.

As East European economists and most politicians readily acknowledge, these "problems" became far more serious—reached crisis proportions—by the time of Gorbachev's accession to power in 1985. The main reasons were the following:

Among the *objective* reasons was an extraordinary slowdown in economic growth. Keeping in mind, again, that such data are less than fully accurate, the average per capita growth rate for the region as a whole was apparently still a healthy 4.2 percent in 1970–75, but in 1975–80 it was 1.4 percent, and in 1980–85 it was only 1.0 percent. In 1985 there was no growth at all (0.2 percent), and even that figure was but a function of East Germany's still-growing economy (supposedly 2.4 percent that year). Nor did it seem to make much difference whether an East European economy was or was not pursuing reforms. At least in terms of growth, Bulgaria (only very slightly reformed) and Hungary (most reformed) were actually the worst performers. In 1985, the record showed a dismal *minus* 3.3 percent "growth" for Bulgaria and a *minus* 2.3 percent "growth" for Hungary.

Another important indicator—per capita standard of living—pointed toward the same trend. Between the periods 1970–75 and 1980–85, the rates of growth in per capita living standards apparently declined from 3.6 percent to 2.0 percent in Bulgaria, from 2.5 percent to 1.4 percent in Czechoslovakia, from 4.9 percent to 1.6 percent in East Germany, from 3.1 percent to 0.6 percent in Hungary, from 4.6 percent to 0.5 percent in Poland, and from 4.0 percent to 1.2 percent in Romania. And these were official figures; Western analysts suspected—mainly because of "hidden" inflation—that there was an absolute decline in living standards in several if not all of the countries of Eastern Europe.

Meanwhile, Eastern Europe's net hard-currency debt to the West dramatically increased over the years. Outside the Soviet Union, the region's total debt (in current U.S. dollars) was only $4 billion in 1970; it jumped to $26 billion by 1976 and to $60.7 billion by 1981. In 1989 it was about $90 billion and rising. Especially Poland (whose Western debt approached $40 billion in 1989) and Hungary (about $20 billion) were in bad shape. Poland could not meet its interest payments, while Hungary has had to borrow more to avoid rescheduling or default. Both countries lived on borrowed money and borrowed time; they could afford to import less and less of the technology they needed and popular (Western and Japanese) consumer goods they wanted. Hungary would have needed a surplus of about $1 billion from its hard-currency trade every year just to pay interest on its outstanding debt; the comparable figure for Poland was over $2 billion. Even if they had been able to manage that—and they could not—their total outstanding debts would only have stopped increasing.

Such poor performance, and poorer prospects, "feel" even worse in the context of prevailing *subjective* economic circumstances.

Of these circumstances by far the most upsetting has been mentioned. It is the comparison the average East European makes with the prosperity he knows about—or thinks he knows about—in Western Europe. These comparisons were becoming particularly painful by 1980 or so, a time of renewed economic health and prosperity in Western Europe. In 1980, for example, the average East European GNP per capita (expressed in U.S. dollars and representing no more than an informed estimate) was about $4,000, while the corresponding figure for West European members of NATO was $7,000. Although the level of economic development of Czechoslovakia and Austria was about the same on the eve of, and right after, World War II, in 1980 Czechoslovakia's GNP was about $4,700 while Austria's approximated $8,500.

The second subjective circumstance is implicit in the figures cited above. It is the contrast East Europeans draw between their improving living standards in the first half of the 1970s (made possible, in part, by Western credits) and the current situation. What amounted to an economic upswing in the early 1970s—especially in Poland but also in East Germany, Hungary, and Bulgaria—is now seen to belong to the distant (but well-remembered) past. East Europeans feel that the "good times" are gone, perhaps forever. And when the future seems bleak, the present is all but unbearable.

Mainly for these reasons there was talk of economic change in Eastern Europe well before Gorbachev's call for perestroika in the Soviet Union. What did these changes set out to do? What can be said about the "reform" of Soviet-type economic systems in Eastern Europe?

It is important to make some distinctions. First, there has always been much more *talk* of change than change. Second, *policy change*—also called perfecting or streamlining the existing system—has always been permitted, at times encouraged. Third, *reform* or *partial reform* of the Soviet-type systems (see below) was officially discouraged; until 1985–86 even the word "reform" was banned. Fourth, the term *radical reform*, which was made palatable by Gorbachev only in January 1987, has come to signify a comprehensive overhaul of the region's economic and political systems.

Even a "pure" comprehensive reform would of course retain state ownership of the major means of production. But, in Ed A. Hewett's words,

> A truly comprehensive reform of this system would affect all the institutions simultaneously: the hierarchy, the information system, and the incentive mechanism. A comprehensive reform designed to enhance the role of the market and increase the autonomy of the enterprises would simultaneously change the price system so that prices could move more freely to reflect shifts in supply and demand; change the financial system to give more authority to banks to decide on competing applications for funds to finance working capital and investment needs; change the wage system to enable enterprises to compete more freely for labor and to allow wage rates to reflect more accurately the supply of, and demand for, various kinds of labor; and change the role of the party so that enterprises could operate in search of higher profits without party interference. The legal system would require a massive overhaul in which much of the law on enterprise rights and obligations would have to be resolved; and an entire new section of the law relating to monopolies, unfair competition, price gouging, and so on would have to be developed.[2]

---

2. Ed A. Hewett, *Reforming the Soviet Economy: Equality versus Effi-*

In the 1980s, only Hungary and Poland can be said to have come close to adopting a "comprehensive reform" so defined, but even they did not fully implement it. Elsewhere—such as in Bulgaria, and lately in the Soviet Union, too—there were "partial reforms"—the introduction of one or more parts of the comprehensive reform—but most countries experimented only with "policy changes" that sought to improve the existing system.

While broad conclusions about reforms should not be drawn on the basis of one country's experience, the Hungarian case shows both the advantages and the limits of reforms. Though the reforms offer no panacea, they are certainly helpful. Introduced in 1968, Hungary's New Economic Mechanism (it could not be called a "reform" at that time) had several ups and downs. Because of political concerns about inequality and the rise of a so-called "petit-bourgeois mentality," as well as Soviet pressures, the reform process was interrupted in the early 1970s; because of the economic cost of retrenchment, however, it was allowed to start again at the end of the 1970s. Generally, NEM was considered a success in the late 1960s and early 1970s; in terms of such indicators as the availability of food and consumer goods, the Hungarian economy proved itself superior to all of the neighboring economies for many years.

The Hungarian economy appears to have come to a dead end in the 1980s. The reforms probably *did not go far enough* to keep improving living standards, to reduce Western indebtedness, to produce sufficient economic growth, and to make the quality of Hungarian products competitive in world markets. Conversely, the reforms probably *went too far* to make it advantageous or profitable for Hungary to continue trading extensively with the Soviet Union and other members of CMEA. While the reform's emphasis on qualitative improvements and market mechanisms made a Western trade

ciency (Washington, D.C.: The Brookings Institution, 1988), p. 16.

orientation feasible, trade with the East called for the opposite approach—for stressing quantitative growth (partly because of the commodity composition of CMEA trade) and for a more centralized economic structure (because of CMEA's long-term plans for foreign trade transactions). In very simple terms, then, the Hungarian experience suggests that (a) market and plan do not easily coexist in a reformed economy and (b) foreign trade relations can suffer when significant disparity develops between the trading partners' economic structures and needs.

Consider now the case of Romania, which, even after Ceauşescu, has the least reformed economy in the region. If its statistics are to be believed, Romania produced the highest rate of industrial growth in the 1970s. (Internal contradictions in—and hence the inaccuracy of—Romanian data are of such magnitude that all that can be stated is that industrial growth might have reached over 5 percent a year.) Yet even if the statistics were accurate, Romanian gains in industry were neutralized by the absence of comparable growth in agriculture and personal consumption. Romania remained a predominantly agrarian country and the people certainly did not benefit at all from rapid industrialization. Moreover, as even industrial growth was financed by Western loans, the economy as a whole cannot be said to have performed well.

In the 1980s Ceauşescu decided to repay Romania's net hard-currency debt, which had reached $10 billion in 1981. No country has ever attempted to do so much in a short period of time. But he did what he had set out to do: by 1987 Romania's debt was under $5 billion—paid for by declining real wages, immense price increases, and drastic cuts in imports—and by 1989 the debt was all but gone. Meanwhile, the Romanian people had little to eat, electricity was often in short supply, especially in the winter, even TV broadcasting time had to be shortened, the streets of Bucharest were at times dark, apartments remained unheated—while, in order to earn hard currency, the country was exporting fuels.

Of course, Romania was not at all typical—it was by far the worst example of conditions characteristic of centralized, Soviet-type economic systems; East Germany and Czechoslovakia have certainly done much better. But the Romanian extreme still illustrates what can happen when a rigid, Stalinist economy undergoes no change and dogmatically rejects reform.

Indeed, only in the 1990s will all East European economies begin to move toward the introduction of free-market mechanisms, led by Poland, which has announced the first major economic program for the post-communist era. How many will do so successfully remains to be seen. Certainly, the transitional years in the early 1990s, during which they will try to combine plan and market, will not yet yield substantial results. For one thing, in order to guide the processes of supply and demand effectively, markets cannot be merely "simulated," they have to exist and function—and that takes both time and a spirit of entrepreneurship. For another, the shortage of capital will hinder genuine marketization. Hence the immediate future—through the early 1990s—looks gloomy; the gap between Eastern and Western Europe is bound to widen. Aware of the political implications of this trend, Gorbachev is no longer known to warn his allies, as he did in 1985, about the dangers of "market mechanisms" and of abandoning "the ship of socialism." It seems that any "ship" is now "socialist"—as long as it does not sink.

The Economics and Politics of Trade

Particularly for non-specialists, it is hard enough to understand the intricacies of "socialist" economics; it is even more difficult, however, to separate facts from rhetoric in the trade relationships between the Soviet Union and Eastern

Europe and among the East European countries. The difficulties only begin with statistics. The problem here is that although each country publishes volumes of foreign-trade statistics, some have proved to be inaccurate, others have been only occasionally reliable, and Romania's has been viewed by Western and even some East European analysts as a pure fabrication. The official data are at times contradictory, too, for what Country A's yearbook reports as export to Country B may not always appear in Country B's yearbook as import from Country A. So far, there has been a little improvement in this respect under Gorbachev.

The pricing mechanism used in foreign trade presents another problem for evaluation. The primary unit for transactions is the so-called "transferable ruble," which was originally intended to provide an alternative standard to the dollar in intrabloc trade. In fact, it is neither a ruble nor is it transferable (or usable as money) within the bloc. And it cannot be converted to Western currencies. It is but a piece of paper—a primitive accounting device—that is used to assign an artificial value to goods exchanged in old-fashioned barter deals. To make things more complicated, the transferable ruble accounts used in intra-bloc trade are supplemented by dollar accounts, which are apparently used for some of the items traded above and beyond those stipulated in long-term trade agreements. Normally, the dollar account is reserved for goods deemed to have a ready market in the West. Although there are plans to make the ruble and some of the East European currencies "transferable" and eventually "convertible," too—the issue is on Gorbachev's agenda—no change is expected to be enacted by CMEA until the mid-1990s. (However, Hungary has declared its intention to use the dollar account as the basis of its future trade relationship with the Soviet Union and Poland.)

How "prices" are thus determined is also complicated, to say the least. To begin with, the actual cost of producing certain goods —especially within an unreformed economy—is not always known; the absence of such "details" is one of the legacies of the Stalin era. Nor do prices reflect what the market can bear—because there is no real market. Hence some of the prices in intra-bloc trade are tied to prices of comparable goods in the world market. This works reasonably well for such natural resources as oil, bauxite, or coal where quality is relatively less important. Accordingly, their price is determined by averaging recent Western prices as reported on the pages of *The Financial Times* of London. But the same method cannot be applied to manufactured goods and especially high technology items, because their particular attributes—especially their quality—define their value. How much should Czechoslovakia pay for Bulgarian software? Should it pay as much as it would have to pay for Japanese software? Should the transaction qualify for entry in the dollar account if Sofia claims to have a Western market for its software? The existing system provides no standard answer to these questions. Prices are as elastic as in a Middle Eastern bazaar. Under Gorbachev, attempts are being made to find answers.

Still another problem that both hinders and complicates the region's foreign trade has to do with translating Soviet and East European currencies into reasonably accurate dollar terms. What East European currencies are really worth is anyone's guess; none of them are convertible into Western currencies. Of course each country has an official rate of exchange for its currency, but its relationship to reality varies from country to country. (For a dollar American tourists in mid-1989 got only about 60 kopeks in Moscow [vs. ten rubles or more from taxi drivers], 12 kronas in Prague, and 58 forints in Budapest. In Warsaw, there were several official exchange rates in addition to those quoted on the black market.) The end result is that any statistic expressed in dollar terms is even less accurate than a statistic reported in Soviet or East European currencies.

Despite immense difficulties of this sort, and the resulting distortions, there are still certain identifiable facts and trends about the nature, volume, and composition of trade within the Soviet bloc.

(1) It is clear that nearly all trade is conducted on a *bilateral basis*. "Bilateralism" means trade between two countries, and in practice it also means barter deals: Country A sells certain goods to Country B in exchange for which Country B sells certain goods for Country A. No money changes hands. To repeat, the "transferable ruble" is only an accounting device.

In economic terms, an important concern in such bilateral trade is the reduction and preferably the elimination of imbalances over a period of time. The ideal is a "break even" situation or something close to it because the surplus cannot be used elsewhere. Imports by Country A from Country B are therefore based less on what Country A's domestic market needs or could absorb than on Country A's export capacity to Country B. The result is that trade turnover is likely to reflect the export capacity of the weaker of two trading partners. In the event, it makes little difference that the "weak partner" has a good market for the other's products.

Nor does it much matter that the "weak partner" (Country A) has a trade surplus with a third country (Country C). Such surplus from that third-country transaction is not transferable and thus cannot buy products elsewhere (in Country B). If, for example, Bulgaria has a trade surplus with Romania, it cannot use that surplus to buy computers in East Germany (let alone West Germany). Indeed, Bulgaria will not want to have a trade surplus with Romania at all, because it gets little or no interest on the credits it grants (via the surplus) and because it cannot use that surplus to settle its purchases from any other country. In addition, the ultimate value of the surplus is uncertain; it depends on what Romania will be willing to sell Bulgaria to settle it. This is why bilateralism impedes the growth as well as the efficiency of trade among the CMEA countries.

To say the least, then, foreign trade in Eastern Europe is thus a very cumbersome and old-fashioned way of conducting business. As individual enterprises are at best only "consulted"—even about their own transactions, nearly all of which are still government-to-government transactions— market mechanisms are effectively prevented from playing any role. Moreover, intra-bloc trade effectively curtails trade with the West because surpluses in the region's inconvertible currencies cannot be applied to import Western products.

(2) The problems just discussed are all the more serious because the *volume of trade* is very high. Ballpark figures indicate that approximately two-thirds of the total Soviet trade turnover—exports and imports—is with Eastern Europe. East Germany and Czechoslovakia are Moscow's two leading trading partners in the world. Of the total East European trade turnover, about 40 percent is with the Soviet Union and 25 percent is with other CMEA members, while trade with less-developed countries accounts for about 10 percent and with the industrialized West about 25 percent of the total.

Such general, area-wide figures do not show individual variations in the trading volume of the several East European countries. Hidden, for example, is the difference between Czechoslovakia— whose Western exposure is low but whose Eastern exposure is high—and the rest of the region. Nor do these regional percentages show the impact of growing Western indebtedness on Poland and Hungary—both of which have had to reduce their Western trade exposure significantly in the 1980s. (The value of exports by the non-communist industrial countries to Poland dropped from $6.3 billion in 1980 to $3.1 billion in 1985; and exports to Hungary declined from $3.2 billion to $2.8 billion during the same time period.) Finally, the percentages cannot show how much CMEA trade matters to countries for whom foreign trade is of critical importance (about half of Hungary's national income involves exports or imports) and others (such as the Soviet Union) for whom foreign trade makes but a minor contribution to the national economy.

Still, the large volume of trade, especially between the Soviet Union on the one hand and East Germany and Czechoslovakia on the other, suggests that economic interdependence has become a way of life over the years. Eastern Europe desperately needs Soviet fuels; the Soviet Union depends on East European manufactures whose technological level is well matched to Soviet circumstances. Thus, even though the 1989 political miracle has reduced Moscow's controlling influence over Eastern Europe, bilateral trade (its volume reduced) is likely to continue.

(3) The relationship will continue mainly because of the *composition of trade*, whose essential feature—to repeat— is that the Soviet Union supplies Eastern Europe with most of the energy the region needs in exchange for East European manufactures. In a sense, the composition of trade reflects a relationship between a developing country rich in vital natural resources and a more developed region capable of producing machinery and consumer goods that meet Soviet specifications—but might not always meet Western needs or tastes. The products include Polish ships, East German computers, Czechoslovak nuclear power plants, and Hungarian busses.

The commodity composition of Soviet–East European trade shows that for several decades, with only minor variations from year to year, about half of Soviet exports have been fuels and primary products. Yet that continuity is more apparent than real. For while in the mid-1950s approximately 80 percent of that total comprised primary products and only 20 percent fuels, by the late 1980s 80 percent was fuels and 20 percent primary products. The reason is obvious: Eastern Europe is energy hungry, and its growing, energy-inefficient industries consume ever-increasing amounts of Soviet oil and gas. As for East European exports to the Soviet Union, the share of manufactures has grown from about 60 percent in the mid-1950s to more than 80 percent in the 1980s.

Given its weight in the composition of trade, *Soviet energy supplies* to Eastern Europe deserve special attention.

The point of departure here is the doubling of Soviet fuel deliveries in the 1970s. Because of that increase, and because the world price of energy so suddenly and so dramatically shot up at that time, changes in the terms of trade (i.e., changes in export prices relative to changes in import prices as compared to some "base" year) eventually resulted in windfall gains for the Soviet Union—and still further problems for Eastern Europe in a few short years. During the decade that began in 1974, the Soviet terms of trade with Eastern Europe improved by about 50 percent.

Another way to explain the problem is to focus not on total trade—where increases in the prices of some East European imports are partly compensated by increases in the prices of some East European exports—but on the "terms of exchange" between single important import and export commodities. The following illustrates the extraordinary change that has taken place in the "terms of exchange": To pay for one million tons of Soviet oil, Hungary sold Moscow some 800 "Ikarus" busses in 1974. By 1981 it had to sell 2,300 such busses for the same amount of oil. By the mid-1980s the "price" of one million tons of Soviet oil was over 4,000 "Ikarus" busses.

Did the Soviet Union take advantage of Eastern Europe's great appetite for energy? Alternatively, did the Soviet Union allow the price to rise only gradually, over a period of years, in order to limit the damage to the region's economies—and, hence, help reduce political tensions?

The question of whether the Soviet Union extended *implicit subsidies* to Eastern Europe was first raised in a study published in 1983 by Michael Marrese and Jan Vanous. Others, including Paul Marer and Raimund Dietz, have addressed the issue since then. At least one East European economist, the Hungarian András Köves, has also joined the debate. The issue is both complicated and significant; it has much to do with the politics of Soviet–East European economic relations.

In their original study, Marrese and Vanous concluded that in the 1970s—from 1971 to 1980—the Soviet Union provided a subsidy of about $80 billion to Eastern Europe. In a subsequent study, this time using 1984 dollars, they concluded that between 1970 and 1984 the subsidy amounted to $118.2 billion. Reduced to simple terms, their calculations were based on two considerations: (1) Since the price of Soviet energy sold to Eastern Europe did not keep pace with rising world market prices, the East Europeans paid *less* than they would have had to pay had they bought energy in the open market. (2) Concurrently, the East Europeans got *more* for the manufactures they sold to the Soviet Union than what Moscow would have paid had it bought these manufactures in the West.

The "implict subsidy" was therefore the difference between what Moscow would have been paid for its energy in the West and what it would have paid for comparable Western manufactures, on the one hand, and what it was paid for its energy by the East Europeans, on the other. However, according to Marrese and Vanous, the subsidies were "implicit" because the Soviet Union granted them surreptitiously— hidden from the Soviet people—in order to keep this potentially controversial domestic issue "under the table," so to speak. (It should be pointed out that other Western scholars, like Paul Marer, suggest that the subsidies resulted mainly from the so-called "Bucharest pricing formula," which links CMEA trade to world market prices of an agreed-upon *earlier* period. Together with several other considerations, this, according to Marer, explains the relatively cheap price of Soviet energy and hence the "subsidies.")

Neither Marer nor Marrese and Vanous addressed the broader meaning of Soviet subsidies. Indeed, Marrese and

Vanous stressed that their data did not constitute a "judgment of the extent to which individual CMEA countries are better off owing to CMEA association with the Soviet Union." Nevertheless, their readers could not help but reach a conclusion "implicit" in their data: that Eastern Europe was an economic burden for the Soviet Union, and that Moscow—in order to maintain a semblance of stability there—bailed out the region for political reasons.

Both the data Marrese and Vanous presented and their "implicit" conclusions have generated much controversy. Marer, for example, questioned the amount, though not the existence, of Soviet subsidies. He found the Marrese-Vanous estimate of East European underpayment for energy in the 1970s "acceptable." However, he viewed the estimate of Soviet overpayment for East European manufactures to be "unacceptable" because of "statistical uncertainties, upward biases, and omitted compensatory gains to Moscow." Marer came up with subsidies for the years 1971–78 of $14 billion, which was only a third of the Marrese-Vanous figure of $42 billion for those years. Equally important was his conclusion that since the subsidies related almost exclusively to the energy crisis of the 1970s, they can be said to have effectively ended in 1982–83.

The Austrian scholar Raimund Dietz shared Marer's conclusion that the Marrese-Vanous estimates were greatly exaggerated. Dietz's calculation, made in transferable rubles (TRs), produced a Soviet subsidy of TR9.8 billion for the years 1973–78. As the Marrese-Vanous study had also provided estimates in transferable rubles for 1973–78, Dietz could be compared with Marrese-Vanous for the same years. The Marrese-Vanous estimate was TR29.1 billion. Thus the Dietz's figure, like Marer's, was only about a third of what Marrese-Vanous had found.

A devastating critique of the whole idea of calculating Soviet subsidies to Eastern Europe came from an East European economist. In an article published in 1983 in the Hun-

garian journal *Acta Oeconomica*, András Köves put forth the
important point that "advantages and disadvantages resulting from economic relations should not be judged only on the
basis of foreign trade prices." In a remarkably candid (if cumbersome) passage, he identified what he considered the miss-
ing issue in the Western debate, alluding to the compulsory
nature of the Soviet–East European economic relationship:

> No doubt, it was very advantageous to buy oil from the USSR
> at half of world market prices—and against ruble payment—
> but if this oil is used for example as the fuel for [Soviet] trucks
> whose specific consumption is about double of the average in-
> ternational [Western] consumption level, then this advantage
> will disappear. Of course, it is also true that in the short run
> the trucks available in a country should be filled with the
> cheapest possible fuel. But, in the longer run, trucks with high
> fuel consumption (in general terms, a less efficient energy con-
> sumption and a too energy-intensive economic structure) are
> a consequence of the same system of economic relations that
> enabled buying oil cheaper than on the world market.[3]

In plain language, Köves argued that Soviet price support for
energy must be seen in a broader political and economic context, the main aspect of which was that Moscow, having imposed an unworkable economic structure on Eastern Europe,
had kept the region from adopting and developing its own
economic order according to its own traditions, customs, and
needs. The Soviet trucks symbolized the damage caused by
the CMEA relationship, while the short-lived subsidies
merely reflected Moscow's interest in mitigating the political
consequences of the economic damage it had done to Eastern
Europe since World War II.

  It is clear, then, that there are at least two ways to look

---

3. A. Köves, "'Implicit Subsidies' and Some Issues of Economic Relations within CMEA (Remarks on the Analyses Made by Michael Marrese and
Jan Vanous)," *Acta Oeconomica* 31, No. 1/2 (1983), p. 127. For more details,
see also A. Köves, *The CMEA Countries in the World Economy: Turning In-
wards or Turning Outwards* (Budapest: Akadémiai Kiadó, 1985).

at both the subsidy issue and—more generally—the Soviet–East European economic relationship.

If one takes pre-1989 political realities as a given, there is no question that Eastern Europe has benefitted from the Soviet economic connection in recent decades, especially in the 1970s. How much the region benefitted from cheap Soviet energy is debatable; that it did is not.

If, on the other hand, one does not take pre-1989 realities as a given—if one assumes an Eastern Europe without Soviet hegemony—then there is room for speculation and doubt. Suppose Stalin had not exploited Eastern Europe to the tune of about $14 billion after the war. Suppose the region had not been required to emulate the structure of the Soviet economy, to invest so heavily in the building of heavy industry for which it lacked natural resources, or to collectivize agriculture. Suppose Eastern Europe did not have to buy inefficient Soviet trucks. Instead, assume that Eastern Europe developed along the lines of such "capitalist" welfare states as Finland or Austria. Would its economy be in better shape? Would it need so much energy to maintain inefficient and unprofitable heavy industries? Would East Europeans be so dissatisfied with their economic conditions that they would need extensive foreign loans and subsidies?

Köves, and apparently most East Europeans, seem to take it for granted that all would be well—or at least better—if only they were free to choose their own economic and political institutions. In that case, would not Poland do as well as Finland, Czechoslovakia as well as Austria, East Germany as well as West Germany? In the early Gorbachev era, the question about the past became relevant because it reflected a widespread East European view—that the region's dismal economic condition was due to its place in the CMEA orbit. However, the question is more relevant, if as yet unanswerable, when rephrased to confront the central issue for the 1990s: "Will post-communist Eastern Europe repair the economic damage left behind by the Soviet connection, rescue itself from the dependency signified by Moscow's 'implicit subsidies,' and then begin to match its Western neighbors' impressive achievements?"

Why CMEA Does Not Work

Tired of hearing of so many "problems" and even "crises" in the East European economies and in the Soviet–East European trade relationship, the Western reader may well ask at this point: "What about the Council of Mutual Economic Assistance? Isn't Eastern Europe served by the vast market CMEA offers? Can't the region's economies benefit from the division of labor and the moves toward integration that CMEA has attempted? Isn't it possible that, especially under Gorbachev's vigorous leadership, CMEA could yet become the East's Common Market—the Soviet/East European response to the West Europeans' impressive European Economic Community (EEC)?"

Formally, CMEA is often presented as a rough equivalent of the Common Market. Founded under Stalin in 1949, it was in fact a dormant organization until Khrushchev made an attempt to give it a mission in the late 1950s and early 1960s. That mission was to develop multilateral economic ties, encourage the "socialist division of labor" among member states (meaning that each country would specialize in what it can do best), and move toward "socialist integration." Alas, none of these goals could Khrushchev realize. CMEA's multilateralism, in Robert L. Hutching's apt phrase, still amounts to no more than "multiple bilateralisms." Division of labor has foundered on account of national or nationalist suspicions. Integration has signified but a few joint projects.

CMEA has been an institution with a large bureaucracy and large headquarters in Moscow. The number of its committees and the frequency of their meetings, together with ambitious declarations about the promise of "socialist economic integration," create the impression of an active organization that promotes fresh initiatives and new ideas for the benefit of its members. In fact, the yearly or bi-yearly sessions of the CMEA Council, its policy-making body, are quite predictable. Normally, a Soviet leader unveils a grand, "long-term" proposal. In the debate that follows, it will be applauded for the acuity of its vision and reduced to broad generalities. Once the meeting is over, implementation will suffer from the members' overriding interest in their national priorities.

Khrushchev, for example, pressed for the adoption of a new charter (1960), followed by a more detailed statement on "The Basic Principles of the International Division of Labor" (1962). The emphasis at the time was on the coordination of national plans, which was expected to lead to a better division of labor. However, the call for a division of labor was perceived by some of the less developed CMEA members, notably Romania, as an attempt to justify and retain the developmental status quo. As each country was to do what it could do well, Romania was asked to concentrate on agriculture, food processing, and the like; in the meantime, the more advanced industrial countries, such as East Germany and Czechoslovakia, would further develop their industrial base. The gap between the region's northern and southern tiers would deepen. In the event, Romania not only vetoed Khrushchev's plans, but—by 1964—it also took a more general position in defense of its national interests and sovereignty, a position that effectively countered the Soviet-sponsored idea of multilateralism, division of labor, and integration. Indeed, the original source of differences between the Soviet Union and Romania in the 1960s was Khrushchev's initiative to give content to CMEA.

Years later it was *Brezhnev's* turn to try. His 1971

proposals—called "Comprehensive Program for the Further Extension and Improvement of Cooperation and the Development of Socialist Integration by CMEA Member Countries"— had as their main objective the development of joint investments in general and of Soviet energy resources in particular. To obtain broad support for his proposals from all members, including Romania, Brezhnev introduced a new mechanism—the so-called "interested party" rule. It meant that only those member states would participate in a particular joint investment project that had an interest in it. At the same time, those who declined to take part in such a project did not have the right to veto it. In effect, while a few useful— and essentially bilateral—projects could thus get underway then, the Romanian concept of "sovereignty" was preserved and the Soviet concept of "socialist integration" received a setback.

Following the adoption of the "Comprehensive Program," Brezhnev did obtain East European participation for a few— *only about ten*—joint investment projects. The largest such project was the building of the Orenburg natural gas complex in Siberia, together with a pipeline from the complex to the Soviet-Czechoslovak border near Uzhgorod. Though Romania played only a limited role, all member states made a contribution to the project. Jointly financed at a cost of about $5–6 billion, and jointly built, the facilities belong to the Soviet Union alone. Moscow keeps the profits too. Eastern Europe benefits as the Soviet Union makes a guaranteed supply of natural gas available.

CMEA was also instrumental in creating a few joint companies in Eastern Europe whose activities range from the production of cotton yarns (the "Friendship Mill" in Poland) to computer programming ("Interprogramma" in Bulgaria). There are only about a *dozen* such companies, none very large or significant, and participation in almost all cases is limited to only two CMEA countries.

Chernenko also tried to bring CMEA to life. He had Sofia

host a summit of party general secretaries (rather than only prime ministers) for a meeting of the CMEA Council—the first such summit in a decade and half. The "Basic Guidelines" (1984) adopted at that meeting made some (largely verbal) concessions to the more reform-minded members (particularly Hungary), which had sought to encourage enterprise-to-enterprise rather than only government-to-government trade within the CMEA framework. But the main purpose of this high-level summit was to provide Chernenko with an opportunity to remind the East Europeans of their obligation to "supply the USSR with the products it needs" and thus "create economic conditions ensuring the implementation and continuation of deliveries from the USSR of a number of types of raw materials and energy. . . . "

Chernenko's warning reflected Moscow's growing economic nationalism, which stemmed from dissatisfaction with the poor quality of products Eastern Europe was selling to the Soviet Union (while offering the region's better goods for sale in the West) and from impatience with late deliveries. Ironically, it may even be that Western studies of "implicit subsidies" had awakened the Soviet leadership to the possibility that it was not getting a fair deal from its junior allies in Eastern Europe. While the issue had more to do with bilateral than multilateral relations, the CMEA Council was a convenient forum for airing Soviet complaints.

If viewed as a multilateral organization, the CMEA that *Gorbachev* inherited was an institution that could not boast of any major achievement. It was a framework without much substance. As an economic institution, it facilitated East European participation in the development of Soviet natural resources. As a political institution, it provided a convenient framework for Moscow to insist on bloc cohesion and unity. Ideologically, CMEA sought to project a spirit of cooperation within the region and abroad, encourage "socialist interdependence," and uphold the idea that benefits accrue—or will accrue—from a joint future.

It is quite understandable, then, that Gorbachev, not un-like his predecessors, has been profoundly dissatisfied with CMEA's largely symbolic role and minimal accomplish-ments. Soon after his accession to power in 1985, another session of the CMEA Council was devoted to a discussion of Gorbachev's "Comprehensive Program for Scientific and Technical Progress" (1985). As the title of this latest CMEA program suggested, the task for member states was to over-come technological backwardness. Gorbachev focused on five areas where speedy action was needed: electronics, robots, nuclear energy, research and development of new technolo-gies, and biotechnology. In effect, the program was meant to extend the Soviet Union's "scientific-technological revolu-tion" to the member states of the CMEA. Again, a number of committees and even a few new, smaller organizations were created to implement the proposals that were intended to bear fruit by the year 2000. What will actually come of them remains to be seen.

Meanwhile, Gorbachev's major preoccupations appear to be somewhere else. First and foremost, he is concerned with perestroika in the Soviet Union itself. While the enormous So-viet subsidies to Cuba, a CMEA member, continue to the tune of perhaps as much as $4.5 billion a year, East European members of the CMEA get stern lectures from Gorbachev, as they did from Chernenko, about their obligations and respon-sibilities. Moscow is known to have already rejected inferior East European products, and it has called for penalties for late deliveries. It has also concluded literally hundreds of new, so-called "Specialization Agreements" with CMEA members in order to assure the supply of products it needs and to make CMEA members dependent on the Soviet market for years to come.

These agreements have produced no results so far. As a matter of fact, the volume of Soviet–East European trade failed to increase in the second half of the 1980s. The East Eu-ropeans have not been able to buy either more energy and raw materials or high technology goods from the Soviet Union. Perhaps because it is now looking out for its own interests more than it ever had before or since the Stalin years, the Soviet Union has not offered "hard goods" for additional purchases. Instead, it has put considerable pressure on Eastern Europe to deliver more. At the end of the 1980s, the value of what even (poor) Poland was exporting to the Soviet Union was thought to exceed Polish imports from the Soviet Union. Hungary found itself in the same position.

Perhaps most troubling for at least some East Europeans, the Soviet Union is also asking for a different mix of products from its allies to satisfy its current and changing needs. Instead of machinery, Moscow—at the July 1988 meeting of CMEA, for example—expressed interest in importing food and food-processing equipment, light consumer goods, and "products that are made with the application of high technology" from Eastern Europe. The new Soviet shopping list presents immense problems for the East Europeans because they would have to modernize and expand old facilities, and build new ones, to satisfy Soviet needs. They lack the necessary money both in their own currencies and, especially, in the hard currency needed to import Western equipment and know-how. The deeper problem is that most of the items Moscow now wants—food and food-related products in particular—would have to be sold below the already very cheap prices that Soviet customers pay for their (subsidized) food. The purchase price would be considerably below the world-market price, and hence the East Europeans could not make a profit on the deal.

Implicit in the new Soviet shopping list and the continued absence of a realistic CMEA pricing mechanism are two new problems that are surfacing under Gorbachev. One is the inflexibility of the CMEA economies, a particularly acute problem today when perestroika calls for new investment priorities at home and new trading mechanisms abroad. As years of misspent investments and the old, artificial pricing system cannot be quickly or easily remedied, the region's as yet centrally planned economies find themselves unable to meet the new requirements of their trading partners.

The broader controversy stems from *growing economic incompatibilities* in the region. Economic structures—some unchanged, some streamlined, and some partially reformed—are out of sync; interaction within CMEA suffers from significant domestic disparities. While past difficulties had to do with the coordination of long-term plans among member states, resistance to Soviet-inspired multilateralism and integration, and different levels of economic development between the more advanced and the less advanced countries, now, in addition, diverse domestic economic structures make intra-CMEA trade quite disadvantageous for several of the member states, especially those that embarked on the road to reform in the 1980s.

This calls for explanation. A reformed economy whose enterprises are becoming autonomous is reluctant to enter into long-term trade agreements with countries whose enterprises are still centrally run. An autonomous enterprise wants to get the best possible price for its products at home, in the West, in the Third World, or in the bloc. Once the government enters into a long-term agreement with another CMEA government, the autonomy of the enterprise is curtailed. It has to deliver at a price specified in the agreement. Its flexibility is gone. Its ability to earn hard currency is gone. It cannot increase its profits by taking advantage of changing world market conditions.

With one foot in a real market and with another in the world of CMEA, reformed economies as a whole cannot function efficiently and continue the reform process beyond a certain (admittedly undefinable) point. The requirements of the two markets are vastly different. As long as CMEA trade remains predominant and hard currency earnings are therefore limited, the East Europeans can neither repay their debts nor modernize their facilities. To repay debts, modernize facilities, and raise living standards, comprehensive reforms—including tough austerity measures—are needed. But if CMEA members do not all follow the same path, the unreformed economies, by insisting on old-fashioned trading patterns that suit their needs, will stifle the reform process everywhere. In other words, CMEA as presently constituted hinders the introduction of a truly comprehensive reform in any one CMEA country alone, for unless all members begin to adopt such reforms none will be able to do it well.

This is not to say that the reformed economies cannot benefit at all from the extensive ties they have with each other and with the Soviet Union. In the short run, they often do. In the long run, however, the lack of a real market (something like the European Economic Community) in the CMEA orbit curtails innovation and such other measures as Eastern Europe would need for even a chance of closing the gap with its Western neighbors. More realistically, the gap that must be closed first is that between the reformed and unreformed economies.

For CMEA to be more than a framework for consultation—and, increasingly, a debating society—*all of its members, including especially the Soviet Union*, must not merely pay lip service to, but must implement, "radical reforms." Indeed, as the acute problems of the already reformed Hungarian economy demonstrate, these reforms must be truly comprehensive. In the realm of foreign trade relationships, for example, they must entail the replacement of bilateral barter deals with:

(a) rapid progress toward introducing a truly transferable ruble;

(b) a decision to make national currencies eventually convertible into hard currencies;

(c) the adoption of foreign-trade prices generally in line with those that prevail in world markets;

(d) the extension of the rights of enterprises in different countries to trade with one another; and hence

(e) the opening of domestic markets to competition from other CMEA producers.

Gorbachev's chances of persuading his CMEA allies to enact such changes are discussed below.

Summing Up and Looking Ahead

The empty house that CMEA has built is not a proper measure of the Soviet–East European economic relationship. The best signpost is bilateral trade, which constitutes over 95 percent of all trade transactions among CMEA members.

Most East European and Western analysts agree that there has come to exist a natural trading relationship between the Soviet Union and Eastern Europe. So energy-thirsty, Eastern Europe cannot help but welcome Soviet energy supplies. Needing manufactures, consumer goods, and food, the Soviet Union cannot help but welcome East European products suited to Soviet requirements. A condition of interdependence, one from which each side benefits at least for now, has come into being. In particular, each side has gained a steady market for its exports, some of which could not be easily sold elsewhere.

Under Gorbachev, and perhaps starting under Chernenko, Eastern Europe has lost some of the benefits it once enjoyed. Whatever the precise amount of implicit subsidies in the 1970s, Eastern Europe got a "good deal" at that time. Due to the decline and apparent disappearance of Soviet energy subsidies since 1983 or 1984, however, the overall amount of implicit subsidies has diminished if they still exist at all. Concurrently, the steady deterioration in the terms of Soviet–East European trade until 1986 or so has meant that the East European countries have had to sell much more to the Soviet Union in exchange for the same amount of goods— mainly fuels—than they received from the Soviet Union. An additional major problem now is that the East Europeans are unable to get more of what they really need from the Soviet Union.

From a purely economic point of view and especially from a Soviet perspective, at least some of the changes Moscow is introducing into the Soviet–East European trade relationship are justified. As Gorbachev has made it clear, the Soviet Union must cope with its own serious economic stringencies now and at the same time finance its still-expensive military establishment as well. As the availability of cheap Soviet energy is on the decline and the cost of producing new Soviet oil is rising, why should Moscow not receive the world market price for the energy its Warsaw Pact allies so desperately need? And why should it not receive goods of higher quality from Eastern Europe? The answer from East Europeans—as suggested by András Köves's statement (quoted earlier in this chapter)—is that Moscow bears responsibility for having made this unfortunate region, in Seweryn Bialer's phrase, the Soviet Union's "co-stagnation sphere." Irrespective of whether the Soviet–East European economic relationship has since evolved into a natural relationship, Eastern Europe must somehow try to make the best of a condition not of its own making.

Can Gorbachev make a difference? Under his guidance, will CMEA develop into a genuine multilateral organization, one that will encourage rather than hinder reforms?

It is perhaps of some significance that at the July 1988 session of the CMEA Council, all members except Romania resolved to work toward the "gradual formation of conditions for the free movement of goods, services, and other production factors, with a view toward forming a unified market in the future." The new CMEA policy goal thus broke with tradition by promising to replace central controls with the mechanisms of the market. When read carefully, however, it is clear that CMEA was alluding only to the "formation of conditions" to accomplish this goal—in the long run. By referring to the period 1991–2005, even the title of the document ("Collective

Concept for the Socialist International Division of Labor for 1991–2005") indicates a distant goal. Moreover, as the fate of past resolutions of this kind suggests, the document is unlikely to be implemented.

Especially in the post-communist era of the 1990s, Gorbachev's vision of a unified CMEA market is unrealistic. If Soviet perestroika begins to yield results at home, the mixed East European economies will still maintain a mutually beneficial, if limited, *trade relationship* with a reformed Soviet economy. By bringing an end to government-to-government barter deals—and replacing them with enterprise-to-enterprise trade, realistic prices, convertibility at least within CMEA, and hence with a competitive, market-oriented economic environment—Gorbachev can look forward to continued foreign trade with the East Europeans. Even under such optimum circumstances, however, *integration* is almost certainly a dead letter, because both popular sentiment and the region's economic needs indicate a strong westward draw.

Worse yet, if perestroika fails to make headway in the Soviet Union, and the Soviet and the East European economies further diverge, the possibility for the marketization of CMEA and of the Soviet–East European trade relationship will simultaneously disappear. In that case even the volume of bilateral trade will decline. So will any realistic hope for reversing the conclusive separation of the Soviet Union, and to a lesser extent the whole CMEA region, from the industrialized West. Indeed, as CMEA and most of its constituent economies are entering the 1990s as beggars, they will be as unable as ever to offer an alternative to the Common Market and its visionary plan for a "Europe without frontiers" in 1992. Vlad Sobell explained it well:

> The EEC intends to abolish all the remaining barriers to the uninhibited movement of goods, services, labor, and capital among its members [by 1992]—a move that may eventually entail such forms of economic integration as the creation of a com-

mon West European currency, a European central bank, and the harmonization of monetary policies. The CMEA, on the other hand, is merely beginning to plan the introduction of preconditions for such a final goal. After all, the CMEA's member economies are not even market economies; their prices (as well as intra-bloc prices) are not real prices and their currencies are not convertible; and the movement of goods, capital, and labor within CMEA is completely subjected to bureaucratic agreements. In short, the CMEA is light years behind the EEC; and the prospect of a unified CMEA market is a very long way off indeed.[4]

In the final analysis, only full participation in a competitive world economy is likely to narrow the gap—that gap of such great political significance—between the two halves of Europe.

---

4. Vlad Sobell, "The CMEA's Goal of a 'Unified Market'," *Radio Free Europe Research*, July 12, 1988.

V

MILITARY RELATIONS

Defense against Whom?

LIKE MANY European philosophers and politicians before him, Gorbachev is also fond of invoking the idea of one Europe. Speaking in Prague in 1987 and echoing French President Charles de Gaulle's vision of the 1960s of a "Europe from the Atlantic to the Urals," the Soviet leader called for a "'common European home' [which] assumes a degree of integrity, even if its states belong to different social systems and opposing military-political blocs."[1] What kind of Europe did Gorbachev have in mind? When did he envisage a new Soviet concept of European security that would entail the dismantling of the Wall and the Curtain? Or did Gorbachev merely revive his predecessors' old hope that Western Europe would prod the United States out of Europe, leaving Moscow in charge of the security of the "common European home"?

Even as late as 1988, Europe—in the vivid phrase of *The Economist* of London—was but "a pair of semi-detached houses, in which two different sorts of people live two different kinds of life."[2] The partition that Stalin built still stood. True, there was much more contact, more high-level visits, trade, tourism; almost all East German TV sets brought in West German programs, and Austrian television enjoyed con-

---

1. Gorbachev, *For a "Common European Home,"* p. 28.
2. *The Economist,* April 23, 1988, p. 13.

siderable popularity in the western parts of Czechoslovakia and Hungary. Also, the East European people took an extraordinary interest in "rejoining Europe." As part of that interest, the ideal of *Mitteleuropa*, which upholds the common heritage and spiritual unity of the peoples of Central Europe, began to fill many a page in unofficial and even official publications. Still, such expressions of longing for one Europe notwithstanding, the political and military map of Europe—until the very end of 1989—continued to show the old continent split into East and West, East and West Germany, the Warsaw Pact and NATO.

More than anything else, security and defense concerns still explained the division of Europe into a "pair of semi-detached houses." Consider that in the late 1980s, four and a half long decades after the end of World War II, there were still *three million* Soviet and East European troops—about 145 divisions—in central Europe (East Germany, Czechoslovakia, Poland, and Hungary) and in Moscow's so-called western military districts, located in the European part of the Soviet Union.

The estimated breakdown even during the "later" Gorbachev era is as follows:

• Thirty *Soviet* divisions (about 565,000 troops) are deployed in central Europe and 70 divisions (about 1,400,000 troops) in the western military districts—for a subtotal of 100 Soviet divisions or almost two million troops.

• Of the *East European* troops, all of which are stationed on their home territory, there are 295,000 Poles under arms, 150,000 Romanians, 145,000 Czechoslovaks, 123,000 East Germans, 105,000 Bulgarians, and 83,000 Hungarians—for a subtotal of 45 East European divisions or about 900,000 troops.

• Of the total of 145 *Soviet and East European* divisions or three million troops in Europe, approximately half are deployed in Eastern Europe and the other half in the European part of the Soviet Union.

• In the critical central European region only, the comparison with NATO shows that the Warsaw Pact's manpower advantage is about 2 to 1. As for armaments, the Warsaw Pact has 2,650 fixed winged aircraft vs. NATO's 1,250; the Warsaw Pact has 16,700 main battle tanks in units vs. NATO's 7,800; the Warsaw Pact has 9,200 artillery pieces vs. NATO's 3,000; and the Warsaw Pact has 5,000 anti-tank missile launchers vs. NATO's 2,000. When comparable figures are considered for all of Europe (from the Atlantic to the Urals rather than only in the central region), the ratios are similar.

Western assessments vary *significantly* about what these figures actually mean, because the numbers by themselves—the "bean counts"—cannot predict either victory or defeat in an actual conflict. Much depends on the combatants' level of readiness, the quality of their equipment and training, logistical support, leadership, motivation, command, control, communications, and intelligence capabilities. The effects of a surprise attack are also incalculable. In 1940, Germany reached the English Channel in four weeks despite the fact that a numerical count had shown its forces to be roughly equal to those of France and England combined. If one reduced the conventional balance to "bean counts," how would one explain Israel's 1967 victory over the numerically superior forces of Egypt, Syria, and Jordan?

Yet, looking only at the raw numbers, no one can deny that the conventional balance strongly favors the Warsaw Pact. Therefore, the question is pertinent: Why are all these Soviet troops and armaments still in the heart of Europe? Three explanations are current, some complementary, some not.

(1) The Soviet and East European official explanation is that they have been there for the *defense* of the Soviet Union and Eastern Europe—defense against NATO's "aggressive designs" and West German "revanchism." From Stalin to Chernenko, and to a lesser extent under the early Gorbachev, too, Moscow claimed that it was only because of the mighty forces of the Soviet Union and its allies that the West

refrained from marching east and overthrowing one or several communist regimes. Stalin is known to have expected a Western attack especially around 1950, at the height of the cold war. The fear of Germany was always widespread in Russia and perhaps still is in the Soviet Union, in Poland, and in Czechoslovakia. Reinforced by Soviet propaganda, the memory of the Nazi invasion and brutalities during World War II is particularly vivid. Call it political paranoia, realism, or good memory, there is genuine fear that under certain circumstances German militarism could revive once again.

On the other hand, considering NATO's fundamentally defensive strategy and deployments as well as West Germany's devotion to detente since the late 1960s, it is difficult to see the source of Soviet anxiety. Was an unprovoked Western attack on Eastern Europe and the Soviet Union ever conceivable? Even if Western aggression has been only "unlikely" rather than "inconceivable," does the Warsaw Pact need three million troops to fulfill its defensive mission?

(2) By contrast, the usual Western explanation is that the heavy concentration of Warsaw Pact troops and armaments indicates *offensive* goals *vis-à-vis* the West. Whether these goals are primarily military or political is in dispute.

The argument that the Soviet threat has been primarily military rests on numbers, on the steady modernization of Soviet (and to a much lesser extent East European) offensive weapons, on the concentration of offensive military deployments in the central region (primarily in East Germany), on aspects of Soviet strategy, and on the history of Soviet foreign policy. In the official Western view, only NATO's deterrence has contained Soviet military expansion.

The (much more complex) view that the Soviet threat has been primarily political—that the Soviet goal has been to divide and intimidate rather than to attack Western Europe—rests on the Soviet conventional buildup. In this view, the implicit Soviet purpose was to force NATO to choose between two politically equally unpopular options. One option was to match the Warsaw Pact's conventional strength. This is not only a very expensive proposition, of course, but it would also require the introduction of additional U.S. and other NATO troops into the Central European theater (which is already one of the world's most heavily militarized regions). The second option—based on the doctrine of "flexible response"—was to counter the Pact's conventional strength by relying on short-range nuclear weapons for the defense of Western Europe and asserting NATO's willingness to use such short-range weapons first if necessary.

Followed by NATO since the 1950s, the second option is both cheaper and politically more acceptable to the U.S. and to European governments. On the other hand, it is a major source of strong anti-nuclear and anti-American sentiments in Western Europe. Instead of, or in addition to, blaming Moscow for having prompted this nuclear strategy by its conventional buildup, many West Europeans ask, "Why should Europe become the 'first candidate' or the testing ground in a nuclear war? Why does the U.S. introduce or seek to modernize such short-range nuclear weapons in Europe that would limit the damage only to Europeans while leaving the United States safe and secure?"

Whether Moscow had anticipated its conventional buildup to cause division in NATO cannot be known. What is clear is that Soviet policies even in the early Gorbachev era had the effect of exacerbating political differences within the alliance.

(3) The last Western explanation is that the primary mission of Soviet forces was to *police Eastern Europe*. Readers of this book need not be reminded of Moscow's traditional unpopularity in the region, nor of the burning East European desire for independence and even neutrality. Afghanistan aside, moreover, only in Eastern Europe has the Soviet Union had to use its military might directly since World War II. So-

viet troops and tanks had to be called in to put down popular uprisings in East Berlin (1953), Hungary (1956), and Czechoslovakia (1968).

Consider, too, the region's importance to the Soviet Union. What Brezhnev so bluntly told the reformist leadership of Czechoslovakia in 1968 still held as late as 1988—even if history has of course disproven his last sentence.

> Your country lies on territory where the Soviet soldier trod in the Second World War. We bought that territory at the cost of enormous sacrifices, and we shall never leave it. The borders of that area are our borders as well. Because you do not listen to us, we feel threatened. In the name of the dead in World War Two who laid down their lives for your freedom as well, we are therefore fully justified in sending our soldiers into your country, so that we may feel fully secure within our common borders. It is immaterial whether anyone is actually threatening us or not: it is a matter of principle, independent of external circumstances. And that is how it will be, from the Second World War to "eternity."[3]

Accordingly, it is the combination of East European anti-Sovietism and the Soviet commitment to keep the Warsaw Pact alive that has propelled Moscow to keep some of its best troops—those with the highest level of readiness—in Eastern Europe (rather than attempt to police the region from the nearby military districts in the western part of the Soviet Union). Their presence in Eastern Europe was needed because, as the case of Romania suggests, the complete *withdrawal* of Soviet troops (1958) provides an opportunity for assertions of limited independence (since 1964). Whether a somewhat smaller Soviet contingent could also accomplish the task of policing Eastern Europe is, of course, another question.

In the final analysis, however, all three objectives can be assumed to have played a role in Soviet calculations and de-

---

3. Mlynář, *Nightfrost in Prague*, p. 240.

ployments. How much importance one assigned to each objective was always a matter of judgment. In this writer's view, Moscow's professed concern about *defense* was both out-of-date and exaggerated. In the absence of Soviet provocations and particularly in an era of East-West detente, the very idea of a Western attack on the Soviet Union has been no more than a flight of fancy. A Soviet-led *offensive* military operation against Western Europe has been another unlikely Soviet motivation—so long as NATO maintains a credible deterrence and so long as Gorbachev's first priority is the rebuilding of the Soviet economy.

Hence the most compelling, though certainly not the only, reason for the continued presence of Soviet troops in Eastern Europe was to *police Eastern Europe*, including East Germany. Soviet contingents were particularly needed between 1985 and 1988 because of growing uncertainty about the applicability of the "Brezhnev Doctrine" (see Chapter 3). These contingents were needed at that time to make sure that East Europeans did not interpret Gorbachev's opening to the West, the growing autonomy of the region's communist parties, and other expressions of change and retrenchment in Soviet policy to mean that Moscow was prepared to sacrifice Eastern Europe on the altar of domestic perestroika and East-West detente. Stationing Soviet troops in East Germany, Czechoslovakia, Hungary, and Poland was the most credible signal of a Soviet commitment to protect vital Soviet interests. Their presence served as a powerful deterrent, making a politically costly military intervention in the future less likely.

With the "Brezhnev Doctrine" apparently still on the books at this time, the question posed at the beginning of this chapter—"Defense against whom?"—thus lent itself to an answer that was as clear as it was incongruous: With its allies unable to obtain popular approbation, the Soviet Union still had to commit tremendous resources to defend them not so much from the West as from the peoples of Eastern Europe.

The East European Militaries

Under Gorbachev, especially, policing Eastern Europe was a task that the Soviet Union would rather let the East European militaries perform. Ideally, they should be able to maintain or restore domestic order in their own countries and make a greater contribution to the Warsaw Pact's collective military missions as well. Before Gorbachev, these Soviet goals could not be achieved. However much Moscow tried to improve the national armies—through joint exercises and by training their officers, for example—their effectiveness and reliability were in doubt.

Consider first the past performance of the East European militaries—as summarized by Ivan Volgyes[4]—when faced with *internal disturbances*:

• *Pilsen, 1953.* The Czechoslovak military refused to suppress the riots.

• *East Berlin, 1953.* Some East German army units would not leave their barracks when ordered to stop the demonstrators.

• *Poznan, 1956.* When the Polish army failed to disperse the workers, the authorities had to rely on the (secret) security police to put down the riots.

• *Budapest, 1956.* After a short period of hesitation, the Hungarian army refused to defend the old Stalinist regime, supporting instead the revolutionary government of Imre Nagy.

• *Prague, 1969.* After the Soviet invasion, the majority of young Czechoslovak officers—those under thirty—resigned.

• *Gdańsk, 1970.* While the Polish military was instrumental in suppressing the demonstrations, it refused to follow an order to use "overwhelming force" against the workers.

---

4. Cf. Ivan Volgyes, *The Political Reliability of the Warsaw Pact: The Southern Tier* (Durham: Duke University Press, 1982), p. 9.

• *Łódź and Warsaw, 1976*. After General Jaruzelski, then Minister of Defense, stated that "Polish soldiers will not fire on Polish workers," the regime cancelled the price increases that had prompted widespread work stoppages.

• The eighth case—the Polish army's behavior during the "Solidarity" era of 1980–81—calls for a somewhat more detailed treatment. In this case, the military declared and then supervised the implementation of martial law. Had the Polish military not acted, the Soviet Union would have had to intervene. Contrary to widespread Western impressions, however, the Polish military played a lesser role—and assumed that role more reluctantly—than it would subsequently claimed to have done.

At the beginning of the crisis (August 1980), when the government was in the process of concluding the "Gdańsk accords" with the workers, the commander of the Polish navy urged approval of the accords, adding that Polish troops would not apply force to end the shipyard workers' strike. On December 13, 1981, when the military—after months of hesitation and several postponements, and now under immense Soviet pressure—finally declared martial law, it found it necessary to leave enforcement and implementation largely in the hands of the small but reliable security forces. As Dale R. Herspring described the situation,

> . . . military involvement was minimal. Regular military units were often not even aware of the declaration of martial law. Furthermore, I am not aware of a single incident in which regular military units were involved in the use of force against civilians. The task of implementing the more onerous aspects fell on the shoulders of the security forces, in particular the dreaded ZOMOs. Military participation in the early days was limited to actions such as manning checkpoints on highways and at main urban intersections; conducting two or three soldier patrols in major cities; transporting ZOMOs around the country (by the air force); providing communications support to the media; or occasionally driving past key points in

tanks or similar equipment in an effort to intimidate the populace.[5]

The conclusion to be inferred from the eight cases is that the region's professional security forces—the much-hated KGBs of Eastern Europe—played a key role in maintaining domestic order; their loyalty to the local regimes and to the Soviet Union should not be doubted. Yet their effectiveness in the face of *large-scale* riots and disturbances has been and is still limited. On their own, or even in combination with the so-called "worker's militias," their numbers were, and probably remain, insufficient to contain or suppress major popular uprisings.

This is why the proprietors of power in Eastern Europe and in Moscow must seek to obtain the active support of the region's militaries, which are generally far more reluctant to use force against their fellow countrymen. This is particularly true of conscripts, who make up more than half of the national armies. Their pay is very low, and they receive no unusual benefits (such as special housing and access to special stores). Their average length of service is only two years, and hence their views tend to reflect the dominant political values of their families and friends. "Order" and "stability," values which inform the professional soldier's world view, mean less to conscripts than nationalism and loyalty to one's home environment. To ask an East European conscript to fire on people of his country is to ask him to turn against his family. Some have done it under fear of retribution and will do it again; many cannot and will not.

As for *external disturbances*, only in one case have the East European armed forces been ordered to go abroad to suppress

---

5. Dale R. Herspring, "The Soviets, the Warsaw Pact, and the East European Militaries," in William E. Griffith, ed., *Central and Eastern Europe: The Opening Curtain?* (An East-West Forum Publication; Boulder: Westview Press, 1989), p. 142.

an enemy. That was in 1968, when five Warsaw Pact member states intervened to end Czechoslovakia's "Prague Spring." During the night of August 20–21, the 24th Soviet Tactical Air Army occupied Czechoslovakia's major airports. The important task of sealing the Czechoslovak–West German border was assigned to four Soviet tank divisions and one East German division. The next most important task—that of encircling and occupying Prague—was left for five additional Soviet divisions to accomplish. In the meantime, four Soviet divisions from the western military districts, along with Polish soldiers, moved in to take up positions along the Czechoslovak-Soviet and the Czechoslovak-Polish border, while Soviet, Hungarian, and Bulgarian troops occupied much of Slovakia. In the end, twenty-three Soviet divisions, two East German and two Polish divisions, one truncated Hungarian division, and a Bulgarian brigade participated in the invasion.

In contrast to the 1956 Soviet intervention in Hungary, this time it was a multilateral Warsaw Pact force which was dispatched to subdue Czechoslovakia's experiment with "socialism with a human face." In reality, however, this was not a collective or multilateral military action either. Romania refused to take part in the invasion. Hungary reluctantly agreed to contribute fewer than 5,000 troops while Bulgaria sent a token contingent. Given Gomulka's and Ulbricht's anxiety about the erosive effect of "Prague Spring" on Poland and East Germany respectively, the size of the Polish and East German forces were larger. Whether or how well they would have fought will never be known, however. They did not have to fight, and hence their reliability was never tested. Nor did they stay long. All the East European troops were withdrawn from Czechoslovakia within weeks after the invasion, while five Soviet divisions—none of which had been stationed in that country prior to 1968—have stayed on to this day. (They are scheduled to leave by 1991.)

It seems that Moscow did not ask the East European militaries (except perhaps the Romanians) to make a greater contribution to the defense of the "gains of socialism" in Czechoslovakia. Nor did the East European militaries volunteer on their own to make a greater contribution.

Causes of Tension in Military Relations

What are the main reasons for the inadequate performance of the East European militaries and the poor state of Soviet–East European military relations?

(1) Both before and under Gorbachev, East European perceptions of the *identity of the enemy* have been fundamentally different from Soviet perceptions. The Soviet Union, a superpower, is concerned with NATO in general and the United States and West Germany in particular; its smaller allies have been more concerned with their traditional adversaries. For Bulgaria, these are Turkey and Yugoslavia; for Hungary it is Romania, and for Romania it is Hungary; for Poland, it is neighboring East Germany more than faraway West Germany. Only East Germany—the communist regime, not the people—felt threatened by West Germany, and even that threat was perceived to be more political than military. Worst of all, all East Europeans seem to know that they have little to fear from their Western neighbors and much more to fear from their large Eastern neighbor.

As a result, it would be far easier to mobilize Romania against Hungary than against NATO, Poland against East Germany (a "fraternal" ally) than against West Germany (a "revanchist" foe), and any East European country—especially Poland, Romania, and Hungary—against the Soviet Union than against the United States.

(2) *Soviet domination* of the institutions of the Warsaw Pact has been another source of friction in military relations.

Under the Political Consultative Committee (discussed in Chapter 3), control over the Warsaw Pact and hence the East European militaries has been exercised by the Joint Command. All the chiefs of staff of the Joint Command are, and have always been, Soviet officers. Only Soviet marshals have served as the Pact's commanders-in-chief. No East European officer has held an operationally significant, top-level position in the Pact. While each member state's Deputy Minister of Defense is concurrently the Pact's "deputy commander," his main responsibility is to convey orders from the Joint Command to his defense ministry at home. In peacetime, organizational subordination to the Soviet command is all but complete; in time of war, it is complete.

The main critic of Soviet domination of the Warsaw Pact was Romania. Since the mid-1960s, it has significantly reduced its participation in the Pact's activities: Romania did not permit troop maneuvers to be held on its territory, and it did not participate in joint exercises of combat forces in other countries. Romania has pressed for an East European voice in Warsaw Pact decisions about nuclear weapons, and it has proposed a system of rotation for the position of the Pact's commander-in-chief. It is a fair guess that on at least a few of these issues, the Romanian position expressed the unspoken opinions of other Warsaw Pact countries as well.

(3) The region's military establishments have been resentful of the *inferior equipment* they have had in comparison with what Moscow provides for its own troops. Moscow has supplied the most up-to-date weapons to (in descending order) the East Germans, the Czechoslovaks, the Poles, the Bulgarians, the Hungarians, and then the Romanians. Thus the countries of the Pact's northern tier (East Germany, Czechoslovakia, and Poland) are far better equipped than their neighbors in the southern tier, but all East European countries—even East Germany—have been denied access to the latest Soviet weapons. At a time when the Soviet armed forces and even Soviet client states such as Syria receive

modern equipment (including new tanks, self-propelled artillery, and sophisticated air defense missiles), the arsenals of the East European militaries still include obsolete weapons and weapon systems from the 1950s and 1960s. Needless to say, it has been very difficult to motivate ill-equipped armies.

Of the many reasons for Moscow's refusal to supply the East Europeans with more modern weapons, three were given by an East European specialist on military affairs (in a private conversation): "First, the Soviets want to make money off the sale of weapons and we don't have the hard currency. Second, they don't think we will do our part in an East-West conflict and don't want to waste the weapons. Third, they don't trust us and are afraid some of our pilots, for example, will defect to the West with the latest equipment."[6] The fourth reason was Moscow's concern that, in a potential conflict between the Soviet Union and an East European country, some of the best Soviet weapons could be used against the Soviet Union.

(4) Another source of tension in Soviet–East European military relations has had to do with *military expenditures.* Military budgets have always been among the most tightly held secrets throughout the region. They are hidden under so many categories in the various budgets that usually well-informed Soviet scholars and even some East European Politburo members claimed to have no knowledge of what the military really costs. The official figures, which appear to be understated, range from about two to six percent of the gross national product; some, though not all, Western estimates are higher.

Even during Gorbachev's era of glasnost, the only certainty was that (a) East European expenditures continued to lag behind Soviet expenditures significantly (in terms of GNP per capita); (b) the Soviet Union believed that its allies spent

---

6. Ibid., pp. 145–146.

too little; and (c) the East Europeans believed they were spending too much. In 1978, when Moscow demanded substantial increases in defense spending, Romania's Ceauşescu responded by saying that the socialist countries "should offer an example to all peoples: not to choose the road of augmenting military expenditures but, instead, of inducing a strong current of opinion for their reduction." Ten years later, in 1988, Iván T. Berend, President of the Hungarian Academy of Science and a member of the party's Central Committee at that time, publicly complained that Hungary spent as much on the military as it did on health, education, and research together, and he called for a review to see if the military budget could be reduced. A more widely voiced East European complaint was that, because of excessive secrecy, the civilian economy did not benefit from research conducted for the military sector. Indeed, civilian research actually suffered—it became less productive and more expensive—when the best minds and the best available technologies were used for military purposes.

With the Warsaw Pact thus beleaguered by a variety of psychological, structural, political, technological, and economic difficulties, the Soviet Union was left to ponder this question: "Given the relatively poor performance of the East European armies both at home and in the region over the years, is there any reason to believe that they would perform better against NATO?" If the answer was negative, as it probably was, the next question was this: "Is there anything the Soviet Union can do to make the Warsaw Pact more effective as an instrument of Soviet policy in Eastern Europe and as a counterweight to NATO?"

Gorbachev's Choices

Before attempting to answer these questions, we should stress that—before the revolutionary upheavals of 1989—the military alliance with Eastern Europe still offered the Soviet Union both tangible and symbolic benefits.

In a strictly military sense, having Eastern Europe as a buffer zone was seen as providing for advance warning in case of Western aggression; as permitting the forward deployment of Soviet forces in Europe; and, given the subordination of East European armies to the Soviet high command, as putting these armies side by side with the Soviet Union in a potential East-West conflict—at least as long as the Soviet side is the winning side.

Symbolically, the alliance was seen as helping reinforce the image of the Soviet Union as a military superpower and indeed as the major European power. Politically, the alliance allowed Moscow to advance various security-related proposals on behalf of a group of European states in the Warsaw Pact rather than on its own behalf alone.

In related areas, the Soviet Union benefited from close cooperation with East European military intelligence, particularly in the realm of illegal technology transfer from the West. With Poland, East Germany, and Czechoslovakia among the top fifteen arms exporters in the world, East Europeans also promoted Soviet military objectives in the Third World. Another Soviet-sponsored activity was the training of pro-Soviet security forces in countries such as Nicaragua, Ethiopia, and South Yemen. (The secret police forces trained abroad by East Germans, who took the lead in this activity, were dubbed in the West as the "Red Gestapos" of the Third World.)

Notwithstanding such real or perceived benefits, the problem remained: How could Moscow make the national armies more effective, if not fully reliable, in joint operations? What were Gorbachev's options to remedy the situation?

(1) His first option—the "radical reform" of Soviet–East European military relations—was to entail an effort to begin to *dilute* Soviet domination of the Warsaw Pact, giving the national commands more control over their forces. By concurrently making modern weapons available to the national ar-

mies at reasonable prices, Gorbachev would move the Soviet Union toward a decentralized and more voluntaristic military alliance with Eastern Europe.

In the resulting atmosphere of growing camaraderie, the national officer corps might develop a larger stake—and take greater pride—in their work; their nationalism could then be exploited to promote rather than hinder Soviet policies. While Moscow would retain its "leading role" in the Warsaw Pact and still obtain most of what it wants and needs, the contribution of the East Europeans would also increase because the officers, and perhaps the conscripts, would have gained a sense of identification with the alliance.

(2) The opposite, old-fashioned option was to *strengthen* Soviet domination of the Warsaw Pact and at the same time further *weaken* East European command over the national armies. There is no question that this was the "early" Gorbachev's approach to Soviet–East European military relations. The evidence suggests that Moscow was merely doing more of what it had done under previous leaders. As identified by Dale R. Herspring,[7] these were some of the (old) policies that Gorbachev also pursued:

• All top-level command positions in the Warsaw Pact were still held by Soviet officers. With a secret 1979 statute ordering the transfer of effective control over the East European militaries to Soviet command, "the ability of an East European national command to obviate Soviet orders" was still all but nonexistent (except in Romania).

• Even when East Europeans received the same weapon systems as their Soviet counterparts, certain advanced features were usually withheld so as to ensure Soviet superiority as well as a continued reliance on Soviet supplies. At times it was difficult for the East European militaries to hold exercises without Soviet participation or supervision because not

_____

7. Ibid., pp. 146–148.

enough ammunition was available. Moreover, both multilateral and unilateral (Soviet) military exercises were used to stifle tendencies toward autonomy in the East European armed forces.

• Soviet military doctrine provided exclusive guidance for the Warsaw Pact's activities; Russian was the Pact's operational language. The political literature offered to the several armies was aimed at reinforcing the Soviet view of international events in general and of the identity of the enemy in particular. An apparently large number of East European officers were invited to study at Soviet military academies; the purpose was to develop a pool of Soviet-trained officers throughout the region. Attendance at Soviet military schools was also used to recruit reliable cadres ready to report to and work for the Soviet Union.

Given the tendency toward political decentralization under Gorbachev, it is not quite clear why the East European militaries were not given a greater measure of autonomy— why the first option mentioned above ("radical reform") was not adopted. Perhaps the best answer is that Gorbachev needed more time to overcome decades of hegemonical habits and pursue an uncharted and potentially dangerous path— all in exchange for an uncertain outcome that could have very negative consequences for Soviet security. He needed time to convince his military to take a chance. In Soviet eyes, diluting Soviet domination of the Pact in the hope of improving East European military performance was initially considered too risky. Finally, the (Western) idea that a more voluntaristic alliance is normally stronger than its individual components was long regarded by Soviet military authorities as strange, far-fetched, and probably wrong.

For the time being, then, Gorbachev opted for policies whose obvious goal was to intensify Moscow's ability to control and indeed dominate the Warsaw Pact. Concurrently, the Soviet Union apparently abandoned all efforts at improving the effectiveness of the East European militaries as a means of making them more reliable. The key distinction here is between the minimal goal of *availability* and the more ambitious goal of developing the *capacity* for joint action. In simple terms, availability means presence or readiness for use, while the capacity for joint action entails, inter alia, motivation, a commitment to fight. As the various Soviet policies (as listed above) were almost exclusively compulsory, they ensured only East European availability in a potential conflict. They had little to do with motivation—with the goal of generating active and competent East European participation—which would have to stem from a common purpose and shared responsibilities, as well as at least a modicum of national autonomy in military matters.[8]

For Moscow to be satisfied with an East European military that is merely available for, but is not necessarily committed to engage in, joint action suggests that the "early" Gorbachev was already aware of the limits of East European contributions to the Warsaw Pact. It is almost as if he resigned himself to the fatalistic conclusion that, while the Soviet Union might be able to lead the East European armies to the battlefront, under no circumstances could it make them fight well.

Courting Trouble

Gorbachev's initial course in Soviet–East European military relations was thus cautious and circumspect. His objectives were limited: he was interested in improving existing mechanisms.

---

8. Along similar lines, Christopher D. Jones has written: "The purpose of the military-administrative structure of the Warsaw Pact is to fragment national command over national armed forces. The fragmentation of East European military organizations does not solve the problem of the reliability of East European military personnel. It solves the problem of availability." See Christopher D. Jones, "Agencies of the Alliance: Multinational in Form, Bilateral in Content," in Jeffrey Simon and Trond Gilberg, eds., *Security Implications of Nationalism in Eastern Europe* (Carlisle Barracks, Penn.: U.S. Army War College, 1985), p. 164.

It was already obvious during the reformist era of 1985–88 that Gorbachev's approach to the Warsaw Pact—the "second option" he adopted—would not serve Soviet interests well. Once a larger number of Soviet troops was withdrawn from the region, the need for a reliable and effective East European military would become paramount to deter or confront political trouble. Without such reliable East European military forces, it was simply much more likely that the Soviet Union would either abandon its empire or else be obliged to return to protect the East European regimes from popular challenges to their authority.

Consider that after mid-1986 Gorbachev put forth several new ideas about the East-West conventional balance in Europe. Reduced to their essentials, they pointed to a Soviet interest in a military doctrine that was oriented less toward offense (and was therefore less threatening to the West) than the Warsaw Pact's current military doctrine. As Gorbachev argued in his book *Perestroika*, it was "time the two military alliances amended their strategic concepts to gear them more to the aims of defense." In accordance with this change in strategic doctrine, Gorbachev announced in his December 1988 speech at the United Nations that the Soviet Union would unilaterally withdraw 50,000 of its 565,000 troops from East Germany, Czechoslovakia, and Hungary. In the spring of 1989 some Soviet forces actually left Hungary.

These proposals and measures, however, were definitely out of sync with Gorbachev's early approach to the Warsaw Pact. The conventional arms measures, by reducing Soviet military strength in Eastern Europe, made it imperative that the region's military forces develop their own capacity if they were called upon to maintain order. Yet the initial Soviet policies toward the Warsaw Pact had the effect of weakening the self-reliance and hence the effectiveness of the East European militaries.

Put another way, it was clear in 1988, at the time of Gorbachev's adoption of a Soviet "defensive doctrine," that by itself it would not have a direct impact on Eastern Europe. But what would inevitably follow—*substantial reductions* in manpower and armaments—would have a direct and indeed significant impact. Even the partial withdrawal of Soviet forces would have two major consequences for Eastern Europe:

First, the news and especially the sight of Soviet troops leaving the region would generate new popular pressures for fundamental political change. Rightly or wrongly, East Europeans would assume that military retrenchment signified political retreat, that the Soviet commitment to preserving the "gains of socialism" in Eastern Europe was on the wane. Second, it would become clear that, since security forces alone cannot contain *major* disturbances, it would be left for the individual East European militaries to maintain order. However, in the face of massive demonstrations, without Soviet troops at hand to back them up if necessary, would the East European militaries stand up and be counted? Would they obey civilian (communist) authority? Might they possibly opt for military rule?

Would they be neutral? In 1988, no one could predict the scope or intensity of popular risings under such circumstances, or precisely where they might occur. Nor could anyone be sure about the behavior of the East European militaries. What was certain was that the expected reduction of Soviet troops would mark the beginning of a new political ball game in Eastern Europe. With the people on the offensive on one side and the regimes on the defensive on the other side, the East European militaries would either act as powerful referees—unless they wanted Moscow to return—or stay in their barracks.

In the original draft of this chapter, written *before* the remarkable uprising of 1989, I concluded this way:

"Will the region's armed forces face up to the challenge of their new responsibilities? In their present condition, they are *available* to do the job; their presence is a deterrent. But it is doubtful that they are *capable* of reestablishing order, for they are not motivated enough to be reliable defenders of Soviet-type systems. Only Gorbachev's "first option"—which he has not adopted—would prepare the East European militaries to take proper precautions, to develop appropriate capabilities, and to acquire the political finesse necessary to handle such a new and complex task.

This is why Gorbachev's military approach to the Warsaw Pact, effective as it may be in Soviet foreign policy toward the West, is not so realistic or useful in other respects. For, to repeat, even the partial withdrawal of Soviet troops will expose the region's communist regimes to unparalleled challenges to their authority and also present the East European militaries with a complex assignment that they might well find 'mission impossible.' Under such circumstances, the Warsaw Pact's principal mission—policing Eastern Europe—would be once again left for the Soviet Army to carry out."

In the end, as we shall see in Chapters 6 and 7, the surprise was that Gorbachev abandoned the Pact's de facto "principal mission." His troops stayed put. What was not surprising was that the East European militaries stayed in their barracks—except in Romania, where they supported the people's cause. In any case, the military alliance Stalin welded together was now in shambles.

Part Three

THE ERA OF REVOLUTIONARY CHANGE, SINCE 1988

VI

MOSCOW RETREATS

From Reform to Revolution

"THE MOST DANGEROUS TIME for a bad government," according to Alexis de Tocqueville, "is when it starts to reform itself." His time-honored observation has come to apply to the Soviet Union. But for Moscow's imperial domain in Eastern Europe —for the bloc that failed—a variation on de Tocqueville's theme is closer to the truth: For bad governments whose survival depends on a foreign protector, the most dangerous time is when their protector has begun to retreat.

In 1988, the Polish and Hungarian regimes began to respond both to growing domestic challenges to their rule and to mixed signals from Moscow. By July of that year, Zbigniew Brzezinski, formerly national security adviser to President Carter, identified the region's condition as "prerevolutionary."[1] Phrasing more cautiously, I also noted at the end of 1988 that as the ideological "foundation of the East European alliance is sinking [and as] the edifice of its socialism is cracked," the Soviet bloc has turned into "a shadow of its former self." Even "the term 'Soviet bloc' is becoming a political misnomer," I added.[2] Gorbachev's speech at the United Nations in December 1988, announcing that Moscow would unilaterally

---

1. Zbigniew Brzezinski, "Special Address," *Problems of Communism* 37, No. 3–4 (May–August 1988), pp. 67–70.
2. Charles Gati, "Eastern Europe on Its Own," *Foreign Affairs* 68, No. 1 (America and the World 1988/89), pp. 99–119.

withdraw some of its forces from Eastern Europe independent of any corresponding measures by NATO, was particularly illustrative of the fading of Moscow's imperial aspirations.

The Soviet military decision to retrench contained a critical political message to the region's communist leaders: *The Soviet Union would no longer protect unpopular East European regimes from their own peoples.* Once that message was conveyed and absorbed, reformers and diehards alike were left with the choice of either making the best deal they could with their own populations or using force to break the people's will.

The Romanian, Bulgarian, Czechoslovak, and East German regimes—the region's "gang of four"—opted to maintain repressive, one-party rule. Their decisions were based on their desire to stay in power. Mistakenly, they assumed that they had greater popular support than in fact they did; they certainly did not regard the political situation in their countries as explosive or, in Brzezinski's phrase, "prerevolutionary." Even without Soviet protection, they believed that they could handle what they assumed was a small minority of oppositionists seeking radical change. At any rate, they expected that Moscow would change its hands-off postion if faced with an actual anticommunist revolution. They convinced themselves that Gorbachev or his successors would inevitably revert to the principles of the "Brezhnev Doctrine" rather than permit large-scale defections from the communist fold.

The less rigid Polish and Hungarian communist regimes interpreted the Soviet message to mean that they, like Gorbachev, should reassess the past, blame current problems on their predecessors, and proceed toward the implementation of radical, if unspecified, reforms. Unlike Gorbachev, however, they entered into formal discussions, first in Poland and later in Hungary, with leaders of the democratic opposition. Although their original intention was no doubt to coopt the opposition into the existing governments and thus to create the appearance of power-sharing, the roundtable discussions eventually produced the transformation of one-party rule under peaceful, if often contentious, conditions. Hence these reform-minded communist regimes ended up with changes far more extensive than the ones they had originally intended to make.

Gorbachev's motives for letting his East European allies fend for themselves remain controversial and, indeed, unclear. His preoccupation with Soviet domestic problems was undoubtedly a compelling factor. Other factors included his desire to reduce the Soviet military budget and in service to that goal, to withdraw Soviet forces from the region. Yet these eminently sensible and rational motives must be viewed in the context of Gorbachev's personal frustration with the "gang of four" and their resistance to his own perestroika and glasnost. As the ambitious Soviet leader of a huge empire, Gorbachev could ill afford to tolerate a Ceauşescu, Zhivkov, Honecker, or Jakeš forever.

Whether Gorbachev fully anticipated the consequences of his decisions remains uncertain as well. It is quite possible that he misjudged East European popular sentiments by assuming that his version of reformist communism would take root in the region. Deluded by shouts of "Gorby! Gorby!", he may well have confused the East Europeans' genuine respect for his personal courage and for what he was doing in the Soviet Union with their support for reform-communism in Eastern Europe. While Gorbachev may have expected his policies to prompt the reform of the region's orthodox communist regimes, he may not have foreseen revolutions against communism itself.

In the end, most of Eastern Europe experienced a series of stunning revolutions rather than step-by-step reforms. The changes came about in this manner not only because the old regimes had delayed making the concessions necessary to appease their peoples but also because both Moscow and the

East European regimes had seriously underestimated the passions emerging among the East European peoples, mistaking their past apathy for permanent acquiescence. The Soviet leadership, in particular, failed to anticipate that the East Europeans would interpret Soviet military retrenchment as political retreat and would press for a change in the system rather than replacement of the current regimes.

Although it does not speak well for Gorbachev's prescience that he failed to discern the region's anticommunist, prerevolutionary condition, it is to his credit that he refused to fight fire with fire. Indeed, in October 1989, when East Germany's Honecker recognized that only massive force could stem the tide against communism in his country and directed his security forces to shoot at the demonstrators in Leipzig if necessary, it appears that Moscow actually encouraged Egon Krenz, the second in command in East Germany, to countermand Honecker's order. At this critical juncture, Gorbachev had decided to allow the reform he had hoped for to turn into revolution. Elsewhere, too, Gorbachev refused to be drawn into a costly and potentially dangerous effort to save his dominion. Even when, in November, the Berlin Wall was breached and thus the most vital of all Soviet geopolitical interests was threatened, Gorbachev was silent. He may well have believed that in the end the East European revolutions would not damage his country's long-term interests and, indeed, that they might even improve his own position.

One of the first clues to Gorbachev's so-called "new thinking" about Eastern Europe emerged in April 1988, when the CPSU abolished the old Department for Liaison with the Communist and Workers' Parties of Socialist Countries. At the same time, the Politburo created a Commission on International Policy and appointed Aleksandr N. Yakovlev, one of Gorbachev's closest advisers, as its chairman. The purpose of the newly created commission was to coordinate Soviet foreign policy in Eastern Europe and around the world. The organizational change had the effect of lessening the importance of the region, signaling that it would no longer be treated as a special case. Moscow's East European policy was henceforth to be made in the context of global and geopolitical rather than ideological considerations.[3]

No comparable organizational changes occurred in the Ministry of Foreign Affairs in 1988 or thereafter. However, the role of the ministry in handling East European affairs has markedly expanded from handling routine matters to becoming an active participant in both making and implementing policy. The department responsible for East European affairs has been upgraded within the ministry. The growing importance of the Ministry of Foreign Affairs in matters relating to Eastern Europe, as well as on all issues of foreign policy, appears to stem from the position that Politburo member and Foreign Minister Eduard Shevardnadze has come to occupy in the Soviet hierarchy.

Another early clue to Soviet intentions that appeared in early- and mid-1988 was a series of what were termed unofficial interviews, articles, and comments about the region by Soviet foreign policy specialists (see also Chapter 3). At the

---

3. In practice, it remains unclear how responsibility for Eastern Europe is divided among the several Central Committee commissions and departments. While the Politburo has retained responsibility for making basic decisions, of course, it appears that policy originates either in the CPSU's International Department (which operates under the Yakovlev commission) or in the Ministry of Foreign Affairs. Since mid-1988, the International Department has been headed by Valentin M. Falin, a German specialist and member of the Central Committee. Of the three First Deputy Heads in his department, only one—Rafael P. Fedorov—deals with Eastern Europe. His staff includes specialists on the East European countries, who perform the functions of the formerly separate Liaison Department.

There are others with East European expertise within the Central Committee apparatus. The Ideology Commission, led by Politburo member Vadim Medvedev, the former director of the Liaison Department, remains a key player. There is also Gorbachev's "personal advisor" on Eastern Europe, the highly regarded political scientist, Georgi Shakhnazarov. Since early 1989, whenever Gorbachev has met with the head of an East European communist party, only Shakhnazarov has accompanied him. Together with Yakovlev, but not Medvedev and Falin, Shakhnazarov is known to belong to Gorbachev's inner circle of like-minded officials.

time, it was unclear whether these observations (by Academician Bogomolov, Fyodor Burlatski, and others) reflected official thinking. When they declared the "Brezhnev Doctrine" "dead," but the official spokesmen of the Soviet government had not yet done so, Western analysts were uncertain whether this was merely the wishful thinking of individuals. However, by the time a long, substantial, and strikingly self-critical assessment of past Soviet policies toward Eastern Europe was published in July 1988 (see Appendix), there was a growing sense in the West that its authors—staff members of the Institute of Economics of the World Socialist System—represented either the official position or the dominant official position. But important differences of opinion remained. In February 1989, when Academician Oleg Bogomolov asserted that even Hungarian neutrality would not necessarily represent a threat to Soviet security interests, his statement was disavowed by a high-ranking Soviet official. Bogomolov subsequently issued a professed retraction that turned out to be no retraction at all.

Only in retrospect has it been possible to confirm that, with the Politburo undecided and Gorbachev still deflecting questions about the history and the future of the "Brezhnev Doctrine," wide-ranging debates over Moscow's East European policy were taking place throughout 1988. Officially, the new policy began to take shape only in the immediate aftermath of Gorbachev's United Nations speech of December 1988, when the Soviet leader announced that by the end of 1990 some 240,000 men, 10,000 tanks, 8,500 guns, and 820 combat aircraft would be withdrawn from Eastern Europe and from the European regions (the so-called western military districts) of the Soviet Union.

More than any other single event, that announcement set the stage for the dramatic developments of 1989. By suggesting that Moscow was prepared to remove Soviet forces from its East European dominion, Gorbachev put the region's communist leaders on notice that Soviet tanks would no longer protect their rule. It did not take long for the peoples of Eastern Europe to understand that their leaders were therefore vulnerable—that some of them were, in effect, on the run.

From Poland to Romania

It was the Jaruzelski regime in *Poland* that first responded to the implications of the new Soviet position. After its long history of denigrating Lech Wałęsa and dismissing "Solidarity" as a relic from the past with no significant popular support, the Polish government reconsidered its position at the very end of 1988 and accorded legal status to the independent union in January 1989. Fearful of losing their privileges and unwilling to give up their "leading role," many party leaders so strongly opposed the move that Jaruzelski and his three closest advisers threatened to resign if the party failed to follow their recommendation.[4]

Having swallowed its pride, the Jaruzelski regime also agreed to hold free elections in June 1989 on the condition that the communists and their parliamentary allies, who were nominally noncommunist and until then insignificant, could remain dominant in the Sejm, the lower chamber of the legislature. The results of these partly free, partly arranged elections turned out to be as unexpected as they were stunning. In the new upper chamber, the Senate, "Solidarity" won all but one seat (99 out of 100). In the Sejm, all but two of the thirty-five top party and government officials who had run unopposed (as a result of the deal between the government and "Solidarity") lost their seats when more than half of the voters crossed out their names.

Nothing like this had happened in Eastern Europe in four

---

4. The change was very sudden indeed. Only a few months earlier, in mid-1988, one of the three told me that he would rather cut his own throat than negotiate with Wałęsa.

decades. The novelty of the situation provoked considerable tension as well as the reemergence of political maneuvering. For example, in order to avoid a crackdown by the communists and the secret police, "Solidarity" supporters in the new legislature helped reelect Jaruzelski as president, albeit by only one vote. Sensing the direction of the political winds, the former allies of the communists—the obedient fellow-travelers who had supported every twist and turn in Polish politics since the late 1940s—rediscovered their democratic past and joined the noncommunist side. With that move, "Solidarity" became the majority force in the legislature.

In August 1989 President Jaruzelski had to decide who would be Poland's next prime minister. Because many party hardliners opposed the appointment of a representative of "Solidarity" to the post, and because their consent was deemed essential for a peaceful transition, Gorbachev made a critical telephone call to Mieczysław Rakowski, the party leader. Given the party's subsequent decision to abide by the will of the people and the legislature, the tenor of Gorbachev's message seems clear. He presumably told Rakowski that the Soviet Union would accept a Polish government with a communist minority. The man who was then appointed prime minister, Tadeusz Mazowiecki, was a prominent Catholic intellectual and senior "Solidarity" leader. The communist were allowed to retain control of defense and internal affairs in the new government.

There were many reasons why the Polish communists agreed to hold largely free elections. The polls they had commissioned, publicized, and may even have believed did not indicate that they would be swept away. At the end of 1988, for example, their polls revealed that popular support for "Solidarity" had waned as Jaruzelski's personal popularity had increased. Thus, although the communists did not expect to win the elections, they believed they would receive one-third of the vote in the Sejm. If their calculations proved accurate, they would be able form a government with the help of the allied parties and deliver a crushing blow to "Solidarity" and its Western supporters. At worst, they would grant "Solidarity" a few insignificant cabinet posts and thus create the illusion of a coalition government. But their polls completely misinterpreted the popular mood. As it turned out, only the preelection deal and tactical considerations by the "Solidarity" leadership after the elections saved the communists and Jaruzelski himself from being completely eliminated from Polish politics.

The ultimate decision to abide by the results of the election may have been prompted in part by Gorbachev's telephone call, coupled with increasing *public* hints in mid-1989 that the Soviet leadership was utterly serious about retreating from Eastern Europe. Speaking to the Council of Europe in Strasbourg on July 7, 1989, a time of postelection maneuverings in Poland, Gorbachev went further than ever before to emphasize "new thinking" in Soviet policy toward Eastern Europe. While maintaining that "existing realities" in Europe must be respected and that Western attempts at "overcoming" socialism in Eastern Europe would provoke "confrontation," his central message was a firm rejection of the "Brezhnev Doctrine":

> Social and political orders in one or another country changed in the past and may change in the future. But this change is the exclusive affair of the people of that country and is their choice. Any interference in domestic affairs and any attempts to restrict the sovereignty of states, both friends and allies or any others, is inadmissible.[5]

Another consideration undergirding the Polish communist decision to respect the election results was the condition of the economy. With good reason, many party members assumed that no Polish government would be able to cope with the problems ahead. If a "Solidarity"-led government were to

---

5. *The Economist*, July 15, 1989, p. 53.

introduce austerity measures, or if prices were to increase, factories close, and unemployment develop, the people would blame whatever party was in power. Why not, these communists reasoned, permit "Solidarity" to try—and then to fail? In the meantime, the communists would have the opportunity to regroup by shedding the communist name and re-emerging as social democrats. In their new guise, they would support some austerity measures and oppose the most unpopular ones, while pointing out that they were responsible for neither the high prices nor unemployment. They would thus await their turn. Moreover, by remaining in charge of the main sources of power (such as the presidency, defense, and internal security), they were not without options—even if, to the extent these options entailed the use of force, they would result in a civil war. For after all that had been gained, the Polish people would not easily relinquish what they had achieved.

As in Poland, the first major step toward democracy in *Hungary* was taken in January 1989, when the parliament approved several bills legalizing the right of assembly and association. In February, the ruling party, abdicating its leading role, also approved the creation of independent political parties. Unlike in Poland, however, the pressure for change originated primarily in the communist party, formally known as the Hungarian Socialist Workers' Party (HSWP). The opposition, while vocal, was initially small and isolated; it also lacked a leader of Lech Wałęsa's stature and broad appeal.

The struggle for supremacy within the party set two factions in contention. One, led by General Secretary Károly Grósz, was kept on the defensive by reformers and their rapidly rising star, Imre Pozsgay. Of the many issues debated, a question of particular importance was that of the party's past in general and, specifically, its role in the 1956 revolution. In February, the party resolved that its historic position on the upheaval of 1956 as a "counterrevolution" had been wrong and that what had taken place should instead be regarded as a popular, national uprising against oppression. Without explicitly stating it, the document produced by the party under Pozsgay's guidance also rejected the party's earlier positions accepting and justifying the Soviet intervention.

How a communist party evaluates its past may not, at first, seem to be of practical importance. But in Hungary the issue helped mobilize the public against Grósz and his followers. Responding to the popular mood, the majority of his Central Committee colleagues disassociated themselves from Grósz's more orthodox values. He suffered a striking political setback in June when, with the participation of the party's reformist wing, the Committee for Historical Justice (a newly formed independent group) arranged for a ceremonious reburial of the leaders of the 1956 revolution. Broadcast live on Hungarian radio and television, reported around the world, and attended by hundreds of thousands in Budapest's Heroes Square, the event showed that freedom of association was a reality and not merely a hypothetical right. Although Grósz retained his post as the party's general secretary, he was demoted. In the newly created four-member party presidium, Party Chairman Rezső Nyers became first among equals; the other three members were all dedicated reformers.

No week in 1989 passed without some significant sign—be it a statement, a demonstration, or an actual measure—of the dismantling of the old order. In May, for example, the government began to disassemble the barbed-wire fence and electronic devices—the paraphernalia of the iron curtain—along its border with Austria. The same month, in an interview with *Magyar Hirlap*, the official daily, Pozsgay acknowledged for the first time what had been obvious to all but never conceded by the party: that competition with other parties "entails the possibility of losing [the monopoly of] power." In principle (although not yet in practice as in Poland), the HSWP was thus moving well beyond a Gorbachevian "reform" or "democratization" and on toward the introduction of a multiparty political system and a true, mixed economy. Many thought and even more hoped that a new Hungary would eventually follow the Austrian model.

For a brief moment in July, it seemed that the HSWP's reformist wing might still play an important, if no longer dominant, role in Hungarian politics. The reformers were doing well in the public-opinion polls; their democratic opponents, largely unknown, were not. The death of János Kádár on July 7, 1989, offered the party the opportunity to blame him for the country's problems, and indeed for the crimes of his thirty-two–year rule. But the moment of political opportunity passed quickly. The fragmented party, divided against itself, could neither take advantage of the popularity of some of its leaders nor adequately disassociate itself from Kádár's legacy.

Not that the party did not try to increase its popular support. In September, for example, the government—still controlled by the party—made the unprecedented decision to allow tens of thousands of vacationing East German tourists to leave Hungary for West Germany, in clear violation of Hungary's treaty with East Germany. The purpose of the decision was to demonstrate to the Hungarian public as well as to Western public opinion, and particularly to the West German government, that Hungary was different; that it would apply the Helsinki Accord's provision concerning the free movement of people even to the citizens of another state. The intended effect at home was to encourage the Hungarian public to view the party and the government as its own. West German opinion was important as well because West Germany was, and remains, Hungary's most generous economic benefactor. What is not known is whether the Hungarian authorities made their decision in collusion with the Soviet Union. If they did, an additional purpose of the move may well have been to undermine the Honecker regime by depriving East

Germany of precisely those citizens who could afford to travel and who thus tended to be members of East Germany's professional elite.

But despite this extraordinary gambit, which would lead to the fall of the Honecker regime in East Germany, the Hungarian communist party continued to lose ground. At its extraordinary congress in October, the HSWP not only abandoned Leninism and declared itself in favor of "democratic socialism," but it also ended its existence as the Hungarian Socialist Workers' Party and reconstituted itself as the Hungarian Socialist Party (HSP). What mattered, in practice, was that party members were asked to reenroll in the party, a decision that was intended to emphasize the difference between the new HSP and the old HSWP. But the decision turned out to be a major blunder. Of the approximately 700,000 party members, only 30,000 chose to join the new party. Even several members of the government, including a deputy prime minister and the minister of justice, failed to reenroll. Prime Minister Miklós Németh, although a party member, subsequently resigned from the HSP's presidium. Even more ominous for the party, the hardliners who had supported Grósz denounced the HSP for embracing "bourgeois democracy"— and then recreated the old HSWP to compete for the very small leftist vote.

By the end of the year, as the communists grew weaker, the opposition parties quarreled among themselves. Although all were agreed that parliamentary elections would be held in early 1990, they were divided over whether the country's president should be elected before or after the parliamentary elections. Hoping to get a head start and seeking to take advantage of Pozsgay's remaining popularity, the Hungarian Socialist Party sought an early date for the presidential elections. The Hungarian Democratic Forum, the largest opposition party at that time, agreed, partly because it was not entirely opposed to Pozsgay's candidacy, but mainly because it wanted an elected rather than an interim president to occupy the office as soon as possible. On the other hand, the Association of Free Democrats and the Young Democrats, the most consistently pro-Western of the Hungarian parties, feared that Pozsgay as president would manage to dominate the political scene before parliamentary elections. To widespread surprise, they collected enough signatures to hold a popular referendum on the issue, and, although only by a small margin, they won. As provided in the constitution and validated by the referendum, an elected parliament—the main source of legitimate authority—would thus choose Hungary's next president.

The issue was significant because it demonstrated the HSP's inability to achieve its goals even with the active backing of the major opposition party. Even Pozsgay, who was "Hungary's Gorbachev" years before Gorbachev's own perestroika and who was far more radical than the Soviet reformer, could not overcome his communist past in the eyes of the electorate. The referendum also demonstrated the atomization of Hungarian politics on the eve of free elections. Indeed, the country was in a state of great anxiety. The most persistent fear was that Hungary might experience the syndrome long associated with Italian politics: serial governments, each attempting to cope with the country's problems and only briefly in power.

A more optimistic, and perhaps even more accurate, interpretation would emphasize that in 1989 Hungary underwent only the first phase of its peaceful revolution. That phase signified the destruction of the old system, which was accomplished without violence or bloodshed. The second phase, begun in 1990, would entail the construction of a democratic, pluralistic political and economic order. Given the need for harsh austerity measures in the economic realm and the prospect of continued discord in the political realm, this phase also promised to be difficult, if ultimately successful. For despite disagreements over details, there was a broad consensus among Hungarians that the historic opportunity of the moment, a unique chance to be independent and to build lasting democratic institutions, could not and should not be missed.

In *East Germany*, the first phase of the revolution took no more than a few weeks. After eighteen years in power, and faced with massive demonstrations and considerable Soviet pressure, Erich Honecker stepped down as president and party leader on October 18, 1989. His initial replacement, a Politburo member and the former security chief, Egon Krenz, resigned forty-six days later, on December 3. During his tenure, on November 9, 1989, a day that will be long remembered, East Germany effectively dismantled the Berlin Wall by physically removing sections of it and allowing unrestricted travel from East to West and from West to East.

Yet even this extraordinary measure failed to help Krenz and his party. The communists were already so discredited that they chose as their next leader a political unknown, Gregor Gysi, while another reform-minded communist from Dresden, Hans Modrow, became prime minister in a cabinet still dominated by communists. Even so, Honecker's old guard was gone, expelled from the party they had served for decades. Some were sent to jail, while others were placed under house arrest, awaiting trial on charges of corruption. In a matter of days, the East German communist system collapsed.

Erich Honecker, as the self-appointed chief of the "gang of four" and the rigid guardian of communist orthodoxy, a supporter of Romania's Ceauşescu, and the only Warsaw Pact leader to condone China's brutal oppression of the pro-democracy movement at Tienanmen Square in the summer of 1989, had been a Stalinist in Brezhnevite clothes. He had paid lip service to perestroika but did not practice it. He kissed Gorbachev on both cheeks, as he had Brezhnev, but ideologically he kept his distance. He ruled East Germany as if he could both defy Gorbachev and depend on the 360,000-strong Soviet garrison stationed in his country to preserve his rule.

Honecker's calculation was not without merit. He may even have expected that Gorbachev would one day attempt to replace him with a younger and more reform-minded leader. But he could not imagine that the Soviet Union would acquiesce in the dismantling of the Berlin Wall or consider the reunification of Germany under West German auspices and thus, in effect, relinquish without a fight or even a serious complaint its most valuable parcel of land in Europe. Had it ever dawned on Honecker that this could happen, this ever-suspicious Stalinist might have concluded that Gorbachev was a renegade who had set out to undermine communism from within.

The ultimate challenge to Honecker and indeed to the East German regime came from an unexpected source. When Hungary allowed about 60,000 East German tourists to leave for the West, thousands of other East Germans flooded Prague and Warsaw as well. To stop these refugees from escaping, Honecker would have had to seal his country's borders with Czechoslovakia and Poland and thus transform all of East Germany into a prison. While under normal circumstances he might well have ordered a new "iron curtain" between East Germany and its socialist neighbors, he was reportedly bed-ridden from late July to September and thus took no action to stop the flood of refugees.

The sight of so many East Germans escaping to the West prompted massive demonstrations for free travel and other human rights throughout the country. It is difficult to identify a particular day as the one on which the revolution against the old order began, but if there was such a day it was October 7, 1989, when Gorbachev attended the fortieth anniversary celebration of the foundation of East Germany. In his speech, Gorbachev did not praise Honecker; he praised perestroika. Ten days later, Honecker resigned. The party was over. His departure only encouraged the oppositionists to increase their demands. Led by the New Forum, a new and amorphous political group, they pressed for free elections and the complete removal of the Berlin Wall. As the new leadership promised to consider reform, including more permissive travel regulations and election laws, growing numbers of East Germans joined the protest movement. By now de Tocqueville's formula fully applied: the promise of reform by the regime sparked the promise of revolution by the people. The post-Honecker regime was on the defensive. On November 4, a crowd of half a million people demonstrated in East Berlin while an additional half million turned out in other cities throughout the country. Five days later, the Berlin Wall was open.

By the end of 1989 new political parties and movements had appeared on the East German political scene. While some advocated a united Germany, others preferred a separate East German entity. More East Germans sought a new economic order that would combine the productivity associated with capitalism with the security associated with socialism. All, however, desired political pluralism. In the upcoming elections, the social democrats appeared to have the edge.

Although communists still controlled the government, the government no longer controlled the population. In fact, the popular revolution against the communist system—and not only against the Honecker regime—proved victorious. With the press already free, travel unrestricted, and genuine, parliamentary democracy within reach, the most serious issue remaining on the agenda (see Chapter 7) was the future of East Germany and the rise of a new German state, an issue that involved the future of all of Europe.

Until its stunning and successful transition from dictatorship to democracy in November 1989, *Czechoslovakia* had been an anachronism in Gorbachev's world of reform and renewal. In political, cultural, and economic matters, orthodoxy prevailed. The main roadblock was the leadership's need to defend and justify its old policies. Before he retired in 1988, for example, Politburo member Vasil Bil'ak spoke for the entire leadership when he stated that the only policies that should be adopted were those that demonstrated "the strengths and advantages of socialism." He repeatedly warned against what he termed the "opportunistic" emulation of Gorbachev's program, emphasizing the lessons of "the struggle against the enemies of socialism in the 1960s." In an earlier speech, he had reaffirmed the validity of a resolution adopted by the Czechoslovak Central Committee in December 1970 which had laid out the country's harsh, oppressive course since the 1968 "Prague Spring." "There are those," said Bil'ak, alluding to Gorbachev, "who would like to have that document nullified, but this will not be done."[6]

As early as 1987, Moscow sought to discredit and even to dislodge the very leaders it had put in power after the 1968 Soviet intervention. Gorbachev visited Prague in the spring of 1987 and was asked by Western reporters to clarify the difference between Dubček's "Prague Spring" and his own perestroika and glasnost; his spokesman, Gennadi Gerasimov, replied in two memorable words: "Nineteen years." But Gorbachev himself shied away from openly criticizing Brezhnev's protégés in Prague. At that time, he was guided by the belief that extending his process of renewal to Czechoslovakia might destabilize that country. That is why Gustáv Husák, who resigned as party leader in December 1987, remained president, and why his younger replacement as head of the party, Miloš Jakeš, was equally hardline.

Only in the summer and early fall of 1989 did overt signs of increased Soviet concern about the Czechoslovak leadership begin to emerge:

• On August 8, *Izvestia* carried a long interview with Ru-

---

6. *The Washington Post*, March 18, 1987.

dolf Hegenbart, then head of the Czechoslovak Central Committee's Department for State Administration and thus the party's direct supervisor of the secret police. The interview was unusual in that Hegenbart had taken a most critical view of Czechoslovak conditions. Because they did not reflect the party line, Hegenbart's remarks were not published in the Prague press, as would have been customary, and he was reprimanded by his Politburo superiors. Since Hegenbart's position in the Czechoslovak party suggested that he was closely associated with the KGB and since the interview appeared in the Soviet government's official daily, it is quite likely that he was encouraged by Soviet officials to state the views he voiced.

• In an interview broadcast September 4 on Hungarian television, Kiril Mazurov, a former candidate (or associate) member of the Soviet Politburo, expressed regret over the 1968 Soviet intervention. This was another extraordinary interview because Mazurov also revealed that, under the pseudonym "General Trofymov," he himself had led the Warsaw Pact forces against Czechoslovakia in 1968. Mazurov also stated, "In my view, the old guard [in Prague] should, without any special fuss, step down from the stage of politics."

• On September 17, *Izvestia* published a letter to the editor from Jiří Hájek, Dubček's foreign minister, doyen of the Czechoslovak democratic opposition since 1968, and a political *persona non grata* in Prague. In his letter, Hájek clarified Dubček's role during the "Prague Spring." In Czechoslovakia itself, even the publication of Hájek's name had been forbidden since 1968.

• In the second half of September, a Soviet television crew appeared in the Slovak capital of Bratislava for a long interview with the great hero of the "Prague Spring," Alexander Dubček. Although Czechoslovak authorities are said to have protested the crew's presence, excerpts from the interview were broadcast on Leningrad television in October.

Such evidence in the public record thus demonstrates that in August 1989 Moscow began a persistent campaign against the post-1968 leadership in Prague. By the end of September, it was clear both to leaders of the opposition and to party officials as well that the country's old guard did not have Moscow's support. Jiří Dienstbier, a leading member of the opposition who was to become Czechoslovakia's foreign minister in December 1989, told me at that time: "The party is dead, but we don't know yet when the corpse will be buried."

The corpse was buried far sooner than anyone, including Dienstbier, had ever expected. By October, the party found itself caught between its habit of using force and its fear of confrontation without Soviet backing; it appeared divided and hesitant. With the danger of arrest or injury thus diminished, Czechoslovaks took to the streets in ever greater numbers. They were also encouraged by the sight of so many East German refugees in their midst and, especially, by the breaching of the Berlin Wall. If the East German regime was as helpless and as vulnerable as it appeared to be, then surely the Czechoslovak regime could not last much longer either.

Another demonstration, on November 17, turned into a final attempt by the Prague regime to use force in defense of its waning authority. But by then it was too late. Three days later, in response to police brutality, 200,000 people massed in Prague's historic Wenceslaus Square to demand free elections and the resignation of the communist leadership. Czechoslovakia's momentous revolution of 1989 had begun.

General Secretary Jakeš, who resigned on November 24, was replaced by Karel Urbánek, a man not widely known, and therefore not widely hated. Prime Minister Ladislav Adamec resigned on December 7 and was replaced by a communist reformer and political novice, Marian Čalfa, whose coalition government included more independents than (reform) communists. On December 10, at last, President Husák also resigned. The new president, Václav Havel, a playwright, was the brave and cultivated leader of the post-1968 Czechoslovak opposition who had spent years in prison for his political activities. His countrymen as well as many in the West considered him the conscience of democratic Czechoslovakia.[7]

In addition to Havel, Czechoslovakia's new leadership included Dubček, the hero of 1968, the man who returned from oblivion to become head of parliament; Dienstbier, the new minister of foreign affairs, who, when not in prison for political activities, had for years earned his living as a coal stoker; First Deputy Prime Minister Valtr Komárek and Deputy Prime Minister and Minister of Planning Vladimir Dlouhý of the Academy of Science's Institute of Forecasting, who would both soon resign from the communist party; Minister of Finance Václav Klaus, lately of the same institute, an economist who had long been unemployed for his role in the 1968 "Prague Spring" and who converted to the free-market philosophy of Milton Friedman; and—still another political miracle—Jan Carnogurský, put in charge of internal affairs and thus also of the police, a Slovak Catholic who was in prison for his human rights campaign until only two weeks before his appointment to the cabinet in November.

The background of such leaders and the relative ease with which the new political order was born were favorable signs for Czechoslovakia's future. Divided and defeated, the communists still retained a few government posts, but they

---

7. If the spirit of the East German revolution was captured by an unnamed young man cheerfully riding his bicycle at the top of the Berlin Wall one night in November 1989, the symbol of the Czechoslovak revolution was Václav Havel. Yet I must also recall here an incredibly moving scene broadcast at that time from Prague's old Symphony Hall. There, the conductor— a bearded man of middle age—led the country's symphony orchestra in a performance of Beethoven's Ninth Symphony. The house was packed, and the audience included President Havel. As the fourth movement began and led into the "Ode to Joy," the television camera showed the conductor leading his orchestra with tears pouring down his face. It occurred to me that even though the cheerful German bicyclist and the tearful Czech conductor were separated by hundreds of miles, they both managed to convey the same feeling of joy shared by all East Europeans and indeed by all who valued freedom.

had in fact lost all credibility. The working-class support they had counted on never materialized. Moscow welcomed developments in Prague by endorsing the Czechoslovak party's latest position on the "Prague Spring" and thus, finally and formally, renounced the "Brezhnev Doctrine":

> In 1968, the Soviet leadership of that time supported the stand of one side in an internal dispute regarding objective pressing tasks. The justification for such an unbalanced, inadequate approach, an interference in the affairs of a friendly country, was then seen in an acute East-West confrontation. We share the view of the Presidium of the Central Committee of Czechoslovakia and the Czechoslovak Government that the bringing of armies into Czechoslovak territory in 1968 was unfounded, and that that decision, in the light of all the presently known facts, was erroneous.[8]

If Czechoslovakia experienced a peaceful, successful, and profoundly democratic "revolution with a human face" in 1989, what happened in *Bulgaria* was essentially a Soviet-inspired "palace revolution." For the day before Todor Zhivkov's dismissal as head of the party on November 10, his long-serving minister of foreign affairs, Petur Mladenov, was in Moscow, holding talks with high-level Soviet officials. In Moscow, he learned of the accommodating Soviet attitude toward the breaching of the Berlin Wall. On his return to Sofia, the Central Committee elected Mladenov—immediately and unanimously—to be the party's new leader.

Before his ouster, Zhivkov had attempted to save his regime by agreeing to implement some of the reforms he had long promised to introduce. After he assumed power, Mladenov also promised immediate, if moderate, reforms that would guarantee freedom of expression, the separation of the functions of the party and the state (and thus a larger role for parliament), and the gradual decentralization of the economy. Initially, the new Bulgarian leader was not prepared to relinquish the party's leading role, and he rejected

---

8. *The New York Times*, December 5, 1989.

calls for a multiparty system. But as the news of momentous changes in East Germany and Czechoslovakia reached the Bulgarian people and as the crowds at the opposition rallies grew, the Gorbachev-like reforms that Mladenov had promised proved insufficient to satisfy the country's increasingly radical mood. The various independent groups, all small and ineffectual individually, created a new umbrella organization, the Union of Democratic Forces, which demanded greater concessions. By mid-December, with the communist party in disarray, Mladenov acceded to some of the demands by announcing that competitive elections would be held in the near future.

In effect, Bulgaria was following a reform-communist course on the Soviet pattern. By comparison to Poland or Czechoslovakia, the changes were limited. Yet the potential for further progress was also considerable. With Zhivkov and several of his colleagues facing trial on charges of corruption, the Bulgarian palace revolution against the old communist order had succeeded. Meanwhile, another—popular—revolution against the new, reform-minded communist system had begun. As the country entered the 1990s, it seemed that although several transitional regimes might well come and go, Bulgaria would not remain far behind in the East European surge toward political and economic pluralism.

Bulgaria's neighbor to the north, *Romania*, experienced the last and the only violent revolution in Eastern Europe. The reasons for its being the last and for its violence were one and the same: Nicolae Ceauşescu. His resistance to change over the years and his order to shoot demonstrators in the Transylvanian city of Timisoara in mid-December unleashed national passions of hatred and vengeance against him, his family, and communist rule.

The immediate cause of the Romanian revolution was Ceauşescu's decision on December 15 to arrest a Protestant minister, László Tőkés, a champion of the rights of the two million ethnic Hungarians in Romania. Tőkés sought refuge in his Timisoara parish, which his followers surrounded in order to prevent his arrest; agents of the Securitate, the notorious secret police, attempted to remove him by force. In the ensuing riots, Securitate forces opened fire on the crowd, killing hundreds and giving rise to a local rebellion. Within hours, all of Romania was inflamed.

In the capital city of Bucharest, Ceauşescu made an ill-fated attempt to mobilize his supporters. At a rally on December 21, 1989, he demanded an end to the "counterrevolutionary" uprising. In a barely veiled reference to Moscow, he railed against "foreign conspirators" who were supposedly trying to overthrow his "socialist" regime. As his obedient followers in the square applauded his words on command, a few courageous students suddenly interjected shouts denouncing the egomaniacal ruler. They were immediately arrested, but, because the event was being broadcast live on television, millions of Romanians witnessed the incident. The long-sustained myth of Ceauşescu's invulnerability was shaken, and an uprising against his despotic rule swept the entire country.

With the Ceauşescu family in flight from Bucharest, desperate Securitate agents, fighting for their lives, took on both the army and the revolutionaries. Ferocious battles were waged in the streets, in secret tunnels under the capital city, at the Bucharest airport, and especially near the radio and television station. On Christmas Day, an unrepentant Ceauşescu and his wife, both captured two days earlier, appeared before a military tribunal which found them guilty after a short trial and ordered their execution. Two hundred soldiers reportedly vied for the privilege of participating in the firing squad.

There were many unanswered questions about the Romanian uprising. It was unclear who ordered the army to join the revolutionary side and why that order was so promptly and widely obeyed. It was unclear what role a group of reform-minded, anti-Ceauşescu officials (who had previously served his regime) had played in instigating the revolt, and how they then seized its commanding posts. It was also unclear, finally, whether the Soviet Union had communicated with and had encouraged these officials who so promptly formed a provisional government under the auspices of the newly established Council of National Salvation. One tentative answer was that in 1989 Romania had simultaneously experienced both a popular revolution, there for all to see, and a "palace revolution" that had taken place behind closed doors.

Because the revolution against the Ceauşescu regime had been decisively won, there was much to celebrate. No European regime in recent decades had been more oppressive, more brutal, more corrupt, more oblivious to international standards of behavior, or more self-righteous than the one the Ceauşescu family had established and controlled. Its immediate successors in the provisional government, who appeared to be transitional figures, would be expected to shed Ceauşescu's legacy and, indeed, lead Romania from dictatorship to democracy.

Summing Up

The East European revolutions of 1988–89 may be classified and analyzed according to the following categories and considerations:

Time. If one thinks of the Polish revolution as having begun with the founding of "Solidarity" in August 1980, then it took Poland *nine years* to reduce the communists to a secondary role. If the the Hungarian effort to replace "goulash communism" with pluralism began with Kádár's resignation in May 1988, it took Hungary *two years* to eliminate the communists' monopoly of power. If the East German revolt began with the removal of Erich Honecker from leadership in October 1989, it took East Germany *three months* to move toward a competitive political order. If the Bulgarian revolt against Todor Zhivkov's despotic rule began with his ouster in November 1989, it took *one month* for his successors to promise free elections. If the bloody Romanian uprising began with the clash in Timisoara in December 1989, it took *ten days* to remove the Ceauşescu family (and one month for the new provisional government to call for competitive elections). Finally, if the Czechoslovak pro-democracy movement can be said to have registered its first major achievement with the resignation of Miloš Jakeš in November 1989, it took *four days* for that country to scrap the communists' leading role (and one month for Václav Havel to become president of Czechoslovakia).

Internal causes of the revolutions.   In the events leading up to the momentous changes of 1989, what mattered most in *Poland* were the rapidly deteriorating condition of the economy (shortages of consumer goods and inflation in particular), universal contempt for the communist party, the continuing appeal of the Catholic Church, deep-rooted anti-Sovietism, and Lech Wałęsa. What mattered most in *Hungary* were the early collapse of communist unity and the rise of a sincerely reformist and thus disruptive faction led by Imre Pozsgay, a nationalist revival prompted by concern over the fate of ethnic Hungarians in Romania, persistent anti-Sovietism, inflation, and the growing realization that communism could not be reformed. What mattered in *East Germany* were the Berlin Wall and what it signified, a fierce hatred of the secret police, and a rapidly declining standard of living in the 1980s. What mattered in *Bulgaria* were thirty-five years of one-man rule, widespread knowledge of corruption among the political and economic elites, and strong nationalist sentiments that the Zhivkov regime could not effectively harness. What mattered in *Romania* were Ceauşescu and all that he and his family stood for, including, especially, the Securitate's persistent terror against the population, and a degree of economic deprivation (such as the absence of food and heat) otherwise found only in the poorest Third World countries. And what mattered in *Czechoslovakia* were shame about this once highly advanced country's condition after forty years of communist mismanagement, the official lies about 1968, the party's total and often brutal rejection of diversity, a feeling that Czechoslovakia was and should once again belong to Central Europe, and leaders of the stature of Alexander Dubček and Václav Havel.

The Soviet role. Through his telephone call to Rakowski in August 1989, Gorbachev played a direct and critical role in convincing the *Polish* party to step aside. As early as May 1988, Gorbachev encouraged the removal of Kádár from the leadership of the *Hungarian* party and thus unwittingly contributed to the process of that party's subsequent dispersal. By permitting Krenz to countermand Honecker's order to fire on the protesters in October 1989 and by remaining silent and inactive when the Berlin Wall was breached, the Soviet leader effectively withdrew Moscow's support from the *East German* regime, thus assuring its collapse. By inviting Mladenov to the Soviet Union one day before an important *Bulgarian* Central Committee meeting in November 1989, Gorbachev signaled Moscow's strong dissatisfaction with the Zhivkov regime. By his longstanding and barely veiled contempt for *Romania's* Ceauşescu, Gorbachev on more than one occasion conveyed Moscow's position to the Romanian people. By his spokesman's 1987 allusion to the similarity between perestroika and the "Prague Spring," and by a series of unmistakable signals to the *Czechoslovak* regime in August and September 1989, Gorbachev undermined the Czechoslovak communist party's unity and thus its ability to resist change.

The Western role. Prior to 1989, the West in general and the United States in particular gave moral and material support to "Solidarity" for many years. Hungary, because of its early reformist course, was granted most-favored nation (MFN) status by Washington and generous credits by Bonn.

The United States' policy of "differentiation," of favoring those East European countries that embarked on the road to democracy, clarified the American position to pro- and anti-reform governments alike. Yet far more important than what the West *did* was what it *was:* free and prosperous. The sharp contrast between East and West was a powerful message to all East Europeans, perhaps the East Germans in particular. That message reached them by growing contact with West Europeans, by Western radio broadcasts, and even by Western television programs that could be seen in many parts of the region. *Since 1989,* Poland and Hungary have both received considerable Western assistance, the purpose of which has been to aid the transition from economies based on the plan to economies based on the market, and thus to help reduce the threat of political turbulence.

Results so far.   While the old regimes have been crushed everywhere, it seems that the countries of Central Europe (Czechoslovakia, Poland, Hungary, and East Germany) have moved ahead of the two states in the Balkans (Bulgaria and Romania). Politically, the *Polish* coalition government is in noncommunist hands, although at the beginning of the 1990s the country's president as well as its ministers of defense and internal affairs were still communists. Representatives of a number of independent *Hungarian* political parties have entered parliament, and several ministers belong to no party at all. In *East Germany,* eight political parties have joined that country's reform-communist government, with the social democrats apparently setting the agenda. Forthcoming elections in *Bulgaria* and *Romania* are expected to produce coalition governments in which communist influence will undoubtedly decline. As to *Czechoslovakia,* its coalition is a shining example of how to build a democratic government based on principle and consensus. Economically, only *Poland* and to a lesser extent *Hungary* have taken significant steps toward eliminating the legacy of the command economies of the past and embracing the free-market economies of the future. Elsewhere, similar measures are to be adopted later in the 1990s.

The question that remains to be raised again (see also the beginning of this chapter) is why the revolutions all occurred in 1988–89. Why not earlier? After all, the Polish economy was already in desperate straits many years ago. Division in the ranks of Hungarian communists has long been the norm rather than the exception. The people of Czechoslovakia have known for decades that they were falling behind Western Europe. East Germans have never enjoyed living in a cage behind the Berlin Wall. Romanians have always despised Ceauşescu and communism, and it did not take the Bulgarians thirty-five years to discover that Zhivkov, who had once promised to make their country "the Japan of the Balkans," was a fraud.

Although the answer to the question "Why now?" is unsurprising and, indeed, self-evident, it is important enough to bear repetition: Overwhelmed by an extraordinary domestic crisis in 1988–89, the Soviet Union lost its ability to sustain its imperial domain in Eastern Europe. Resorting to the use of force under the circumstances would have called into question the very survival of the Soviet Union. On the other hand, the indication that it would not use force on behalf of its allies effectively undermined the region's communist regimes, not only members of the "gang of four" but the reformist contingent as well, thus revealing that all East European communist regimes lacked legitimate authority.

Moscow's inability to use force unwittingly sparked the fire next door. "Unwittingly" because the Soviet Union could not have wished to reduce its role in Eastern Europe to that of an interested bystander; Gorbachev's colleagues did not knowingly select him to preside over the dissolution of the Soviet empire. Indeed, the Soviet goal was to replace orthodoxy with reform and to replace its sphere of domination based on the imposition and exercise of force with a sphere

of influence based mainly on voluntary concessions and mutual interests. To have failed so completely to achieve this
goal suggests that the goal itself was unrealistic, the result of
a historic miscalculation in Moscow about East European
conditions and aspirations.

Yet neither the Soviet domestic crisis nor Soviet foreign
policies born of that crisis were the original causes of the East
European revolutions. The region had always smoldered with
rage beneath the surface; that it would ignite one day was
never in doubt.

VII

THE BRAVE NEW WORLD
OF EASTERN EUROPE

THE SOVIET BLOC has passed into history. Although democracy
has yet to be learned, lived, and thus won, East European independence, after four harsh decades of alien rule, is within
reach. From now on, the region's future will be decided in
Warsaw and Prague and Bucharest rather than in Moscow.
Having neither recent experience nor truly comparable models elsewhere to guide them, East Europeans must now learn
for themselves the skills and values needed for self-govern-
ance: how to cope with diversity, how to assume personal
responsibility, how to conduct themselves democratically.

The widely shared East European goal of achieving "capitalism with a human face" will require drastic austerity measures and therefore tremendous sacrifice. Destructive political quarrels will inevitably follow, because economic
hardship and the resulting social tension will be made more
acute by the legacy of intolerance. It will be a long time before a democratic mentality takes hold.

Yet, because they are independent, the East Europeans appear to have a reasonably good chance to solve many of their
problems in the 1990s.

The Soviet Factor

The major cause for cautious optimism is that communist
Eastern Europe as a geopolitical and ideological entity has
ceased to exist. The Warsaw Pact and CMEA may remain as

forums for the exchange of views, but as time passes, there will be even less business to discuss and fewer decisions to make than in the past. On the military agenda, there will be the question of what tasks to assign to the Warsaw Pact when Moscow no longer considers either NATO or an uprising in Eastern Europe a potential challenge to Soviet security. The economic agenda will include the issue of what tasks to assign to CMEA at a time when its members, including the Soviet Union itself, are in the process of expanding both their multilateral and bilateral ties with the West rather than with one another. On the political and especially on the ideological agenda, the issues have all been decided.

Thus, as Eastern Europe enters the constructive stage of its revolution—as it begins to build new institutions of economic and political pluralism that will resemble those created in Western Europe after World War II—the Soviet Union will find itself with nothing of significance to contribute to the region's emerging order. Its political system has been in disarray. Its economy has become bankrupt. Its ideology, discredited at home, has lost its appeal even in the Third World. It has retained the means to remain a military power, but military power by itself will not readily translate into political influence. Most East Europeans seem to have concluded that they need not fear Moscow's wrath.

Thus, with little leverage left, the Soviet Union may have missed the opportunity to do what it could and should have done earlier and what most East Europeans would have gladly accepted in the past: to transform its sphere of domination into a sphere of influence.

In an acceptable sphere of influence, both sides must be ready to make concessions. Specifically, the strong state settles for being influential rather than dominant, because the price for hegemony, which normally entails the use of force, is far too high. The weak state, in turn, accepts to be influenced rather than insisting on full sovereignty because the price for full independence, which normally requires armed resistance, is too high.

Thus, steering carefully between that which is desirable (full sovereignty) and that which is unacceptable (domination), the weak state settles for partial satisfaction. It thus accommodates itself to being in a sphere of influence for fear that the strong state may one day decide to use force to become dominant. In the end, it is that fear of being dominated —the fear of losing all of its independence—that propels the weak state to acquiesce in a subordinate status.

Although Finns strongly resent the word and deny that they have such a relationship with the Soviet Union, the term "Finlandization" is often used to characterize Moscow's implicit understanding with its small Northern neighbor.[1] In practice, "Finlandization" has come to mean a free Finnish political order and an economy based on private ownership, while Finnish foreign policy—irrespective of which political parties currently make up the coalition government—is guided by a firm national commitment to harmonious relations with the Soviet Union. On the whole, despite a few irritating incidents over the years, the formula has worked. Finland has retained some leeway in foreign affairs, while its domestic order has remained free from Soviet interference.

Moscow has been satisfied with the situation as well. During his visit to Helsinki in October 1989, Gorbachev praised the Soviet-Finnish relationship and implied that it might become a model for Soviet ties with Eastern Europe. *The New York Times* interpreted his comments to mean that "'Finlandization' [for Eastern Europe] is OK."[2] Yet, despite Gorbachev's

---

1. Cf. J. P. Vloyantes, *Silk Glove Hegemony: Finnish-Soviet Relations 1944–1974. A Case Study of the Theory of the Soft Sphere of Influence* (Kent: Kent University Press, 1975). For a view that denies that Finland belongs to a "soft sphere" of Soviet influence, see Roy Allison, *Finland's Relations with the Soviet Union* (New York: St. Martin's Press, 1985).

2. November 1, 1989.

apparent endorsement, the "Finlandization" of Eastern Europe was by then an idea whose time had passed. In Eastern Europe, the choice was no longer seen as one between being in the Soviet sphere of domination or in a Soviet sphere of influence, but between domination and independence. With Soviet troops withdrawing from the region—and with Moscow anxiously attending to disorder at home and so deeply preoccupied with the very survival of the Soviet Union itself—East Europeans saw no reason to exchange subservience for subordination. With the lessening of the old, pervasive fear of Soviet intervention, "Finlandization," once seen as a respectable formula for a relationship based on mutual concessions, has come to be regarded in Eastern Europe as a needless compromise.

Thus, having finally ended forty years of Soviet rule in 1988–89, few East Europeans consider "Finlandization" an appealing alternative. Gorbachev's personal popularity notwithstanding, they want nothing to do with either the Soviet Union or with those whom they regard as the local beneficiaries of forty years of Soviet domination. Simply put, East Europeans have no use for communism, socialism, "reforms," or indeed for the Soviet Union.[3]

When their passions subside, East Europeans will come to realize that their dependence on the Soviet Union must continue for years, if only for one reason: the region's need for energy. Until Eastern Europe can afford to buy energy with hard currency, there will be no alternative to reliance on Soviet supplies. Hard currency, in turn, will not be available until the generally poor quality of East European goods improves sufficiently to make them competitive in Western markets.

Yet even when the East Europeans succeed in improving

---

3. The small turnout at the Polish election and the Hungarian popular referendum of 1989 suggests a mood of resignation about politics in general and political parties in particular—as if the anticommunist parties were cut from the same cloth as their communist predecessors.

the quality of their products, another problem will confront them. The Soviet Union, which is by far the largest market for East European manufactures, does not demand high-quality products. Indeed, in most cases the Soviet Union prefers not to purchase high-quality products because it cannot put them to effective use. Under the circumstances, the East Europeans will find it difficult to assemble small quantities of high-quality goods for Western consumption while producing large quantities of similar goods of lesser quality for the vast Soviet market. Given limited resources, relatively small productive capacities, and the initially prohibitive cost that the development of high-quality products will entail, the East European economies cannot efficiently serve these two very different markets.

If the East Europeans were to base their economic strategy on trade with the West, they would eventually achieve independence from Soviet energy. They would also pay a high price for their efforts. During the long process of transition, they would risk losing the Soviet market for their traditional products while seeking, perhaps in vain, Western markets for their new ones. For this reason, most East Europeans will probably decide to continue trading their food and manufactures for Soviet energy.

Still, such continuity in the Soviet–East European economic relationship will begin and end with bilateral trade. There will be no Soviet-dominated coordination of one-, two-, or five-year plans among CMEA members because there will no longer be either a CMEA or any all-encompassing planned economies in the region.

With energy as its sole (albeit compelling) source of leverage, Soviet policy in Eastern Europe is not likely to be reversed. Soviet domestic conditions, in particular, militate against the reemergence of an assertive Soviet foreign policy in the near future. With Stalinism condemned and Leninism rebuked, the Soviet Union will seek to incorporate West European social democracy into its new ideology and attempt to recreate the unity of the socialist movement of the pre-Leninist period. In the political realm, Moscow may soon permit institutionalized (if limited) pluralism and allow the transformation of the Union of Soviet Socialist Republics into something closer to an Association of Semi-Independent Soviet Republics. Economic need would thus leave Moscow with a modicum of influence over Lithuania, Armenia, and the other republics that have so forcefully asserted their national identities.

With or without Gorbachev, it is reasonable to expect major setbacks in the Soviet Union during the 1990s. Although it is unclear where or when, it is certain that Moscow will eventually draw the line on nationalist pressures in order to save the integrity of the Soviet state. Yet even though massive force could be used to restore domestic law and order, the application of sanctions against an East European country has become unlikely. After all, Moscow consistently refrained from using economic sanctions against recalcitrant East European regimes even under Gorbachev's predecessors. (Stalin learned during the Yugoslav crisis of 1948–49 that the harsh sanctions he applied only intensified Yugoslav resistance and were thus counterproductive.)

There are therefore many in the West as well as in Eastern Europe who believe that the Soviet Union has become a "pitiful giant," pitiful even in its own backyard. The available evidence suggests that—as long as Moscow continues to experience such acute difficulties at home—this view may be correct. Confused about its values, overwhelmed by extraordinary pressures from within, and exhausted economically, the Soviet Union appears to have lost its will to pursue its old ambitions and defend its traditional interests. After withdrawing from Afghanistan, the Soviets have retreated both militarily and politically from Eastern and Central Europe as well. At the time this chapter was being written, Moscow indicated its willingness to relinquish its hold over East Germany, its most precious postwar geopolitical acquisition. Indeed, because the Soviet Union is now unwilling to use force abroad on behalf of its interests, it is likely that the Soviet Union will even accede to the reunification of Germany, which will signal the effective absorption of East Germany into West Germany.

As its domestic crisis abates, perhaps in the next century, the Soviet Union may well attempt to regain its military grandeur and corresponding global role in world affairs. However, its condition at the start of the 1990s argues against an early recovery.

Thus, the answer to the question posed in the Preface— "Can there be an Eastern Europe that in its relations to the Soviet Union is cordial but not subservient, independent but not inhospitable, and thus influenced but not dominated by its large and powerful neighbor?"—is that although the Soviet Union will be unable to dominate or even significantly influence the course on which Eastern Europe has embarked, the East Europeans will treat Moscow cordially. They will do so both before the Soviets leave the region completely— mainly to ensure that they actually do leave—and also after they are gone—to ensure that they will not return.

East European Prospects

The chances for the successful completion of the second phase of the East European revolution vary from country to country. To the extent that generalizations apply, however, the transition from independent existence to political democracy and a free enterprise system will depend mainly on each country's management of economic change and the strength of the emerging coalition governments.

In the economic realm, the most difficult dilemma will be how to combine economic productivity and efficiency with social sensitivity and responsibility. Understandably, most East Europeans want the best of both worlds: the economic productivity associated with capitalism and the social benefits associated with socialism. Unfortunately, the models of Sweden or Austria cannot be followed in Eastern Europe: the region's six countries are too poor to subsidize housing, medical care, long maternity leaves, or even public transportation. Extended social benefits will have to result from (and thus cannot precede) economic recovery. Above all, present subsidies to inefficient enterprises— about one-third of the budget of an average East European government—will have to be reduced and eventually eliminated.

The conflict of values and priorities will be unavoidable. On the one hand, the introduction of hard-headed, market-oriented economic policies—such as the reform of prices and the monetary system and a shift from public to private ownership—are both essential and long overdue. On the other hand, social responsibility, coupled with the prevailing sense of egalitarianism, argues for a slow transition to free enterprise in order to minimize the harmful side-effects of a new economic order. If in fact the economic changes are resolutely pursued, the bankruptcies of inefficient enterprises will increase and unemployment will rise. Moreover, if the free enterprise system moves toward greater wage differentiation in order to reward talent and hard work, the income of the average and less gifted workers will fall below the poverty line. If economic policies turn into half-measures, however, the East European economies will do no better than in the past when some, such as Hungary and Poland, unsuccessfully tried to "reform" their economic mechanism without changing the system.

Economic hardships and dislocations, which appear to be inevitable, will have the most serious social and political consequences. Support for political democracy may decline in an economic environment that is perceived to favor the few at the expense of the many. If dissatisfaction gives rise to manifestations of social turbulence such as prolonged general strikes, the struggle for economic recovery and social justice will suffer—and a stable, democratic political order may not long survive.

How the region's emerging coalition governments will handle these problems will mark the difference between order and anarchy, economic advance and economic decay, progress toward democracy and regression away from it. If these governments turn out to be weak coalitions made up of weak parties led by weak leaders, they could even be swept away by a combination of popular rage and populist demagoguery. In that case, they could be replaced by unstable and equally weak coalitions—or by nationalist, populist, or authoritarian regimes.

As Eastern Europe enters the final decade of the twentieth century, it seems likely that in a majority (but not in all) of the region's six countries democratic governments will nevertheless acquire sufficient legitimacy to govern. While the initial coalitions, composed of honest but inexperienced parties and politicians, may not last long, they may be strong enough and resilient enough to undertake the first measures necessary to smooth the way for a relatively peaceful transition to economic and political pluralism.

East Germany, for example, because of its association with West Germany, is a particularly promising candidate for successful transition, as is Czechoslovakia, which has a fine democratic tradition, an economy that is not beyond repair, and Václav Havel—a leader of immense popularity and stature. Hungary, despite its overwhelming foreign debt and contentious politics, has made considerable progress toward dismantling the communist system. The country's entrepreneurial spirit and its highly educated labor force bode well for the future.

It is far more difficult to assess Poland's chances for success. Unable to pay the interest on its debts, the country is bankrupt. Inflation is still unchecked. Its activist industrial working class, which brought the "Solidarity"-led government to power, could also be that government's—and Poland's—undoing. On the positive side of its ledger, Poland has Lech Wałęsa at home and the Pope abroad. It also has an energetic and competent government, which in December 1989 introduced the region's most promising economic program.[4]

While there is no cause for euphoria, then, there is none for excessive alarm. The region's discredited communist parties and demoralized security forces are unlikely to reemerge as a major force on the East European political scene. Despite extensive speculation in the Western press, there are no indications of nationalist rivalries seriously disturbing the region's peace; on the contrary, there are good prospects for the creation of a Central European or a Danubian confederation. Nor have any of the new East European governments prematurely confronted the Soviet Union about withdrawing from the Warsaw Pact or CMEA, although, over time, several will undoubtedly leave both organizations. Popular sentiment favoring neutrality cannot be long denied.

Indeed, the absence of such divisive or violent developments (or even the *prospect* of such developments) offers the best hope and suggests grounds for a cautiously optimistic outlook. Economic, social, and political conflicts notwithstanding, most East European countries may well emulate the examples of Portugal and Spain, which emerged from decades of dictatorial rule in the 1970s to become constructive and stable members of the European community of free and independent nations.

---

4. These forecasts were made in December 1989, in the midst of a revolutionary process. It is too soon to estimate Bulgaria's and Romania's chances for a successful transition from dictatorship to democracy.

Western Concerns

The East European revolution has caught the West by surprise. In particular, earlier West German statements predicting the inevitability of change in Eastern Europe have turned out not to reflect official expectations; they were apparently meant to keep hope alive. When change did occur—when instability turned into revolution, when it became evident that Moscow would not intervene and that communist rule would thus end—there was both incredulity and concern.

Looking ahead, the West will face three major challenges.

The first area of concern is the extent of Western economic assistance to Eastern Europe. Financial constraints will be the first obstacle. The problem is not that Washington, for example, is not sympathetic to East European needs; it is and it will be. The problem is how to determine the criteria for the allocation of limited resources. So-called humanitarian aid aside, is Poland more important to the United States than the Philippines?

Assuming that Poland will continue to receive Western assistance, there will still be heated political debate as to whether assistance should include what that country needs most: debt relief. For if the West decides to give preferential treatment to Poland, will indebted nations in Latin America and elsewhere not ask for and expect similar concessions? Will Poland itself not conclude that its future debts will be forgiven as well? The choice for the West is between financial prudence and political opportunity.

Nevertheless, the West will play an important role in attempting to make permanent the changes that have occurred in Eastern Europe, because these changes serve Western interests and because they conform to Western ideals. Western Europe more than the United States—and West Germany more than any other West European state—can be expected to support particularly those countries that will initiate radical economic and political measures. East European countries with a free-enterprise system will easily persuade private Western firms to invest and do business there, especially if the resulting profit is available in hard currency. East European countries that practice political democracy will persuade Western governments to encourage such business activity and also to remove existing barriers from the free flow of goods, including products that reflect advanced, although probably not the most advanced, technology.

The second Western concern involves the Soviet Union. The problem is that the West does not and will not have sufficient influence to make a significant contribution to the Soviet Union's democratic evolution. For the sake of Western security interests as well as Western ideals, the West has a stake both in what Gorbachev stands for and, indeed, in the rise of an increasingly democratic Soviet political order. Given the limits of outside influence on the Soviet domestic scene, however, the West can do no more than applaud Gorbachev's efforts, conclude arms control agreements that serve the interests of both sides, and ease trade restrictions.

Whether these otherwise important steps will make a difference for Soviet domestic developments is highly doubtful. Almost irrespective of what the West does, it appears that the Soviet Union will encounter greater convulsions in the early 1990s than those experienced by Eastern Europe at the end of the 1980s. For the West, a key issue is determining how to prepare for the international consequences of Gorbachev's probable failure to implement his ambitious objectives.

A third Western concern is the future of European security. That it is a concern is the paradoxical result of the end of the cold war: as the dangers associated with the cold war disappear, the sense of clarity it offered will disappear as well. Being somewhat removed from the scene, Americans, in particular, will no longer be able to distinguish between friends and adversaries, NATO and the Warsaw Pact, democrats and communists. The end of the cold war is a concern, then, because in the 1990s there will be no alternative to exchanging the simplicity of a divided Europe for the complexity of a united Europe. Without the Iron Curtain and the Berlin Wall, novel security arrangements will have to be created, taking into account both the new geopolitical reality and the possibility that a convulsive Soviet Union will turn unpredictable.

While American influence over Soviet domestic developments will be marginal, and while its role in Eastern Europe will be secondary to that of Western Europe, the United States will have to *lead* the West in the search for a dependable and lasting security formula for Europe. As the only superpower in the world of the 1990s, the United States can no more abdicate its responsibility for Europe than it can relinquish its own security interests.

What, in the end, will replace NATO and the Warsaw Pact cannot be predicted. Yet it is clear that, despite Soviet retreat, the new European security formula for the 1990s and for the next century will have to be more than just NATO in a new guise. It will have to provide stability for a new Europe, West and East. To devise such a formula and thus to ease Eastern Europe's reentry into the European community of nations is a task worthy of the legacy of the East European revolutions.

Appendix

A SOVIET VIEW OF EASTERN EUROPE

*By the Staff of the Institute of Economics
of the World Socialist System (Moscow)*

[The following paper was presented at the first conference on Eastern Europe at which American and Soviet scholars discussed the region's past, present, and future problems. Held in Alexandria, Virginia, on July 6–8, 1988, the conference had as its title and subject "The Place and Role of Eastern Europe in the Relaxation of Tensions between the USA and the USSR." The Soviet delegation was led by Academician Oleg T. Bogomolov, Director of the Institute of Economics of the World Socialist System. The American delegation was led by the present author.

Drafted primarily by Vyacheslav I. Dashichev, a prominent Soviet expert on Eastern Europe and East-West relations at the Institute of Economics of the World Socialist System, the Soviet paper was nonetheless a collective work by the staff of the institute (known as the "Bogomolov Institute"). It was subsequently published in the journal *Problems of Communism* 37, Nos. 3–4 (May–August 1988).

The paper is included here for two reasons.

First, it offers an original Soviet overview of East European developments. Although it was written for an American audience and, as of this writing, has not been published in the Soviet Union, it represents the most comprehensive semi-official Soviet perspective on Eastern Europe.

Second, and more specifically, the paper is of great potential pedagogical value for college or university courses dealing with Soviet foreign policy or Eastern Europe. At Georgetown University, for example, it served as the background for an assignment in which students were asked to write an essay in response to the following: "Suppose you are an adviser to an East European party leader. Suppose further that he has asked you to read and study this Soviet view of Eastern Europe. How would you summarize the Soviet position? What are the implications for this particular East European party (or country)? Finally, given the Soviet view, what recommendations would you offer to your boss about the policies he should adopt and follow?" More advanced students were asked to advise two East European leaders—one favoring reform (Poland or Hungary) and one resisting reform (Romania, East Germany, Czechoslovakia, or Bulgaria)—and to state the reasons for different advice submitted to the two leaders.

—C. G.]

The countries of Eastern Europe constitute an international and political community of states marked by contradictions. Not only are they heterogeneous ethnically and linguistically, and in their levels of cultural, economic, and political development, but they lie within a region that has historically been in the magnetic fields of different major powers. This circumstance has imparted particular features to the policies of the East European countries. Over the centuries, they maneuvered between different power centers and blocs and exerted tremendous influence on the destiny of Europe.

After World War II, the East European countries were united by the path of socialist development. But even socialism was incapable of eliminating the region's historical and new interstate contradictions, especially those regarding territorial and national questions. Thus, the administrative-state model of socialism, established in the majority of East European countries during the 1950's under the influence of the Soviet Union, has not withstood the test of time, thereby showing its socio-political and economic inefficiency. Moreover, the Soviet model erected serious barriers to direct communication among the nations of these states, impeding the intertwining of their political, economic, scientific, and cultural interests. The process of reform and renewal of socialism in East European countries was further hindered for a long time by the stagnation of the Soviet system and the related conceptual inertia and dogmatism of Soviet policy in the 1960's and 1970's. As a result, internal socio-political and economic contradictions accumulated in many countries of Eastern Europe and were not resolved in time. This only aggravated previous interstate controversies and domestic problems.

Today, the socialist countries of Eastern Europe are at a turning point in their development—a turning point characterized by societal understanding of the compelling necessity to change radically the political and economic structures, and to undertake profound reforms in all spheres of public life.

The scope of work to be done is enormous indeed. It ranges from the recovery of an economy distorted by the administrative-command methods of the past, to the democratization of a society emerging with difficulty from the suppression of the Stalinist period, to the improvement of cooperation among socialist countries—a cooperation based on true partnership and mutual respect. Not only present-day problems, but those inherited from the past, must be solved.

The profound socio-political and economic reforms that have been started in a number of East European countries are intended to create radically new conditions for economic, social, and scientific-technological progress, and for the free development of the individual. The aim is to create in these countries a qualitatively new model of socialism that would be truly humane in nature. This would lead to drastic changes in the role of these countries in the all-European process and in the system of East-West relations that, in turn, would substantially enhance their importance and influence on international politics.

The USSR and the East European Socialist Countries

The establishment and development of relations between the Soviet Union and its neighbors in Eastern Europe have been complicated and contradictory. The conditions for good-neighborly relations were, frankly speaking, very unfavorable. As is well known, after World War I, the sponsors of the Versailles Treaty system tried to erect a "cordon sanitaire" around the young Soviet Russian state, and the system's bulwark in Eastern Europe was the Little Entente. The anti-Soviet orientation of the ruling circles of the countries of Eastern Europe in the interwar period caused considerable damage to the security of the Soviet Union. Serious collisions and conflicts also took place among the East European countries over national, territorial, and other issues.

A new situation arose in Europe after World War II as a result of the defeat of the Axis powers and the downfall of the pro-fascist regimes in Eastern Europe, creating favorable conditions for a radical reorganization of relations between the Soviet Union and the East European states on the basis of neighborly and mutually beneficial cooperation. The course of events in Europe had been such that conservative bourgeois circles and the capitalist order were seriously discredited. At the same time, there was the unprecedented rise of a mass movement for social renewal, which had its origins in the context of wartime resistance. These two developments placed revolutionary transformations of the socio-economic system of the East European countries on the agenda. Clearly, the sympathy and support of the Soviet Union were with the mass movement; this led at first to the formation of the people's democracy regime, and then to the victory of the socialist system in the countries of Eastern Europe.

Once socialism moved beyond the borders of one country, the issue of the theoretical and practical foundations on which international relations among socialist countries were to rest became a pressing one. The Soviet Union and the other socialist countries faced a number of new and complicated problems which the international workers' movement and Marxist-Leninist theory had not previously encountered. The primary issue was how to align the specific national features and the ensuing political and economic interests of independent sovereign states with the international interests of the community of socialist states as a whole—in other words, how to synchronize the specific interests of individual socialist countries that differed from one another in territorial size; in endowment with natural resources; in national habits, traditions, and historical experience; in the level of development of productive forces, as well as in production relations, social structures, forms of political organization, extent of democratic experience, etc.

In dealing with these problems, the Soviet Union and the other socialist countries embarked on an uncharted path in a difficult "cold war" climate marked by military, economic, and propaganda pressures from the West. It is quite understandable that everything did not turn out well immediately. There were illusions that had to be overcome, and mistakes, sometimes grave ones, were made which had serious consequences. For example, great damage was caused by the naive concepts prevailing in the 1950's and 1960's about the noncontradictory and conflictless character both of the socio-political and economic development of socialist states and of relations among them. The theory of "non-conflict" made it impossible to understand the nature and sources of contradictions and crises in the socialist community, and to elaborate mechanisms and procedures for their timely detection, prevention, and elimination. This, in turn, led to incorrect decisions that brought on deformations in the mutual relations of socialist states.

Still greater difficulties and problems arose in applying the principles of equal partnership among socialist states. For objective reasons, the Soviet Union, as the first socialist state in the world, was in a special position relative to other socialist countries. When the Third International was in existence, solidarity with the Soviet

Union and acceptance of its leading role in the world communist movement was regarded by communist parties as natural. But even at that time, this view hindered the realization of the principle of independence on the part of working-class parties and prevented the understanding of their role as a national force in their own countries. Moreover, it was inadmissible to extend the postulate of the primary role of the Communist Party of the Soviet Union to relations among socialist states. The urge of the Stalin leadership to do so resulted in a conflict between the Soviet Union and Yugoslavia (as well as other socialist states) and affected the entire system of links among socialist countries and communist parties. Closely related to this erroneous policy was the practice of thoughtlessly copying and mechanically transferring the Soviet experience to the different social and historic situations of the East European countries.

The period of the 1940's and 1950's, when relations between the Soviet Union and the socialist countries of Eastern Europe were being established, was unfortunately marked by many of the above-mentioned mistakes and distortions of the principles of socialism, a process aggravated by the voluntaristic practices and violations of law by Stalin. After his death, a process of eliminating deformations and purging the mutual relations of the socialist countries of unhealthy phenomena commenced. The need to observe strictly the principles of full equality, good will, respect for national sovereignty, and consideration for specific national features was acknowledged. The recognition that different roads of socialist development were rightful was also of great significance.

However, the process of "rejecting evil" initiated after the 20th CPSU Congress was of a contradictory nature. It was influenced by a desire to overcome past inertia, by rigid stereotypes, by a dogmatic incomprehension of change and the new requirements for social development. Moreover, this process was interrupted after 1964, when the leadership of Leonid Brezhnev and Mikhail Suslov came to power and the era of stagnant neo-Stalinism began. Even reversion to the past, to Stalinist practices, became noticeable. Major deformations of socialism in East European countries, major mistakes in their internal policies, together with the hegemonic aspirations of the Soviet leadership of that period, were among the main reasons for the deep political crises in Hungary in 1956, in Czechoslovakia in 1968, and in Poland in 1956, 1970, and 1980. These crises acquired an international dimension and seriously tested military and political stability in Europe. The negative consequences of Stalinist distortions in the domestic policies of the socialist countries and in the system of relations among them are being felt even today.

The *perestroyka* initiated in the Soviet Union when the Gorbachev leadership came to power marked not only a drastic turn in Soviet internal policy away from the Stalinist model of state-bureaucratic socialism in the direction of a qualitatively new model of democratic socialism; it also introduced profound changes in the system of political and economic relations among the socialist countries belonging to the Warsaw Treaty Organization and the Council for Economic Mutual Assistance (CEMA). New thinking, free of outlived stereotypes and dogma, underlies the policy of the Soviet Union with respect to the countries of Eastern Europe. The policy is directed toward a harmonious development of true good-neighborliness with these countries; toward a relationship free from dictate, pressure, and interference in each other's internal affairs; and toward strict observance of the principles of equal partnership, independence, and attentive respect for the national interests and the national forms of socialist development of each country. The countries of Eastern Europe now have broad opportunities to realize unhindered their national interests both within the framework of the socialist community and in relations with the West.

Political Perestroyka *of the Socialist System and its Effect on East-West Relations*

In many countries of Eastern Europe, *perestroyka* of the system of political power has begun. The model for the existing system was created in the Soviet Union during the 1930's and 1940's. This model was profoundly influenced by Stalin's perverted concepts of the character of political mechanisms in socialism, as well as by the insufficient political maturity on the part of Soviet society and a lack of democratic traditions and political culture. The administrative-command system of power started in the USSR was replicated in other socialist countries. It was characterized by hyper-centralism, an absolute monopoly on decision-making, monolithic thinking, a disdain for the masses (who were seen as "small crews" and as objects of management), and isolation from the outside world. Political institutions aimed at securing political stability primarily through suppression and the leveling of diversity. This system, which demanded servile obedience, undermined the foundations of societal dynamism and viability.

The pyramidal, monocentric model of power could not help but affect the behavior of socialist states in the sphere of international relations. A similar hierarchic structure, based on subordination of everybody to a "single center," long prevailed in relations among the socialist countries. Development in these countries was undertaken according to the same model; that is, national specificity was ignored. In relations with the West, the administrative-command system of power was oriented first of all toward its own preservation, and toward counteraction and self-isolation. The existence of interests of civilization common to the two systems and requiring their cooperation and interaction was rejected. Dialogue as a form and means of international coexistence was neglected. The principle of *kto kogo* ("who bests whom") was mechanically applied to the external sphere.

The image of the capitalist "enemy" impressed itself on the public psyche. To some extent, this image was used as a means to effect the internal consolidation and mobilization of the masses in individual socialist countries. However, its utilization as the motive force for vital actions undermined the creative stimuli, and the economic and democratic regulators, of socialism. The defensive reaction of the political system long delayed the formation of a civil society in socialist countries, the growth of the political maturity of the masses, and their creative progress. It should be noted, however, that this behavior was due largely to external reasons, to the constant pressure exerted by the West, a genuine external menace to socialism. The perpetuation of the administrative system of socialism was thus, in part, a consequence of the policies of some Western circles and their blatant anticommunism.

The essence of the new model of power can be defined as the delegation of considerable responsibility to the local level, to labor and territorial collectives; the expansion of pluralism in public life; and the democratization of all institutions, including the vanguard party. The aim is to create more effective guarantees against the power monopoly of the layer of managers and professional politicians—against the bureaucratic apparatus.

The process of *perestroyka* is already shaping a new multifaceted political reality, one full of contradictions and conflicts, of collisions of interests of individuals and social groups. The renewal is just beginning, and there is a long road ahead before a new political system will be formed. The resistance of old, but still unbroken mechanisms is quite strong, and the force of inertia is quite great both "at the top" and "at the bottom." But the process of *perestroyka* has been started, and there are signs that it is becoming irreversible, and that a return to Stalinist methods is becoming impossible.

The formation of a qualitatively new political system of socialism is occurring to some extent under the influence of international realities, of the general progress of civilization and technology. In the socialist countries, there is enhanced understanding that it is necessary to promote East-West cooperation to ensure the survival of humanity, and that such cooperation requires mutual confidence between the two systems. This, in turn, calls for a new quality in foreign policy, for a reconsideration of its priorities. This reappraisal is directly linked to the *perestroyka* of the entire system of power. The shift to the new model is intended to bring about not only greater efficiency and effectiveness in political decision-making; it is intended also to create conditions for the democratization of the foreign policy process, its control by society, so as to prevent a repetition of the past, namely, the taking of voluntaristic and, in many cases, quite risky steps in international relations. Legislative and institutional guarantees of public control over foreign policy must be elaborated.

The results of political reform ought to include a more comprehensive evaluation by the socialist countries of the diversity of interests existing in the international arena, of different "balances of forces," and a renunciation of attempts at their equalization so as to preclude the development of hegemonistic intentions on the part of anyone. This stimulates greater flexibility, openness, and tolerance, which also result directly from the new atmosphere in individual countries. A country that rids itself of the command methods of management is unlikely to impose its position on others. This, however, does not mean renouncing one's own ideal values.

In the socialist countries, the formation of a new political thinking is now under way—in particular, the view of the West as a hostile force is being revised. This is reflected in a gradual retreat from the stress on autarky, on the defensive function in exercising power inside the country. Opportunities for exchange of ideas and experience are opening up, and justification of unpredictable actions in both domestic and foreign affairs is being eliminated. If society becomes more transparent, more democratic, if power is controllable, then a basis will be formed for greater mutual understanding in the international sphere as well.

It should be noted, however, that the processes of renovation occurring in the Soviet Union and other socialist countries need suitable international conditions. Pressure, blackmail, derailment of agreements by the Western side can work in favor of the adversaries of *perestroyka*, may lead to restoration of the former order. This would also mean the aggravation of international tensions. For this reason, the successful renovation of socialism is one of the guarantees for the establishment of new international relations, and above all, of a qualitatively new East-West relationship.

Perestroyka *of the Economic Cooperation Mechanism and East-West Economic Relations*

All the shortcomings and difficulties in the development of cooperation among the East European countries within the CEMA framework, as well as in economic relations with the West, stem from the old mechanism of managing the national economy. With slight variations, the mechanism was copied from the Soviet model created in the 1930's and 1940's. Its specific features were rigid centralism; administrative methods of management; arbitrary methods of price formation; the ignoring of the role of the market, of the intimate link between production and consumption, and of economic methods of management; and a primitive and simplified understanding of the character and functions of ownership under socialism.

These features determined the nature of integrational cooperation among CEMA countries. Cooperation was based on macroeconomic decisions made by higher power echelons and, accordingly, on the basis of administrative methods of regulating the integrational processes and economic interaction. This doomed to inertia, passivity, and lack of entrepreneurship the micro-economic units of the economies of socialist countries, that is, the overwhelming majority of working people directly engaged in industry, agriculture, science, and services. This led to an abnormal situation, whereby there existed no direct contacts and business relations between cooperating collectives of enterprises and organizations of the CEMA countries. As a result, there was no real interest in the progress of economic cooperation and in deriving benefits from it. Integration in CEMA took an administrative-bureaucratic route. Instead of working for a true economic partnership leading to the extensive interweaving of genuine economic interests and the creation of cooperative links among basic units of the national economy and the entire social organism of socialist countries, spurious and pretentious measures and projects were substituted by the higher power echelons. The process of integration was reduced to one of bureaucratic organization of economic interaction among the state systems of self-contained individual countries which were separated from one another by virtually insurmountable administrative, financial, economic, legal, and other barriers. With time, these barriers grew even higher. The swollen bureaucratic apparatus could not keep up with, let alone regulate, the growing and increasingly complicated economic ties between individual enterprises, associations, and organizations of the CEMA countries. This led to reduced effectiveness in economic, scientific, and technological cooperation, to growing dissatisfaction with existing economic relations, and to the collapse of CEMA's prestige. In terms of the scale and depth of integration processes and the intensity of the interweaving of economic, scientific, and technological interests and relations, the CEMA countries turned out to be far behind the countries of the European Economic Community.

The main imperative at the present stage of mutual economic cooperation among CEMA countries is to shift from interstate barter to direct commercial links between enterprises as economic entities.

In fact, the process of transforming the directive-distributive model of labor division within the CEMA framework into a qualitatively new model of a market type, including the indispensable "rehabilitation" of price and currency tools, has begun. In this process, the Council for Economic Mutual Assistance should turn into a body maximizing favorable conditions for the realization of direct cooperative relations among enterprises, associations, and organizations in the national economies of the socialist countries. It is necessary to create in all CEMA countries favorable legal, administrative, financial, and other conditions and prerequisites for economic, scientific, and technological contacts at the micro-economic level to match the national economic mechanisms. CEMA should also be sure to remove existing or emerging obstacles and barriers to setting up and realizing direct cooperative links. Special emphasis should be placed on the unimpeded movement across borders of all factors of production, including manpower, commodities, capital, and information.

According to the new model of cooperation, the principals in economic interactions would be the producers and consumers of the supplied products; they would enter into contracts not because of a command from "the top," but because of the mutual expectations of economic benefits. The partners would naturally become the real "subjects" of price formation, setting prices according to contractual principles. The contract price itself, being part of an actual deal, would acquire a structure-forming function that is now lacking, i.e., it would contribute in practice to the formation of a progressive structure of mutual exchanges. Since the contract price would be governed by demand-and-supply relations, this would ensure that only those products that meet real public needs and are manufactured at the lowest possible cost would be involved in mutual trade. The process of forming foreign trade prices would no longer be performed according to a predetermined rigid scheme but would allow for considerable freedom of maneuver.

To ensure the viability of the new price-formation mechanism, the CEMA countries have to introduce radical changes in the monetary sphere of cooperation. First of all, it is essential to introduce mutual convertibility (though limited in the initial stages) of the currencies of the countries concerned, at exchange rates reflecting their real purchasing power. In practice, this will mean the use of national currencies in mutual accounting and in setting mutual trade prices. Under such conditions, a truly unified market of the CEMA countries will begin to take shape with mechanisms for ensuring multilateral (not just bilateral, as things now stand) balancing of commodity deliveries. The need for genuine convertibility of the currencies of the CEMA countries, including convertibility into hard currencies, will grow as their internal domestic mechanisms are rearranged to foster the proliferation of market relations.

The step-by-step implementation of the concept of a CEMA common market should not be seen as economic isolation of its members from the rest of the world. On the contrary, the course of forming such a market and, in the long run, a monetary and customs union of the CEMA countries is related to a considerable extent to the need to involve their economies more effectively in world economic relations. A successful implementation of the commodity-money model of economic interaction among the socialist countries will surely give a powerful impetus to the growth of East-West economic relations.

This model will make it possible to overcome the isolation of the economies of the CEMA countries not only from one another but from the West as well. It will make possible more joint East-West economic ventures. The creation of a market setting in which the actual subjects of external economic activity become the enterprises themselves creates favorable conditions for them to carry out various mutually beneficial transactions with foreign medium- and small-size firms, thus providing truly unlimited opportunities for East-West economic cooperation.

Reform of the economic cooperation mechanism by the CEMA countries will hinge directly on the success of the *perestroyka* of the political and economic system in the USSR and other CEMA members.

The United States and Eastern Europe

The policy of the United States toward the socialist countries of Eastern Europe, both conceptually and in practice, is characterized by a certain contradictoriness. To a considerable extent, this stems from the inconsistent general methodological approach the United States takes to these countries. On the one hand, for nearly three decades, American scholars and politicians have been declaring that diversity and differences are inherent in the countries of Eastern Europe and, hence, that the US approach to each of them should be differentiated. On the other hand, there is an impression that in practice matters are quite different, that Washington takes the same approach to all the East European countries. Since Eastern Europe is, in fact, internationally one political region despite the considerable specificity of each East European country, it objectively forms one sphere for implementing a particular line in the foreign political strategy and tactics of the United States. In this context, it may be noted that there does exist a regional—East European—area in US foreign policy whose specific features are determined by common goals and interests in the approach to all the countries of the region, by an overall policy conception, and by the general doctrinal setup. This does not exclude differentiation in US foreign policy, which naturally occurs in relations with the East European countries. Indeed, to a great extent, it explains the differences that exist in the US approach to the Soviet Union and to other countries of the socialist community.

As is known, the core of the most extensively elaborated, tested, and still operational US foreign policy doctrine of "building bridges" to Eastern Europe is a differentiated, long-term policy whose goal is to develop varied relations of differing intensity with individual states in this region so as to gradually and carefully weaken the ties of the socialist community. This would, first of all, enfeeble the position of the Soviet Union by creating a situation in the East European community that would fully preoccupy the Soviet Union with maintaining its coherence and prevent the Soviet Union from competing with the United States in other parts of the world.

It is frequently alleged in American scholarly literature and the press that the United States has but limited possibilities for exerting influence in Eastern Europe. Hence, the conclusion is reached that it would be advisable to encourage European countries allied to the United States through the North Atlantic Treaty Organization to utilize their long-established and broad contacts with the East European states to exercise influence. Such reliance on Western Europe is hardly warranted. Although the interests of the allies on both sides of the Atlantic do coincide to some extent in this region, there are also significant differences between them. These differences are revealed in the general assessments of both sides concerning the importance of relations with socialist countries (out of security considerations and in terms of economic cooperation), and of such problems of particular importance to Europe as the German issue, the "legacy of Yalta," the varied and contradictory ideas about the restoration on the political map of the European continent of some sort of neutral interstate formation called "Central Europe," the further development of the all-European process and of disarmament, and so forth.

There is a desire on the part of the United States to use the fact that Eastern Europe is, on the one hand, an integral part of the socialist community, and on the other, a part of a European system of ties. The desire is to obtain political advantages in relations with the Soviet Union, which reflects the obsolete stereotype of a bipolar evaluation of global politics. This oversimplified understanding of East-West relations does not correspond to today's complicated international realities.

This US approach is also improper in the sense that it assigns to the states of Eastern Europe the function of serving as a means to exert influence on the main rival of the United States—the Soviet Union. It unilaterally seeks to define the national and state interests of the East European countries, and thereby artificially narrows their positions and restricts their sovereign role in global relations, especially in the socialist community and the all-European process. This approach to Eastern Europe is especially dangerous today, since the present stage of the development of these countries is characterized by considerable difficulties in connection with reforms, aggravation of conflict regarding reform, and, in a number of countries, even crisis tendencies.

In today's era of growing interdependence, no region, and especially not Eastern Europe, should be the arena of interstate rivalry of the two systems, of the two great powers—the USA and the USSR. After all, in Eastern Europe—as in all of Europe—their basic interests coincide, regardless of the acuteness of the contradictions existing between America and the Soviet Union. This confluence of interests derives above all from the need to prevent conflictual processes in international affairs, to maintain stability, and to strengthen international security.

Crises in Socialist Countries and East-West Relations

The experience of recent decades clearly shows that crises in the countries of Eastern Europe have never been confined within the borders of the country in which they originated. Rather, they have quickly drawn into their orbit a whole number of actors on the international scene—first of all, the USSR and the other East European allies who wanted to prevent the military-political, ideological, and economic destabilization of the socialist community. Crises in Eastern Europe also affected the Western powers, especially the United States, which has traditionally viewed the dramatic collisions inside the "Soviet bloc" in terms of the potential damage they might do to the bloc's consolidation and of the opportunities they offered for weakening Soviet positions in this region and/or Soviet control over its East European allies, thus negatively affecting the interests of socialism in Eastern Europe. The clash between the main objectives of the two sides has its origins in the acute military-political, ideological, and economic rivalry of the two social systems that has existed throughout the entire postwar period. This clash was intensified by the nuclear confrontation between the USA and USSR, and by the division of Europe into opposing military and political groupings. Inevitably, this meant that a crisis situation in any East European country was globalized and aggravated, and that it seriously destabilized East-West relations irrespective of whether the international political barometer registered calm or storm when the crisis erupted.

Two vitally important circumstances require that East and West, and the USSR and the USA above all, must thoroughly rethink both the history of past East European crises and their response to present and future crises. First, unfortunately there is no reason to believe that crises in East European countries are a thing of the past. The present period in socialist countries—where the new coexists with the old and the cumbersome but ingrained forms and methods of political and economic activity are still being overcome—is pregnant with crises. Even the reforms as such, which aim at the eventual recovery of society and the improvement of socialism, might become in the course of their implementation new sources of public discontent and conflict.

Second, not the USSR, not the USA, nor any other country can afford to make the success of normalization of East-West relations, dictated as it is by the nuclear imperative, dependent on crisis phenomena in any country—including a socialist one. The stakes are too high. This necessitates an open-minded revision by each side of many aspects of traditional policy behavior during crisis situations in Eastern Europe.

What particular traits of the "crisis" policy of the USA and USSR (as the most representative and influential powers in the two systems) appear from past experience to be most dangerous and destructive for a normal development of relations between the two systems? First, and this applies to both sides, is a tendency toward the excessive globalization and ideologization of any given crisis situation. Both the United States and the Soviet Union have tended in recent years to regard every crisis in the context of their global policies, from the perspective of an inter-bloc confrontation, from the perspective of American-Soviet rivalry. (For justice's sake, it should be noted that in early stages of the existence of the world socialist system, the United States did not exclude the possibility of restoring capitalism in the countries where crises took place.) In their analyses of crisis situations in East European countries, American official circles placed the main responsibility for their origin on the USSR and explained them mainly as a rejection by these countries of the Soviet model of socialism "imposed" on them; they made much less effort to understand the domestic reasons for the crises.

Soviet policy also frequently demonized the "subversive activity" of the opposite side to the detriment of a sober-minded analysis of the reasons for certain conflicts and crises in the allied countries. A dogmatic understanding of the essence of socialism and the fear in the USSR of novel solutions in the course of building socialism prevented the socialist countries from eliminating in time the causes of ripening crises. Once a crisis developed, the role played by the

Western powers, above all the USA, in the situation was exaggerated. The more so when Western countries provided pretexts for doing so.

A specific feature of American policy toward East European crises was not to try to normalize the situation but to maintain a so-called "controlled tension" in close vicinity to the Soviet Union's borders for an extended period. As the situation became aggravated during crisis, a more realistic US policy came to the fore; in the initial stages of crises, however, propagandistic activities of a provocative character were generally carried out (which, by the way, were often resumed when the crises de-escalated). Under present circumstances, such a policy could have a destabilizing effect on the development of Eastern Europe and on the European continent as a whole. It could also result in undesirable complications—for the United States as well—in East-West relations, including in the field of arms control and arms reduction. Such diplomacy also does not correspond to the moral principles and political ethical norms espoused by the United States.

The risks this policy posed for stability in Europe during recent years was well understood by the European allies of the United States. This was clearly evidenced by their markedly different approach to the Polish crisis of the early 1980's. Today, it is quite clear that Central and Eastern Europe, and Europe as a whole, is not the place for experimenting with maintaining a state of tension, especially when this involves countries belonging to different systems and military-political groupings.

Interest in preserving peace, a prerequisite for which is the positive development of relations between the two systems, necessitates that new political thinking guide the policies of the great powers with respect to crisis situations in the whole world, including those in the socialist countries of Eastern Europe. First, it is inadmissible that either side interfere in the internal problems of a country finding itself in a difficult position. Second, it is necessary to avoid globalizing crises, or attempting to use them to damage the interests of the opposite side and promote one's own interests.

Should crisis situations develop, they should under no circumstances be allowed to deter progress in East-West relations. On the contrary, improvement of these relations should be the factor that facilitates the quick localization of the crisis. Moreover, cooperation between the USSR and the USA is possible in rendering assistance to East European countries that find themselves in difficult straits. Should this happen, everyone wins: a focal point of potential destabilization in Europe is eliminated, the country more easily comes out of the crisis, and the USSR and the USA expand the sphere of their cooperation—so much needed for the improvement of international relations and the strengthening of peace.

Sources and Suggestions
for Further Reading

A few years ago I asked a friend—a famous scholar of Soviet–East European relations who changed jobs to become a high-ranking official in the State Department—the following question: "Now that you have access to all the secret information our government has, how much more do you know?" His answer was encouraging: "Only some details that add little or nothing to my general assessments." 1 persisted with a follow-up question: "To stay current, what should 1 read?" His reply: "If you regularly read *The New York Times*, *The Washington Post*, *The Economist*, and *Le Monde* [of Paris], you know just about as much as I do."

Since I do not read French, my "basic list"—the way I try to stay current—now includes the two American dailies and the British weekly (which offers in-depth coverage of international events). Next in importance are *The Financial Times*, *The Los Angeles Times*, and the *Christian Science Monitor*. Readers who happen to know Italian will find the Communist Party daily *l'Unita* very informative. For instant analysis, I often watch "The MacNeil-Lehrer Report" on the Public Broadcasting Service (PBS) or listen to "All Things Considered" on National Public Radio (NPR).

Only selected libraries are likely to have the single best source on developments in the Soviet orbit. It is the weekly *Research Papers* of Radio Free Europe, a goldmine of timely information and balanced analysis on all the countries of Eastern Europe. Similar in content and quality, but covering Soviet affairs, is Radio Liberty's *Weekly Report* on the USSR. Most of the reports published in these two bulletins are signed; my favorite authors are Vladimir Kusin (on Eastern Europe) and Elizabeth Teague (on the Soviet Union).

Scholarly or semi-scholarly journals published in English and dealing with the region include *Problems of Communism*, published by the United States Information Agency in Washington, D.C., as well as *Survey* and *Soviet Studies*, both of which are published in England. For an occasional piece on Soviet and East European topics, see the authoritative *Foreign Affairs*, the informative *Orbis*, and *International Security*, all quarterlies of high quality. From a journalistic perspective, the best-written think-pieces can be found in *The New York Review of Books*, *The New Yorker*, and *The New Republic*.

The New York Review of Books quite frequently carries essays by Timothy Garton Ash, a British writer who is one of the most astute observers of Eastern Europe, and Istvan Deak, a professor of history at Columbia University who is an authority on Central Europe (especially Hungary).

There are relatively few books that deal with Soviet–East European relations in the Gorbachev era. The most comprehensive single-authored study is J. F. Brown, *Eastern Europe and Communist Rule* (Durham: Duke University Press, 1988), while the most up-to-date multi-authored volumes are William E. Griffith, ed., *Central and Eastern Europe: The Opening Curtain?* (Boulder: Westview Press; An East-West Forum Publication, 1989), and Nicholas N. Kittrie and Ivan Volgyes, eds., *The Uncertain Future: Gorbachev's Eastern Bloc* (New York: Paragon House, 1988). For a brief, well-informed, and useful account, see Karen Dawisha, *Eastern Europe, Gorbachev and Reform: The Great Challenge* (Cambridge: Cambridge University Press, 1988).

For a more general treatment of the crisis in communist systems in the Soviet Union, Eastern Europe, and elsewhere—a book that is full of insights—I recommend Zbigniew Brzezinski, *The Grand Failure: The Birth and Death of Communism in the Twentieth Century* (New York: Scribner's, 1989). Many books on Gorbachev do not deal extensively with Eastern Europe but may be most useful for an understanding of the problems of reform in Soviet-type systems. There is much to be learned, for example, from the writings of Seweryn Bialer, most notably from his book *The Soviet Paradox* (New York: Knopf, 1986). For a brief introduction that is as tightly argued as it is brilliantly written, see Timothy J. Colton, *The Dilemma of Reform in the Soviet Union*, rev. and expanded ed. (New York: Council on Foreign Relations, 1986).

The issue of perestroika is ably treated by a number of American economists. Focusing on the Soviet Union is Ed A. Hewett, *Reforming the Soviet Economy: Equality versus Efficiency* (Washington, D.C.: The Brookings Institution, 1988). On economic relations between the Soviet Union and Eastern Europe, see Franklyn D. Holzman, *The Economics of Soviet Bloc Trade and Finance* (Boulder: Westview Press, 1987), which is one of many books on the subject offering a rather positive evaluation of trade relations in the region. The old subsidy issue was originally put forth in Michael Marrese and Jan Vanous, *Soviet Subsidization of Trade with Eastern Europe* (Berkeley: Institute of International Studies of the University of California, 1983). For a critique of the Marrese-Vanous thesis, see Paul Marer, "The Political Economy of Soviet Relations with Eastern Europe," in Sarah M. Terry, ed., *Soviet Policy in Eastern Europe* (New Haven: Yale University Press, 1984), pp. 155–188. For a more up-to-date treatment of relations between the Soviet Union and Eastern Europe, see Paul Marer, "The Economies and Trade of Eastern Europe," in Griffith, op. cit., pp. 37–73.

An overview of military developments in the Warsaw Pact is Dale R. Herspring, "The Soviets, the Warsaw Pact, and the Eastern European Militaries," also in Griffith, op. cit., pp. 130–155. For a broad treatment of conventional arms control issues in Europe, see Robert D. Blackwill, "Conceptual Problems of Conventional Arms Control," *International Security* 12, No. 4 (Spring 1988), pp. 28–47. The issue of East European reliability has been treated systematically in Ivan Volgyes, *The Political Reliability of the Warsaw Pact Armies: The Southern Tier* (Durham: Duke University Press, 1982, and in Daniel Nelson, ed., *Soviet Allies: The Warsaw Pact and the Issue of Reliability* (Boulder: Westview Press, 1984). A. Ross Johnson, "The Warsaw Pact: Soviet Military Policy in Eastern Europe," in Terry, op. cit., pp. 255–283, is somewhat outdated but thorough and stimulating. Finally, a controversial book I like for its systematic, hard-headed treatment of the functions of the Warsaw Pact in Eastern Europe is Christopher D. Jones, *Soviet Influence in Eastern Europe: Political Autonomy and the Warsaw Pact* (New York: Praeger, 1981).

Finally, here is a list of seven books on the postwar history of Soviet foreign policy, Eastern Europe, or Soviet–East European relations, focusing on the pre-Gorbachev era:

Vernon V. Aspaturian, *Process and Power in Soviet Foreign Policy* (Boston: Little, Brown and Co., 1971);

Zbigniew Brzezinski, *The Soviet Bloc: Unity and Conflict* (Cambridge: Harvard University Press, 1971);

Charles Gati, *Hungary and the Soviet Bloc* (Durham: Duke University Press, 1986);

Robert L. Hutchings, *Soviet–East European Relations: Consolidation and Conflict, 1968–1980* (Madison: The University of Wisconsin Press, 1983);

Joseph Rothschild, *Return to Diversity: A Political History of East Central Europe since World War II* (New York: Oxford University Press, 1989);

Sarah M. Terry, ed., *Soviet Policy in Eastern Europe* (New Haven: Yale University Press, 1984); and

Adam Ulam, *Expansion and Coexistence* (New York: Praeger, 1968).

And, when all is read and done in English, there is no substitute for knowing Russian or an East European language and for traveling in this rapidly changing region.

Index

Adamec, Ladislav, 180
Aganbegyan, Abel, 105
Albania, 9
Alexandrov, Chudomir, 92
Association of Free Democrats, 174
Austria, 31, 32, 83, 109, 198
Autonomy, 38, 101, 130

Beneš, Eduard, 10
Berend, Iván T., 150
Berlin Wall, 164, 175, 177
Bialer, Seweryn, 65, 133
Bierut, Bolesław, 89
Bil'ak, Vasil, 93, 178
Bilateralism, 116
Bogomolov, Oleg T., 76, 82, 166
Bovin, Alexander, 77
"Brezhnev Doctrine," 47, 71–79, 142, 166, 169, 182
Brezhnev, Leonid: "Prague Spring," 46, 85; "Solidarity," 52–53; socialist internationalism, 73; Gorbachev, 75–76, Czechoslovakia, 89; Polish crisis of 1980–81, 90; CMEA, 125–26; neo-Stalinism, 209
Brzezinski, Zbigniew, 15, 161
Bulgaria: satellization and sovietization, 11–12; perestroika and glasnost, 91–92; resistance to reform, 101–102; economics, 108; repressive regime, 162; revolution, 182–83, 186, 187, 188, 200n
Burlatski, Fyodor, 76

Čalfa, Marian, 180

Carnogurský, Jan, 181
Ceauşescu, Nicolae, 98–99, 150, 183–85
Censorship, 94, 97
Chernenko, Konstantin U.: CMEA, 126–27
China, 100, 175
Committee for Historical Justice, 171
Committee of Foreign Ministers, 84
Communist parties, 15, 25, 88, 101
Communist Party of the Soviet Union (CPSU), 80, 89–90, 98–99, 164–65
Council for Mutual Economic Assistance (CMEA), 20, 124–35, 191–92, 212–15
Cuba, 128
Czechoslovakia: satellization and sovietization, 10–11; "Prague Spring," 43–48, 56, 85; outcome of crises, 57; Gorbachev's early policies, 70; Soviets and personnel matters, 89; perestroika and glasnost, 92–93; resistance to reform, 101–102; economics, 109; trade, 117, 118; military, 143, 146; repressive regime, 162; revolution, 177–82, 186–87, 188; pluralism, 199; neo-Stalinism, 209

Debt, hard-currency, 108–109, 112–13, 117, 201
Dienstbier, Jiří, 180, 181
Dietz, Raimund, 119, 121

Dlouhý, Vladimir, 181
Dobrynin, Anatoly, 80–81
Dubček, Alexander: "Prague Spring," 44, 46; Brezhnev and personnel matters, 89; reformism, 92; revolution, 179, 181

East Germany: satellization and sovietization, 12–13; East Berlin riots of 1953, 31, 32; "Prague Spring," 45–46; perestroika and glasnost, 93–95; resistance to reform, 101–102; economics, 106, 108; trade, 118; military, 143; repressive regime, 162; revolution, 164, 175–77, 185, 186, 187, 188; Hungary and Helsinki Accord, 172–73; pluralism, 199
Economics: sovietization, 20–21; Stalin, 24, 27–28; Soviet policies in post-Stalin era, 34, 58–59; "Prague Spring," 44; East and West Germany, 93; Hungary, 95; Poland, 98; concept of socialism, 104–106; urgency of change, 106–13; politics of trade, 113–24; CMEA, 130–35; interdependence, 132; military expenditures, 149–50; Polish elections, 169–70; revolutions of 1988-89, 188; second phase of revolutions, 197–99; Western concerns, 201–202; perestroika, 212–15
Elections, 167–70, 173–74
Energy, 118–23, 132–33, 194, 195–96
Europe: Warsaw Pact debates, 86; unified, 136–37; West and security, 202–203; Polish crisis of 1980–81, 219
European Economic Community (EEC), 124, 134–35

Falin, Valentin M., 165n
Fedorov, Rafael P., 165n
Finland, 193–94
Foreign policy: Stalin, 8–9; post-Stalin era, 31, 57–58; Warsaw Pact debates, 86; Soviet intentions in 1988, 165–66; Soviet domestic crisis and revolutions, 189–90; political perestroika, 211–12; U.S.-East European relations, 215–16

Geremek, Bronislaw, 66
Germany, 31–32, 139; reunification, 176, 197
Gerő, Ernő, 11
Glasnost, 91–99, 102
Glemp, József (Cardinal), 97
Gomułka, Władysław, 15, 85
Gorbachev, Mikhail: early policies, 65–71, 87–103; socialist internationalism, 73–75; Brezhnev, 75–76; modification of policies, 78; Warsaw Pact debates, 86–87; market economics, 104; CMEA, 127–35; unified Europe, 136; military relations, 150–57; unilateral withdrawal, 161–62, 166; policies in 1988, 163; East German revolution, 164, 176; institutional changes in CPSU, 164–65; Polish elections, 169; Czechoslovakian revolution, 178; revolutions of 1988–89, 187; "Finlandization," 193–94
Grósz, Károly, 96, 170–71, 173
Gysi, Gregor, 175

Hager, Kurt, 94
Hájek, Jiří, 179
Havel, Václav, 92, 180–81, 199
Hegedüs, András, 89
Hegenbart, Rudolf, 178–79
Helsinki Accord, 172–73
Herspring, Dale R., 144–45, 152–53
Hewett, Ed A., 110–11
Honecker, Erich, 93–95, 164, 172–73, 175–77
Hungarian Democratic Forum, 173
Hungarian Socialist Workers' Party (HSWP), 170–75
Hungary: satellization and sovietization, 11; post-Stalin era, 32–33, 34, 35, 37; 1956 revolution, 39–43, 56; "Prague Spring," 45; outcome of crises, 57; popularity of Kádár regime, 67; Gorbachev's early policies, 70; perestroika and glasnost, 95–96; economics, 108–109, 111–12; trade, 117; military, 143, 150; reform-minded regime, 162–63; revolution, 170–75, 185, 186, 187, 188; East German refugees, 176; referendum, 194n; plu-

ralism, 199; neo-Stalinism, 209
Husák, Gustáv, 92–93, 180–81
Hutching, Robert L., 124

Ideology, 22, 24–25, 87–99, 127
Industry, 20, 112, 118–19, 194–95
Institute of Economics of the World
Socialist System ("Bogomolov In-
stitute"), 76, 82, 166, 205–19
Institutions, 26–27, 79–87, 87–99
Intellectuals, 56
Internationalism, 71–72, 208–209

Jakeš, Miloš, 178, 180
Jaruzelski, Wojciech, 54–55, 96–98,
167, 168
Jones, Christopher D., 154n

Kádár, János, 67, 85, 95–96, 172
Kanis, Stanisław, 50
KGB, 81
Khrushchev, Nikita: post-Stalin
struggle for power, 29–30, 60; Yu-
goslavia, 36; Hungarian revo-
lution of 1956, 40, 41–42; CMEA,
124, 125
Klaus, Václav, 181
Komárek, Valtr, 181
Köves, András, 120, 122, 123, 133
Krenz, Egon, 164, 175
Kukliński, Ryszard J., 86n

Marer, Paul, 24, 119, 120, 121
Marrese, Michael, 119, 120–21
Marshall Plan, 16
Marxism, 71–72
Mazowiecki, Tadeusz, 168
Mazurov, Kiril, 179
Medvedev, Vadim, 81, 165n
Michael (King of Romania), 12
Mićunović, Veljko, 41n
Mikoyan, Anastas, 39–40
Military: East-West relations and in-
tervention, 61; Gorbachev on in-
tervention, 75–76; Soviet forces in
late 1980s, 137–38; Soviet objec-
tives, 138–42; Gorbachev, 143–47,
150–54; tensions in relations,
147–50; unilateral withdrawal,
162, 166; future of Soviet policy,
196–97
Ministry of Foreign Affairs, 165

Mladenov, Petur, 182–83
Mlynář, Zdeněk, 89n
Modrow, Hans, 175
Molotov, Vyacheslav, 29

Nagy, Imre, 33, 39–40
Nationalism, 35–39, 58, 127
Nazi-Soviet Pact, 8–9
Németh, Miklós, 173
New Economic Mechanism (NEM),
95, 111–12
North Atlantic Treaty Organization
(NATO), 83, 138, 139–40
Novotný, Antonin, 44
Nyers, Rezső, 171

Perestroika: leaders of Eastern
Europe before 1988–89, 90–99;
fear of instability, 102; CMEA,
129–30, 134–35; Soviet–East European relations, 209–10; political,
210–12; economic, 212–15
Poland: satellization and sovietization, 13; nationalism in post-
Stalin era, 35, 37; "Prague
Spring," 45; crisis of 1980–81, 48–
55, 57, 85–86, 89–90, 219; outcome
of crises, 57; Gorbachev's early
policies, 70; perestroika and
glasnost, 96–98; economics, 106,
108–109; trade, 117, 129; military,
143, 144–45; reform-minded regime, 162–63; revolution, 167–70,
185, 186, 187, 188, 199–200; elections, 194n; Western assistance,
201–202; neo-Stalinism, 209
Polish United Workers' Party, 50
Political Consultative Committee
(PCC), 84–85
Politics: geographical identity of
Eastern Europe, 3–4; pre-communist era, 4–5; Stalin, 24–25,
27; Kremlin power struggle in post-
Stalin era, 60; Warsaw Pact, 83–
84; economics and trade, 113–24;
CMEA, 127; NATO, 139–40; repressive regimes, 162; reform-minded
regimes, 162–63; Poland and
Hungary in 1989, 194n; democracy and economic hardship,
198–200; perestroika, 210–12
Portugal, 200

Pozsgay, Imre, 96, 170–71, 173–74

Radio Free Europe, 67–69
Rajk, László, 19
Rákosi, Mátyás, 32, 33
Rakowski, Meiczysław, 168
Roman Catholic Church, 50, 53, 96, 97
Romania: satellization and sovietization, 12; "Prague Spring," 45; perestroika and glasnost, 98–99; resistance to reform, 101–102; economics, 112–13; CMEA, 125, 126; Warsaw Pact, 148; repressive regime, 162; revolution, 183–85, 186, 187, 188, 200n; Council of National Salvation, 185
Ryzhkov, Nikolai, 81

SALT treaty, 45
Satellization, 9–13, 13–18
Secret police, 19, 26, 144, 145
Shakhnazarov, Georgi, 80–81, 165n
Shevardnadze, Eduard, 81, 165
Shishlin, Nikolai, 80, 81
Slánský, Rudolf, 19
Sobell, Vlad, 134
Social democracy, 39
Socialism, 104–106, 206
Socialist internationalism: Czechoslovakia, 47; Soviet–East European relations, 71–72, 208–209; Brezhnev Doctrine, 73; autonomy of communist parties, 77
"Solidarity": Polish crisis of 1980–81, 48, 49–53, 54; legalization, 98; elections, 167–70
Soviet Academy of Science's Institute of Economics of the World Socialist System, 82
Sovietization, 9, 10, 18–23
Soviet Ministry of Defense, 82
Soviet Ministry of Foreign Affairs, 81–82
Spain, 200
Stalin, Josef: post-war power vacuum, 7; expansion of communism, 7–8; foreign policy, 8–9; satellization, 13–18; sovietization, 18–23; objectives, 23–28; funeral, 29; strategic importance of Poland, 49; attitude, 88–89; economic exploitation, 123; threat from West,

139; Yugoslavia, 196; Soviet model of socialism, 209
Suez crisis, 42
Suslov, Mikhail, 39–40, 45, 209
Sweden, 198

Tito (Josip Broz), 16–17, 36
de Tocqueville, Alexis, 161
Tőkés, László, 183–84
Trade, 99, 113–24, 194–96
Trotsky, Leon, 7–8
Truman, Harry S, 14

Ulam, Adam, 21–22
Ulbricht, Walter, 45–46, 85
Union of Democratic Forces, 183
United States: Stalin, 13–14; nuclear weapons, 140; revolutions of 1988–89, 187–88; Cold War and security, 202–203; Soviet view of relations, 215–17; crises and East-West relations, 217–19
Urbánek, Karel, 180

Vanous, Jan, 119, 120–21
Vas, Zoltán, 14
Volgyes, Ivan, 143
Vyshinski, Andrei, 12

Wałęsa, Lech, 52. *See also* Poland; "Solidarity"
Warsaw Pact: "Prague Spring," 45, 46; Polish crisis of 1980–81, 49–50; institutional framework, 82–87; forces in central Europe, 138; Soviet domination, 147–48; Gorbachev, 151–54, 155; future, 191–92
West: Soviet relations, 60–61, 217–19; Soviet fear of attack, 138–39; Soviet threat, 139–40; revolutions, 200–203; political perestroika, 210–12; economic perestroika, 212–15
West Germany, 45, 86, 93–94, 139, 201–202

Yakovlev, Aleksandr, 80–81, 164
Young Democrats, 174
Yugoslavia, 9, 16–17, 36–37, 196

Zhdanovshchina, 21
Zhivkov, Todor, 91–92, 182–83